CREATING
THE
ENTANGLING
ALLIANCE

Recent Titles in Contributions in Political Science
Series Editor: Bernard K. Johnpoll

Politicians, Judges, and the People: A Study in Citizens' Participation
Charles H. Sheldon and Frank P. Weaver

The European Parliament: The Three-Decade Search for a United Europe
Paula Scalingi

Prelude to the Presidency: The Political Character and Legislative Leadership Style of Governor Jimmy Carter
Gary M Fink

Presidential Primaries: Road to the White House
James W. Davis

The Voice of Terror: A Biography of Johann Most
Frederic Trautmann

Presidential Secrecy and Deception: Beyond the Power to Persuade
John M. Orman

The New Red Legions
Richard A. Gabriel

Contemporary Perspectives on European Integration: Attitudes, Nongovernmental Behavior, and Collective Decision Making
Leon Hurwitz, editor

The Italian Communist Party: Yesterday, Today, and Tomorrow
Simon Serfaty and Lawrence Gray, editors

The Fiscal Congress: Legislative Control of the Budget
Lance T. Leloup

Iran, Saudi Arabia, and the Law of the Sea: Political Interaction and Legal Development in the Persian Gulf
Charles G. MacDonald

Improving Prosecution? The Inducement and Implementation of Innovations for Prosecution Management
David Leo Weimer

Timothy P. Ireland

CREATING THE ENTANGLING ALLIANCE

The Origins of the North Atlantic Treaty Organization

Contributions in Political Science, Number 50

Greenwood Press
WESTPORT, CONNECTICUT

Library of Congress Cataloging in Publication Data

Ireland, Timothy P   1948–
    Creating the entangling alliance.

    (Contributions in political science; no. 50 ISSN
0147-1066)
    Bibliography: p.
    Includes index.
    1. North Atlantic Treaty Organization. I. Title.
II. Series.
JX1393.N67173   355'.031'091821   80-655
ISBN 0-313-22094-8 (lib. bdg)

Library of Congress Catalog Card Number: 80-655
ISBN: 0-313-22094-8
ISSN: 0147-1066

First published in 1981

Greenwood Press
A division of Congressional Information Service, Inc.
88 Post Road West, Westport, Connecticut 06881
Printed in the United States of America

10 9 8 7 6 5 4 3 2

To my family
Robert McLeod, Joan Lucille
and Kathleen Sweeney

Contents

Acknowledgments

My first and most heartfelt word of thanks goes to Robert B. Stewart, dean emeritus of the Fletcher School of Law and Diplomacy. Dean Stewart's death in June 1980 saddened all who knew him. The memory of his kindness, encouragement, and strength continue to be a source of inspiration.

Another grateful acknowledgment goes to John P. Roche, Henry R. Luce Professor of Civilization and Foreign Affairs at the Fletcher School. His sincere interest, strong support, and thoughtful suggestions were the sustaining elements in the completion of this work, and I can only hope his faith was justified.

I also would like to express my deep appreciation to Robert J. Art, dean of the Graduate School at Brandeis University. Dean Art's careful reading of the manuscript and his thought-provoking criticisms and helpful suggestions helped clarify my thinking on many points and contributed significantly to the completion of this book.

Many people have been most helpful to me in my writing, and several deserve special thanks. Robert L. Pfaltzgraff, Jr., awakened an early interest in the Atlantic Community, and Leo Gross, Alan K. Henrikson, W. Scott Thompson, and John S. Gibson offered constructive personal and professional advice. Warnock Davies provided valuable information on the origins of the Revolutionary War alliance with France. I also enjoyed exchanging ideas on the "great debate" with Phil Williams of Aberdeen University in Scotland. I profited from the examples and support of my friends Coit Blacker, Stephen Flanagan, Steven Miller, and Neil Sullivan. The historical offices of the State Department and the Senate Foreign Relations Committee were most helpful in obtaining research materials.

Research on the book was further facilitated by the staff of the Edwin Ginn Library, especially Henrietta Moore and Barbara Boyce. Deborah Louis and Deborah Manning each spent many long hours typing and editing the manuscript. Phyllis Berry Webber, registrar of the Fletcher School, was a source of administrative and personal help. Joe Carriero often provided the lift to keep going. I would also like to thank Mildred Vasan and the Editorial Department of Greenwood Press for their careful editing.

A final word of thanks to Andrea Lynn Gilchrist, who, in addition to reading and editing much of the manuscript, was unfailing in her support, encouragement, and love.

CREATING
THE
ENTANGLING
ALLIANCE

Introduction

On April 4, 1949, representatives of the United States, Canada, and ten countries of western Europe signed the North Atlantic Treaty in Washington, D.C.[1] Two years later American ground troops were assigned to duty in Europe under article 3 of the treaty and as part of the North Atlantic Treaty Organization (NATO) command structure. Today, almost thirty years later, NATO continues to offer the most visible, tangible, and durable evidence of the "revolution" that took place in American foreign policy following World War II.

By accepting the obligations inherent in the North Atlantic Treaty and by assuming a primary role in NATO, the U.S. government broke with two of the most time-honored traditions in American foreign policy: George Washington's Farewell Address dictum against entanglement in permanent alliances[2] and James Monroe's doctrine of the mutual exclusiveness of European and western hemispheric political affairs.[3] Indeed, the strength of these traditions was manifest well into the twentieth century as the United States eschewed membership in the League of Nations following World War I and reverted to a policy of isolation. It was not until the attack on Pearl Harbor forced the United States into World War II that many Americans began to reexamine their traditional foreign policy assumptions.[4] However, even during the years following World War II, isolationist sentiment remained strong among segments of the American body politic that threatened to thwart any new "internationalist" role for the United States.[5] Why, then, did the years following the end of the war witness a fundamental transformation of the guiding principles of U.S. foreign policy through American participation in the North Atlantic Alliance?

This study is designed to answer that question by undertaking a critical reexamination of the process whereby the United States became formally "entangled" in its first extrahemispheric military alliance since the Treaty of Mortefontaine terminated the Revolutionary War Alliance with France in 1800. The purpose of detailing the underlying assumptions behind the original commitment is to shed some new light on the rationale for American participation in the Atlantic Alliance and to demonstrate the strength of the ties binding the United States and western Europe.

Traditionally, in analyses of the North Atlantic Treaty and NATO, American historians have concentrated on the development of the "cold war" between the United States and the Soviet Union. The emergence of the American commitment to western Europe has been viewed as a cause-and-effect relationship in response to Soviet actions in the Near East, the Balkans, eastern Europe, and Germany. Even "revisionist" historians view the creation of the Atlantic Alliance almost exclusively in terms of the cold war.[6]

However, such analyses overlook the fact that the American commitment to western Europe through the Atlantic Alliance was designed to accomplish two goals. The first, short-term goal was to counter the threat of Soviet-sponsored subversion against the war-weakened economic and political institutions of western Europe and to enable that area to recover from the devastating effect of World War II. The second, more long-term goal was to recreate a balance of power in Europe. In this regard U.S. policy was aimed not at directly confronting the Soviet Union with American might, but rather at restoring Europe as a center of international power capable of standing on its own (albeit with American backing) against potential threats from the Soviet Union. In short, the United States hoped to rebuild the war-shattered economic, political, and military institutions of western Europe and to re-create a European balance of power against the Soviet Union, and in so doing it hoped to minimize the cost and duration of the American commitment. This second goal of American policy toward Europe, although often obscured by the pervasive nature of Soviet-American relations, was of critical importance in determining the specific nature of the American commitment to Europe through the North Atlantic Treaty Organization.

The impact of an American policy directed at re-creating a European balance against the Soviet Union was this: in order to restore western Europe as a balancing factor against the Soviet Union, the United States had to press for the inclusion of western Germany in programs for European recovery and defense and, at the same time, to provide France and the other countries of western Europe security against a possible renewal of German aggression. However, the only way the United States could provide adequate safeguards against the fear of German *revanchism* was progressively to involve itself in European affairs. It was this goal that did much to determine the scope and structure of the American commitment to NATO.

Although the United States had fought two world wars to prevent the domination of Europe by a single power, no clear-cut American policy for western Europe emerged during the early months of the postwar period. It was only as American officials recognized the magnitude and implications of Europe's economic devastation and the threat posed to the continent's political stability by the Soviet Union that the primary goal of American foreign policy became the rehabilitation of western Europe. To be more direct, it was not until after the failure of the Moscow Foreign Ministers Conference on Germany in late April 1947 that the State Department focused on European recovery as the cornerstone of postwar American policy.[7] This linkage between the focus on western European recovery and the failure of the four wartime allies to reach agreement on the status of Germany is doubly important because it helps demonstrate the initial significance of the German question in shaping the American commitment to Europe.

Prior to the Moscow Conference, American foreign policy had not dealt directly with the problems confronting postwar Europe. Although the Truman Doctrine of March 1947 was motivated in large part by the relationship between security in the eastern Mediterranean and the stability of western Europe, an analysis of the famous "fifteen weeks" between the Truman Doctrine and Secretary of State George C. Marshall's call for a European recovery program on June 5 suggests considerable uncertainty within the U.S. government as to just what the scope and nature of America's European policy would be. But with the failure of the Moscow Conference on Germany and the implications of that failure for the stability of Europe, the United States began to direct its major postwar efforts toward the rehabilitation of western Europe; a goal that could not be reached without including the western zones of Germany.

As the development of a European recovery program became the major goal of American foreign policy, the United States became involved progressively in the question of western Germany's relationship to western Europe and, ultimately, in the maintenance of European security. This is demonstrated by the fact that at every stage of the evolution of the American commitment to Europe—the Marshall Plan, the Vandenberg Resolution, the North Atlantic Treaty, the creation of an organizational structure for the Atlantic Alliance, and the assignment of ground troops to NATO—the German question played a key role.

The distinction between the cold war and the German question is a subtle one, for clearly the two are closely related. But if the distinction is subtle, it is also important: an American commitment responsive to security concerns other than the particular issues of the Soviet-American rivalry would leave a far different legacy than a commitment shaped solely by the perception of threat from the Soviet Union. Indeed, neither the formulation of a treaty nor the creation of an institutional structure with long-term political and military implications was a necessary prerequisite for an American commitment designed to prevent a Soviet attack. A policy along the lines of a twentieth-century "Monroe Doctrine" for western Europe and the unilateral extension of military assistance—including the dispatch of troops—could have accomplished that purpose. Instead, the "legal" commitment and the organizational structure were largely shaped in order to satisfy the dual goals of providing a framework through which western Germany could be safely integrated into the West and France offered security against future German aggression. This, in turn, gave the American commitment—to use Dean Acheson's words—a "depth and permanence" that would otherwise not have existed.

The legal commitment was, of course, the treaty itself. The treaty formula was deemed necessary in order to give the Europeans assurance of U.S. support for Europe and to dispel French fears of a repeat of the interwar years, when the United States rejected the Treaty of Versailles, withdrew into political isolation, and left France feeling abandoned. The fact that the treaty was signed in Washington almost simultaneously with three power agreement on the Occupation Statute for the Federal Republic of Germany is testimony to the close relationship between the Atlantic Alliance and the German question.

A factor often overlooked in analyses of American participation in the Atlantic Alliance is the distinction between the obligations accepted by the United States when the North Atlantic Treaty was signed in April 1949 and the obligations actually assumed through participation in NATO. Because the U.S. Congress continued to contain important segments of isolationist thinking, the wording of article 5 of the North Atlantic Treaty was framed in order to conform with the "Monroe Doctrine formula" that had already found expression in the Inter-American Treaty of Reciprocal Assistance. As a result, article 5 did not bind the United States to the military defense of western Europe; it was not until U.S. troops were assigned to NATO under article 3 that Europeans were assured of automatic American participation in their defense. And here too, in the transformation from a treaty of guarantee to an organizational structure, the German question played a key role, as NATO's development was strongly influenced by the need to find an organizational structure strong enough to contain West German participation without allowing the Germans to dominate.

Again, and this must be emphasized at the outset, an analysis of the importance of the German question in shaping the American commitment to Europe does not negate the importance of the cold war during the period under study. Indeed, cold war issues often provided the impetus for the United States and western Europe to reach agreement on the status of western Germany and the extent of American involvement in European affairs. Rather, it is the purpose of this book to demonstrate the importance of traditional intra-European politics in shaping the particular nature of the U.S. commitment to Europe through the North Atlantic Treaty and NATO.

But because of the wider implications of the German question in giving the U.S. commitment a more permanent character, it has remained a somewhat hidden issue. In fact, at almost every stage of the evolution of the American involvement, the importance of the German question appears to have been deliberately minimized in order to obscure the long-term ramifications of the Truman administration's actions. The difficulty in dealing with a Congress that retained strong pockets of isolationist sentiment was the motivating factor in this regard, but it prevented any in-depth analysis of the long-term effects of American policies of the early postwar era. This was most true during the so-called great debate over the assignment of American troops to NATO in 1951.

Even today, as such topics as arms control and troop reductions raise questions about the intrinsic relationship of the United States to the security of western Europe, issues other than those directly related to the Soviet-American rivalry continue to receive only secondary attention. It is hoped that by focusing on the importance of the German question in determining the scope and structure of the original American commitment a clearer picture of the rationale behind the continuing U.S. "presence" in NATO will emerge, thereby adding increased definition to the questions currently at hand.

Notes

1. U.S., Department of State, *North Atlantic Treaty*, Treaties and Other International Acts Series, 1964, Pubn. 3635 (1950).

2. Felix Gilbert, *To the Farewell Address* (Princeton, N.J.: Princeton University Press, 1970), pp. 144-47.

3. Dexter Perkins, *A History of the Monroe Doctrine* (Boston: Little, Brown and Co., 1963), pp. 391-93.

4. Alan K. Henrikson, "The Map as an 'Idea': The Role of Cartographic Imagery During the Second World War," *The American Cartographer* 2, 1:19-53.

5. John Lewis Gaddis, *The United States and the Origins of the Cold War: 1941-1947* (New York: Columbia University Press, 1972), pp. 343-46.

6. Robert Hunter, *Security in Europe* (Bloomington and London: Indiana University Press, 1972), pp. 15-16; also, John Gimbel, *The Origins of the Marshall Plan* (Stanford, Calif.: Stanford University Press, 1976), pp. 2-3.

7. John Backer, *The Decision to Divide Germany* (Durham, N.C.: Duke University Press, 1978); Gimbel, *The Origins of the Marshall Plan.*

ONE

A New Direction

Introduction

Although the German question would do much to shape the American commitment to western Europe, it is clear that at the end of World War II the United States possessed no clearly defined or well-thought-out policy for Germany. Initially, the United States hoped to join with Britain, France, and the Soviet Union in administering Germany as an "economic unit." However, once the common goal of defeating Hitler's Germany was reached, the cohesion of the wartime alliance began to dissolve.

At first the chief obstacle to four power agreement was the intransigence of France, but by early 1946 it was apparent that the two main protagonists in Germany were the United States and the Soviet Union. Moreover, U.S.-Soviet disagreements over German policy were beginning to fit into a larger pattern of deteriorating relations between the two superpowers.

The problems facing the United States were further complicated by the fact that western Europe had been devastated by the war. The European economies were in shambles, political chaos was everywhere in evidence, and there was a genuine fear that the governments of France and Italy would fall to Communist-inspired subversion. Yet political stability depended on economic recovery, and economic recovery could not take place until the industrial resources of defeated Germany could be utilized without threatening the rest of western Europe with German domination.

Therefore, as it became increasingly evident that the allies would not reach four power agreement on the future of Germany, it became the task of the Truman administration to develop a foreign policy designed to contain the expansion of Soviet communism and to integrate the western German economy into a larger program for general European recovery.

To be sure, 1946 did witness several efforts to give American foreign policy more definition. Of particular importance were George Kennan's famous "long telegram" of February 22,[1] and Clark Clifford's memorandum to the president that was initiated in the summer and was completed by September.[2] Both documents explained the growing sense of confrontation between the Americans and the Soviets by presenting the latter's actions in terms of a predictable pattern of behavior based on a merger of traditional Russian security requirements and the foreign policy dogma inspired by Soviet communism. In recommending American strategies to counter the Soviet Union, both documents outlined what became known as the "containment policy," and Clifford advocated a global foreign policy that would be shaped by the overriding issue of relations with the Soviet Union.[3] He also proposed a program of technical and economic assistance to strengthen American ties with prospective allies against Soviet expansion.[4]

During 1946 the United States did take several actions that indicated a growing disillusionment with the Soviet Union. In July the United States and the United Kingdom began to take steps leading toward a merger of the Anglo-American occupation zones in Germany. A further step in this direction was taken on September 6, when Secretary of State James Byrnes indicated that, if four power agreement on the unification of Germany was not forthcoming, the United States would move ahead with the unification of as much of Germany as was possible. Moreover, as a result of the Near Eastern crises of 1946 the U.S. government authorized a permanent naval presence in the eastern Mediterranean in order to counter Soviet moves in that strategic area.[5]

However, it was not until the Truman Doctrine of March 1947 that the United States began to formulate a general foreign policy based on the acknowledgment of a disharmony of interests with the Soviet Union. The Truman Doctrine was doubly important in that, by emphasizing the importance of the Mediterranean to the stability of Europe, it helped direct the thrust of American assistance programs toward the rehabilitation of western Europe as a key element in the balance of power against the Soviet Union.

However, in creating a program for the recovery of western Europe, American decision makers soon found that it would be necessary to include Germany, or at least a significant part of it, in any rehabilitation plan. Of course, any such designs raised French fears of possible German *revanchism* and forced the United States to begin to develop procedures whereby western Germany could be included in the restoration of western Europe and France offered security against a renewal of German aggression.

German Policy

Throughout World War II the common goal of defeating Nazi Germany cemented the tenuous "grand alliance" of the United States, the Soviet Union, and the United Kingdom. Moreover, as the war drew to a close it was also clear that four power attempts to find solutions to questions concerning the occupation and administration of defeated Germany would do much to determine the nature of postwar relations between the allies. However, despite the importance of the German question to allied relations, it is apparent that the U.S. government entered the postwar era without a well-defined German policy. This lack of direction was due to two related factors: interdepartmental disputes over the future of Germany, and President Franklin D. Roosevelt's desire to avoid making political decisions regarding the postwar world while military operations against Germany were still under way.[6]

The intragovernmental debates over German policy centered on the question of whether a policy of repression or one of rehabilitation would best ensure a pacified Germany after the war. The details of the debates between the State, Treasury, and War departments and their effects on German policy have been well documented elsewhere and need only be summarized here.[7]

Briefly, the prevailing view in the State Department was that the rise of Hitler and the outbreak of World War II could be directly attributed to the harshness of the Versailles peace after World War I. Long-range thinkers at State were especially critical of the famous "war guilt" clause and the unduly restrictive nature of allied economic and reparations policies. Therefore, while the State Department favored a policy of demilitarization and denazification, it was the chief advocate of a moderate peace designed to prevent future wars by reforming Germany.[8]

On the other hand, the Treasury Department, led by Secretary Henry Morgenthau, was the chief advocate of repressive postwar policies. Morgenthau and many of his lieutenants felt that Germany was an inherently aggressive nation, and they blamed the leniency of the Versailles peace for Nazism and World War II. The various "Morgenthau plans" that circulated throughout the government during the war best express Treasury Department thinking. These plans, authored by Secretary Morgenthau himself, advocated the total dismantling of the Third Reich's remaining heavy industry and the transformation of Germany into a country "primarily agricultural and pastoral in nature." In short, Morgenthau proposed that a condition of "planned chaos" exist throughout Germany in order to ensure that the Germans could not harness their industrial might for aggressive purposes. The height of the Treasury Department's influence came in late September 1944, when many of Morgenthau's ideas were incorporated in the initial occupation directive issued to the U.S. Army as it moved across western Europe—JCS 1067.[9]

For its part, the War Department, especially the army, was not so much concerned with the impact of American policies on the long-range future of Germany as it was with the short-run problems of military occupation. The soldiers viewed their primary task as the defeat of German armies and were reluctant to undertake what they viewed as the unpleasant responsibilities of administering a defeated enemy's territory. Accordingly, the War Department favored German policies that it felt would guarantee a quick end to occupation duties and a speedy return of American troops to the United States. During the wartime debates, the military resisted the efforts of the other departments—especially State—to influence occupation policies and usually sided with the Treasury Department's repressive plans "as a matter of administrative convenience."[10]

These interdepartmental debates over German policy continued throughout most of the war and were still in progress when the fighting ended in Europe on May 8, 1945. The unresolved nature of the debates was due, in large measure, to President Roosevelt's desire to avoid making decisions on postwar political questions while the fighting continued.[11]

The clearest expression of Roosevelt's desire to limit wartime discussions with the allies to military matters was the doctrine of "unconditional surrender" that he announced at the Casablanca meeting with British Prime Minister Winston Churchill in February 1943. By making it clear to the Germans that peace could only be achieved by the destruction of the German war machine, Roosevelt also assured the Soviets that the Western allies would carry the war to the finish and that there was no danger of a separate peace with Germany.[12]

This is not to say that Roosevelt did not have his own opinions on postwar Germany or that the allies entirely avoided the German question during the war. Because of his personal experiences in Germany as a

youth and his service as assistant secretary of the navy during World War
I, Roosevelt viewed the Germans as a warlike race and was generally
sympathetic to the proponents of a harsh peace.[13] This predilection
toward harshness was reinforced by Roosevelt's desire to preserve allied
unity after the war and to accommodate Soviet Premier Joseph Stalin's
security interests in Germany and eastern Europe. Therefore, at the
Tehran and Yalta conferences, Churchill, Roosevelt, and Stalin devoted
considerable time to the questions of dismemberment of Germany and
reparations policies.

At the Tehran Conference in November-December 1943, the three
leaders talked at some length about the possible dismemberment, and
these discussions mirrored in many respects deliberations within the U.S.
government. Briefly, the major question was whether the partition of the
Third Reich would improve postwar security by weakening Germany or
whether dismemberment would pose an additional threat by providing
a ready-made rallying point for *revanchist* elements in the German popu-
lation.[14] Although the question was not settled at Tehran and was carried
over for further discussion, it is significant that the partition of Germany
into two or more states received serious (and sympathetic) consideration
by the allies, who were by no means tied to the retention of a unified
German state.

At Yalta in January-February 1945, the partition question was discussed again by the "big three" but was overshadowed by the reparations
issue. Reparations was an extremely important question, and the Yalta
talks reflected growing divisions among the allies on this issue. Although
Great Britain and the United States did not expect to claim war reparations, the Soviet Union hoped to extract $20 billion in damages from
Germany. Of that sum, $10 billion was to go to the Soviet Union itself.
Moreover, the Soviets insisted that reparations be given first priority by
the allies without necessarily taking into account the need to prevent
starvation and disorder in many parts of Germany. The British and Americans were especially concerned about the potential for starvation in the
industrialized western occupation zones where food was scarce. While
Roosevelt refused to accept the Soviet figure as final, he did, over
Churchill's objections, agree to use that total as the basis for future discussions.[15]

However, beyond his desire to preserve allied unity after the war and
his general sympathy for a harsh peace, Roosevelt's thinking on postwar
Germany remained "vague," and it is clear that he wanted to postpone

final decisions on partition and reparations until after the war. Then, he hoped that the personal relationship he had developed with Stalin during the fighting would help resolve any differences over allied policy.[16]

Because Roosevelt remained preoccupied with military questions and wanted to avoid making political decisions during the war, he saw no need to take a final stand on the intragovernmental debates over German policy. Unfortunately, his death on April 12, 1945—less than a month before Germany's surrender—ended the personal relationship between the Soviet and American leaders and left the debates within the U.S. government unresolved.[17] Therefore, when Harry S. Truman assumed the presidency, the United States did not possess a clearly defined policy to govern the treatment of the defeated enemy or to guide relations with the allies.

As a result the revised occupation directive that was signed by President Truman on May 11, 1945 (JCS 1067/8), represented a series of bureaucratic compromises that reflected the uncoordinated nature of American thinking on Germany and provided uncertain policy guidance to the U.S. military governor in Germany, Lt. General Lucius Clay.[18] Moreover, the allies had yet to resolve important questions concerning coordination between the allied occupation zones, the level of German industry, the standard of living for the German people, partition, and reparations. These issues headed the agenda when Truman, Stalin, and the new British leadership of Prime Minister Clement Attlee and Foreign Minister Ernest Bevin met at Potsdam in late July and early August 1945.

The reparations issue was the key to the discussions, and after complicated negotiations the three allies were able to establish some general principles for the payment of reparations. In exchange for a provisional Anglo-American offer to recognize the Oder-Niesse line as the Polish-German frontier, the Soviets agreed to forego their demand for a fixed figure of $10 billion in reparations. Instead, the Russians could begin to meet their reparations claims through the removal of industrial goods from their own zone and through a complex system of transfers from the western zones. According to the final agreement at Potsdam, the Soviets were entitled to 10 percent of surplus "industrial capital equipment as is unnecessary for the German peace economy" and an additional 15 percent of such material "in exchange for an equivalent value of food, coal . . . and other commodities as may be agreed upon."[19]

Moreover, at Potsdam the allies decided to treat Germany as an "economic unit." This decision was supposed to lead to the creation of centralized allied agencies operating from Berlin under the general supervision of the Allied Control Council. A large part of the work of these agencies would be to facilitate reparations deliveries from the western zones in exchange for food deliveries from the Soviet zone and to maintain a standard of living throughout Germany "not exceeding the average of the standards of living of European countries" excluding the United Kingdom and the Soviet Union.[20]

Therefore, although none of the allies had expressed a strong commitment to the retention of a unified German state, the Potsdam reparations formula and the decision to treat Germany as an economic unit were important steps in that direction. However, the effectiveness of these arrangements was undermined by the so-called first charge principle.

The first charge concept was a legacy of the American belief that the U.S. taxpayer had been forced to finance German reparations payments after World War I through a series of loans designed to bolster the struggling German economy. Because of its desire to avoid a repetition of that experience and to protect the American taxpayer, the Truman administration insisted that the first charge on German production be used to pay for "essential and approved imports required for the German economy" rather than to provide reparations.[21] This provision, agreed to reluctantly by the Soviets, allowed the individual military governors to control the flow of goods from their own occupation zones and actually went counter to the decision to treat Germany as an economic unit.[22] The American willingness to increase the authority of the U.S. zonal commander at the expense of centralized allied agencies had already been made clear when, on July 29, 1945, President Truman instructed the military "to assume procurement and initial financing responsibilities" for imports into the U.S. zone "whether or not an agreed program is formulated and carried out by the Control Council."[23]

The contradictory nature of American policy toward Germany is thus apparent. On the one hand, the United States sought to prevent future German aggression by crippling the war-making capacity of German industry and by preserving the wartime alliance through the creation of centralized allied institutions that would administer Germany as an economic unit. On the other hand, in order to protect the American taxpayer, the United States favored a reparations policy that was dependent on the capacity of German industry to maintain a minimal standard of living for the German people, to finance necessary imports, and to meet

Soviet reparations claims. In addition the first charge principle insisted on by the Americans at Potsdam actually increased the authority of the American zonal commander at the expense of the Allied Control Council.

Consequently, it is no exaggeration to state that even after the Potsdam Conference American policies for Germany remained tenuous, vague, and uncoordinated. In addition, because of the initial emphasis given to treating Germany as an economic unit, U.S. policy for Germany remained dependent on reaching accord with the other allies. Moreover, the difficulties inherent in achieving agreement among the allies were increased by the presence of France as an occupying power and as a member of the Allied Control Council.

France, although nominally a victor during the war, had suffered a crushing defeat in 1940 and had endured a long and bitter occupation by German forces. The effects of the war and the occupation left France with a fragmented political system containing three main political parties: the Communists (who emerged as the largest political party in the first postwar elections),[24] the Socialists, and the Catholic *Mouvement Republicain Populaire*. The situation was further complicated in early 1946 when wartime hero and provisional president of France, General Charles de Gaulle, resigned from that office and began to develop his own political party, the right-wing *Rassamblement du Peuple Français*. One of the few things these parties could agree on was a harsh policy toward Germany.[25]

Despite the legacy of defeat and the splintering of political loyalties, France's chief aim was to return to the ranks of the great powers after the war, and in this effort the French were supported by both the United Kingdom and the United States. The latter was particularly anxious to restore France so that it might serve as a "bulwark of democracy" in Europe.[26] The French received symbolic evidence of their return to greatness at Yalta when the United Kingdom, the United States, and the Soviet Union agreed to give France a zone of occupation in Germany. This decision was crucial for the future of American policies toward western Europe.

Because of the unstable nature of the French political scene, the Fourth Republic was in constant danger of collapse from within. The American desire to restore France and to prevent such a collapse often meant that U.S. policies for Germany could be held hostage by French political instability. American decision makers constantly had to be on guard against pursuing German policies that could provoke dangerous political turmoil in Paris.[27] Moreover, the French were not invited to the Potsdam Conference, and they quickly registered their displeasure by blocking implementation of decisions taken by the British, Soviets, and Americans at that meeting.[28]

The chief motivation behind France's obstructionist approach to the Potsdam agreements was traditional French fear of a centralized Germany possessing the human and material resources capable of dominating Europe. Moreover, in the aftermath of World War II the French were doubly concerned that a centralized Germany would fall under Soviet tutelage and pose an even greater threat to the stability and security of western Europe. In order to prevent the resurgence of a menacing Germany—especially one within the Soviet sphere—French policy called for a lengthy occupation, heavy reparations, the detachment of the industrially rich areas of the Rhineland and Saar from Germany, and the internationalization of the Ruhr.[29]

Another reason for French intransigence was their bitter memory of the interwar period, when they felt abandoned by the U.S. refusal to participate in the League of Nations and subsequent political isolation from Europe. Again, since the League was supposed to prevent German militarism and contain the expansion of Soviet communism, the French felt doubly betrayed, which made them wary of accepting allied promises and policies without first ensuring that French security would be protected.[30]

A final reason for French obstinacy was their desire to receive substantial coal shipments from Germany in order to ensure the success of their economic recovery from the devastation of World War II. The United States indicated its support for this goal when, on July 26, 1945, in the midst of the Potsdam Conference, President Truman issued his famous coal directive to the U.S. Army. In his instructions Truman directed the American Occupation authorities "to make available for export out of the production of the coal mines in Western Germany a minimum of 10 million tons of coal during 1945, and a further 15 million tons by the end of April, 1946."[31]

The difficulties inherent in such a plan are obvious. Truman's directive meant that in addition to preventing a revival of German militarism, providing reparations for the Soviet Union, securing a minimum standard of living in the American zone, and paying for necessary imports, the army was supposed to ensure that German industry produced enough coal to promote French economic recovery. Of course, Truman's directive soon proved unworkable, and it is estimated that only 8.2 million tons out of the total 25 million were ever exported. As a result of their failure to receive the necessary coal from Germany, the French feared that German recovery would actually outstrip that of France, and throughout 1945 and 1946 they repeatedly criticized allied coal policies.[32]

Consequently, during the early months of the postwar era France remained the chief obstacle to the successful implementation of the Potsdam accords. The French used their seat on the Allied Control Council to veto all attempts at centralization and effectively blocked the creation of an economic unit in Germany. In addition, repeated efforts by General Lucius Clay (and others) to have the Truman administration pressure the French government into more cooperative policies usually had little effect: the State Department feared that too much pressure on the French over the serious German question might lead to the collapse of the Fourth Republic and a Communist takeover in Paris. Moreover, by February 1946 the U.S. government was beginning to view its problems in Germany in light of overall American-Soviet relations.[33]

Although the details of Soviet policy toward Germany are unknown, it is safe to say that their overall thinking, like that of the Americans, was evolutionary.[34] During the war Stalin had expressed some sympathy with plans to dismember Germany,[35] and it is likely that the Russians accepted the economic unity of Germany in exchange for the reparations formula and in the hopes that they might someday be able to incorporate Germany into the Soviet orbit. Some influential analysts in the State Department felt that the *de facto* western acceptance of the Oder-Niesse line, thus depriving Germany of valuable agricultural lands in eastern Prussia, would leave any future unified German state "seriously crippled and unbalanced economically, and psychologically extensively dependent in [the] first instance on the great land power to the east which controls or holds great food producing areas so necessary to [the] German economy."[36] Moreover, by 1946 it was becoming clear to American officials that the Soviets were taking advantage of French intransigence on the Control Council to consolidate their economic and political position in the eastern zone; it appeared probable that they were acting in collusion with the French Communists to prolong the Fourth Republic's internal difficulties and stubbornness on the German question.[37]

Indeed, early 1946 was marked by deteriorating relations between the Soviet Union and the West. On February 9 Stalin told a Soviet radio audience that armed conflict remained an inherent part of the western capitalist system and that future wars could be expected. Then, in a move likened to the "declaration of World War III," the Soviet leader put his country on war footing.[38] Shortly after Stalin's speech, on February 22, George Kennan sent his famous "long telegram" to Washington, which presented a dark picture of the motivations behind Soviet foreign policy and reinforced the growing suspicions in Washington that "you can't do business with the Kremlin."[39] Just over two weeks later, on March 9, Winston Churchill delivered his famous "Iron Curtain" speech at Fulton, Missouri, and according to at least one analyst, the cold war became a reality.[40]

Relations between the West and the Soviet Union continued to deteriorate throughout the year. Disputes over atomic energy and policies in the Near East, eastern Europe, and Asia drove the wartime allies apart. But nowhere were the growing splits more serious than in Germany.

In Germany the main issues were still centralization and reparations. The failure of the four powers to reach agreement on the creation of an economic unit in Germany meant that the Potsdam reparations formula became a dead letter. As the allies deliberated, the Soviets continued to consolidate power in their own zone by stripping the area of its industry and by creating a "rubber stamp" political party through a forced amalgamation of the Social Democrats and the Communists.[41] Meanwhile, they continued to demand $10 billion in reparations from Germany and, in the absence of four power agreement on centralized agencies, withheld food shipments to the western zones.[42] Moreover, in early April 1946 the Soviets refused to implement a common export-import plan for Germany that would have helped ease a growing food shortage in the U.S. and British zones.[43] The deteriorating situation in Germany finally led U.S. Secretary of State James Byrnes to bring matters to a head at the Paris Foreign Ministers Conference.

On April 29, in an effort to force the hands of both the French and the Soviets, Byrnes proposed to the conference a four power treaty that would ensure the disarmament of Germany for a twenty-five-year period.[44] While there would be no official Soviet reply until July 1946, Soviet Foreign Minister V. M. Molotov's initial, unofficial response was that the demilitarization of Germany could not be assured until reparations deliveries had been completed.[45] However, shortly thereafter General Clay made a momentous decision of his own.

On May 2, 1946, Clay ordered a halt to the dismantling of German plants in the American zone and discontinued the shipment of reparations to the Soviets until centralized agencies had been established in Germany.[46] His decision must be viewed in light of several considerations, including the following: the failure of the four powers to reach agreement on the administration of Germany as an economic unit, the failure of the American zone to receive food shipments from the Soviet zone, the army's need to import food and other essential commodities from the United states, the inability of the U.S. zone to pay for those imports because of conflicting restrictions and demands on German industries, and the increased burden being placed on the American taxpayer to support the occupation. In short, Clay's move was administrative, made by a hard-pressed officer in the face of frustrating dealings with the allies, deteriorating economic conditions in the U.S. zone, and unclear policy guidance from Washington.[47] Although his decision did not necessarily preclude four power accord in the future, it signaled the army's abandonment of repressive economic policies in favor of rehabilitation, and it did have far-reaching implications for the future division of Germany.[48]

A major break in four power relations occurred on July 9, 1946, when Soviet Foreign Minister Molotov rejected Byrnes's four power treaty proposal. Molotov's chief objection to the treaty remained that the demilitarization of Germany could not be assured without the completion of reparations shipments.[49] The rejection of the four power treaty by the Soviets after a two-month delay and their continued demands for $10 billion in reparations meant further delay in reaching accord on economic unity and had an immediate impact on the British.

Throughout the postwar period the British Labour government of Prime Minister Clement Attlee and Foreign Minister Ernest Bevin had been in general accord with U.S. thinking on Germany.[50] However, the effects of the war found the British hard-pressed financially. In order to help the United Kingdom through the postwar economic crisis, the United States had extended the British a $3.75 billion loan in late 1945, but by the end of 1946 inflation had largely wiped out the effects of the American effort.[51] Moreover, the efforts of the Labour government to build a welfare state in Britain were being seriously hampered by the high costs of the German occupation. Like the American zone, the British zone was heavily industrialized and was supposed to depend on food imports from the Soviet zone to sustain a minimal standard of living for the population. Yet in the absence of four power accord the food had to be imported from overseas. As was the case in the U.S. zone this placed a heavy load on the British taxpayer, a load the British government was reluctant to ask its citizens to bear.[52] Therefore, following rejection of the four power treaty, Ernest Bevin informed the other allies that the British would be forced to "organize the British zone" and "to produce for export in order to reduce the burden on the British taxpayer."[53]

In order to salvage the possibility of four power agreement, Byrnes immediately called for the other powers to merge their zones with the U.S. zone, but only the British—after considerable thought—accepted.[54] The British and American occupation forces then began working on the institutional arrangements for "Bizonia" (as the Anglo-American zonal fusion was called), which was to come into existence on January 1, 1947, marking the first concrete step to the division of Germany, as well as an intensification of the cold war. A further step in these directions was taken when Byrnes, after consulting with political, diplomatic, and military leaders in Washington, spoke in Stuttgart, Germany, on September 6, 1946.

In his speech Byrnes announced a new U.S. policy for Germany: "If complete unification cannot be secured, we shall do everything in our power to secure maximum possible unification." Byrnes also said that "it is the view of the American Government that the German people throughout Germany, under proper safeguards, should now be given the primary responsibility for the running of their own affairs."[55] In addition, Byrnes indicated that American occupation forces would remain in Germany "for a long period." This statement was critically important in that it involved a major shift in American occupation policy. Originally, American troops were to remain in Germany for approximately two years. However, with Byrnes's statement at Stuttgart it is apparent that the United States was considering a much longer presence for American forces. As John Backer has commented: "The barrier of the Atlantic thus seemed removed and the future of the United States effectively tied to that of Western Europe."[56] While the implications of the linkage between the stationing of American troops in Germany and the American commitment to western Europe were not fully realized until much later, it is important to note that the linkage existed as early as 1946.

Not only was the question of Germany an increasing source of inter-national tension, but also there were strong internal pressures for a resolu-tion of the German problem. The army had long been frustrated in its dealings with the allies and was extremely unhappy with the growing costs and length of the occupation. In addition, the eightieth Congress was beginning to take a hard look at the continuing U.S. responsibilities in Germany.

The 1946 elections returned Republican majorities to both the House and the Senate, and the budget-conscious GOP was anxious to reduce the costs of America's overseas responsibilities. A priority target for reduc-tion was, naturally, the occupation, and many Republican voices were added to those calling for a German policy aimed at the rehabilitation of the former enemy. The Republican argument received ammunition when, in February 1947, former President Herbert Hoover went on a fact-finding mission to Bizonia. After a survey of the situation in the joint zone, Hoover concluded that the "combined zones should proceed immediately to 'build a self-sustaining economic community.' "[57] Hoover's report found immediate favor with the army, as well as with many Republicans in Con-gress. Moreover, because the Republicans hoped to win the White House in the 1948 elections, their attacks assumed added importance.

By early 1947 the rapidly deteriorating situation in Germany was call-ing for a redefinition of American thinking. However, the uncertainty over German policy that had clouded American thinking since the war years still remained. Although many, including the newly appointed secretary of state, General George C. Marshall,[58] were beginning to think that the division of Germany might be the only solution to the German question,[59] further attempts at obtaining four power agreement would shortly be made.

The so-called critical conference on Germany was held in Moscow from March 10 to April 24, 1947 with each of the foreign ministers of the occupying powers present. Marshall was not optimistic about the conference's chances for success; indeed, his fears were confirmed, as the conference failed to resolve the crucial issues that had deadlocked the war-time allies for so long. While some progress was made with the French on the question of the Saar, the reparations questions that split the Anglo-Americans and the Russians proved too difficult to resolve.[60]

With the failure of the Moscow Conference, the allies moved toward the final division of Germany. Yet even before the meeting began, two events occurred that had important implications for the future course of American foreign policy. One of these events was Secretary Marshall's meeting with French leaders in Paris; the other was the announcement of the Truman Doctrine.

While on his way to Moscow, Marshall stopped in Paris to confer with French President Vincent Auriol and other French officials on the German question. Marshall was informed of French concerns about the economic troubles France was experiencing due to their failure to receive adequate shipments of coal from Germany. Unless the French could receive an increased coal allotment from the mines in Germany, French recovery from the war would suffer. They were especially fearful that American plans to create a self-sustaining Bizonia might actually allow German recovery to precede that of France and the other countries of western Europe. The French regarded this as extremely unfair and indicated that the political situation in western Europe was dominated by the issue of Franco-German relations. However, the French informed Marshall that if they could receive satisfaction on the coal issue they would find it easier to support the United States on other problems concerning Germany.[61]

As a result of these conversations Marshall was fully apprised of French economic problems and fears of German domination. In addition it became clear to Marshall that French economic recovery was closely linked to the productive capacity of western Germany's coal industries. Yet, the French feared that the strength of those industries alone would permit western Germany to dominate the rest of western Europe. This meant that, even if the four powers failed to reach agreement at Moscow, concessions still would have to be made to French economic and security interests. Indeed, these concerns did much to shape the American commitment to western Europe through the Marshall Plan, the North Atlantic Treaty, and NATO. However, the first steps in this direction came as a result of events in the Near East and the subsequent Truman Doctrine.

The Truman Doctrine

On Friday, February 21, 1947, the first secretary of the British embassy in Washington, Herbert Sichel, called on Loy Henderson, director of the Office of Near Eastern and African Affairs of the State Department, and presented him with two *aides-mémoire* regarding Britain's position in Greece and Turkey. Briefly, the two documents stated that after April 1, 1947, the United Kingdom would no longer be able to assist the Greek monarchy in its civil war against Communist insurgents nor would it be able to aid Turkey in modernizing its army and resisting Soviet political pressure.[62]

The contents of the *aides-mémoire* were immediately transmitted to Acting Secretary of State Dean Acheson and through Acheson to Secretary of State Marshall and on to President Truman. Henderson and Acheson immediately began work on a plan designed to meet the emergency in Greece and Turkey, and when their proposal was presented to Marshall and Truman the following Monday, it was decided to ask Congress for a "full scale program."[63]

The flurry of activity in Washington after receipt of the *aides-mémoire* is somewhat surprising, considering the fact that the U.S. government was well aware of the deteriorating military and economic situation in Greece, and since October 1946 had expressed (at least in principle) a willingness to assist the British "if His Majesty's Government were unable to supply the essential requirements."[64] Moreover, American reactions to meeting the Soviet challenges in Iran and Turkey in 1946 demonstrated the administration's awareness of the strategic importance of the Near East and the implications of a Communist victory in Greece.

However, given the policy implications of the Kennan telegram and the Clifford memorandum, it was clear that the American response to the British *aides-mémoire* would have a significance far beyond the immediate situations in Greece and Turkey. In short, the real significance of the *aides-mémoire* was that they forced the Truman administration to articulate a new foreign policy for the United States, one that was compatible with the changed nature of the international environment and with increased American responsibilities in the postwar world.[65]

Any new policy developed in response to the British notes had to fulfill three essential requirements: first, it had to meet the immediate needs of Greece and Turkey; second, it had to win the support of Congress and the American people; third, it had to reflect the wider requirements of an expanded American role in world affairs. The first problem was, relatively speaking, the easiest to solve. More difficulty was inherent in the second and third requirements because a policy envisioning greater responsibilities on the part of the United States might not win domestic support. Clearly, if any new U.S. foreign policy was to be successful, the support of the American people would be required, and as David McLellan has

written, "if the American people were to be supportive, a deliberate appeal
had to be made to their moral as well as to their intellectual sense."[66]

The first step taken by the administration to win the support of the
American people was a meeting at the White House of congressional
leaders and President Truman, Secretary of State Marshall, and Dean
Acheson. Marshall, who would soon leave for the Moscow Conference,
spoke first. But apparently his efforts did not convey the force necessary
to create the proper effect on the congressmen.[67]

After the secretary finished, Acheson asked for the floor and spoke in
"ominous" terms, dividing the world into free and totalitarian camps and
emphasizing the strategic importance of Greece and Turkey to three
continents. Acheson was especially mindful of the worsening situation
in western Europe where the large Communist parties in France and Italy
were posing serious internal threats to the governments of those countries.
He drove home the point that the collapse of Greece and Turkey would
damage the morale of prowestern elements in Europe and would seriously threaten the economic recovery of that area.[68] Therefore, at least in
its initial form, the American concern about the Near East developed in
response to a desire to stabilize the situation in western Europe and cannot
be separated from evolving American policies on the continent.[69]

Unlike Marshall's talk, Acheson's appeal had the desired effect on the
congressmen, and Senator Arthur H. Vandenberg (R.-Mich.), chairman
of the Senate Foreign Relations Committee, assured those present that
he would support the administration's effort to deal with the situation.[70]
However, his subsequent statement that it was necessary to "scare the
Hell out of the American people" ultimately meant that the president's
speech to Congress would emphasize the ideological rather than the
strategic aspects of Acheson's exposition to the congressional leaders.

The speech was prepared by the State-War-Navy-Coordinating Committee and, looking toward the public opinion aspect of the moment,
by the Office of Public Affairs of the State Department. An examination
of Truman's speech demonstrates the emphasis given to the "emotional"
aspects of the situation.

Truman addressed the Congress on March 12, 1947, and his speech
incorporated many ideological themes. According to the president, the
world was fast being divided into two opposing camps, freedom was being threatened, and it was up to the United States to defend freedom
whenever that threat occurred. Specifically, the president stated that each
country in the world faced a choice "between alternative ways of life"

and that the choice "all too often is not a free one." Truman then proclaimed his belief "that it must be the policy of the United States to support free peoples who are resisting attempted subjugation by armed minorities or by outside pressure." He closed his address by asking Congress to appropriate $400 million to aid Greece and Turkey and to dispatch "American civilian and military personnel to Greece and Turkey . . . to assist in the tasks of reconstruction, and for the purpose of supervising the use of such financial and material assistance as may be furnished."[71]

By speaking of a world divided into free and totalitarian camps, and by seeking authorization to provide assistance to those countries resisting totalitarian encroachment, Truman set the tone for American foreign policy during the early postwar years: the policy of "containment" of Soviet communism. It was because of the speech's wide-ranging policy implications, reflecting the desire of Acheson and others within the administration for the United States to be more active in its foreign policy *vis-à-vis* the Soviet Union, that Truman's address received so much attention

By and large support for the administration's decision was forthcoming from a wide cross section of the American political spectrum, with only the ideologues of the extreme right and left offering sustained public protest. In this regard Dean Acheson was able to write that "[w]e were fortunate in our enemies."[72] However, if the administration was fortunate in enemies, there were several influential figures who, although generally supportive of a more active foreign policy, were critical of the tone of Truman's speech.

The question of just what the Truman Doctrine did imply for American foreign policy was a vexing one for many people concerned with the decision-making process. Not only did the decision to send American military personnel and assistance to the Near East raise questions about bypassing the United Nations[73] and extending an American commitment to Greece and Turkey,[74] but the universal language used by Truman also opened the administration to heavy criticism.

Chief among the influential critics of Truman's wording was George Kennan, the soon-to-be-appointed director of the State Department's Policy Planning Staff. Although Kennan—because of his "long telegram" and "Mr. X" article in *Foreign Affairs*—has been called one of the architects of the "containment policy," he has subsequently, through the publication of his *Memoirs,* downplayed his role in shaping American policy during the early postwar years. Kennan also has aired specific disagreements with many of the actions taken at that time and has been especially critical of the Truman Doctrine. Specifically, Kennan objected to the "universal language" of Truman's speech and to the "sweeping nature of the commitments which it implied." In addition he did not feel that the situation warranted the inclusion of Turkey in the assistance program.[75]

George Kennan was not alone among high State Department officials who reacted against the language of Truman's speech. Secretary of State Marshall, who, with Charles Bohlen, was in Paris at the time preparing for the Moscow Foreign Ministers Conference on Germany, also expressed concern. According to Bohlen, both he and Marshall were "somewhat startled" by the ideological tone of Truman's speech, and Marshall sent a telegram to the president suggesting that Truman "was overstating the case a bit."[76] Kennan also argues that even Acheson felt the language of the speech "might be subject to misinterpretation." To support this view, Kennan maintains that much of the testimony given by administration witnesses before the Senate Foreign Relations Committee was designed to dispel such thinking.[77]

The record of the Foreign Relations Committee hearings does in fact indicate that Acheson and other administration officials stressed that similar requests from other countries would be handled on their individual merits.[78] This effort to move away from the global implications of the Truman Doctrine supports the view that the real aim of U.S. assistance to Greece and Turkey was to help stabilize the situation in western Europe. The link between the two areas was, in fact, the only valid reason Kennan saw for the approval of aid to Greece, and John Lewis Gaddis has argued that by making that link the Truman administration was backing away from the global implications of the Truman Doctrine toward a "less ambitious . . . [goal] of restoring the balance of power in Europe."[79]

This more limited view of the Truman Doctrine has recently, and correctly, received increased scholarly attention. Because of the strategic importance of Greece and Turkey to western Europe, Robert Art has argued that "[t]he Truman Doctrine was the first postwar manifestation of the domino theory." In Art's view the Truman administration felt that the collapse of Greece and Turkey would have opened the Near East to Soviet penetration and would have threatened the supply of oil from the Middle East to western Europe. Moreover, the failure of the United States to support Greece and Turkey would have strengthened the Communist parties in France and Italy and would have led to the "detachment" of western Europe from the United States and European accommodation to the policies of the Soviet Union. Therefore, according to

Art, "[t]he aid to Greece and Turkey embodied in the Truman Doctrine was thus aimed at influencing political developments in Western Europe."[80]

This view is supported by the fact that when Truman did speak in strategic terms on March 12 he emphasized the importance of the Near East to western Europe. Truman pointed out that if Greece fell it "would have a profound effect upon those countries in Europe whose peoples are struggling against great difficulties to maintain their freedoms and their independence while they repair the damages of war." If the European countries failed, Truman said it would be "an unspeakable tragedy": "If we fail to aid Greece and Turkey in this fateful hour, the effect will be far reaching to the West as well as to the East."[81]

However, despite the clear linkage of aid to Greece and Turkey and the situation in Europe, and the clear intention of the administration to meet specific situations as they arose, Kennan argues with some force that "the misapprehension already conveyed . . . was never entirely corrected."[82] Kennan's position is borne out by the attitudes of several members of the Foreign Relations Committee who, although they supported the bill providing aid to Greece and Turkey, had serious questions about the implications of Truman's speech.

On April 3, 1947, the day that the Foreign Relations Committee issued its unanimous report in favor of S.938, several senators expressed their concern about the ramifications of the action they were taking. Senator Henry Cabot Lodge (R.-Mass.) warned against the creation of a crusade or the waging of a "holy war" against the Soviet Union. However, while he felt that he was on "the horns of a dilemma" about the Truman Doctrine, he believed that the "forces of history" compelled him to go along with the administration's program.[83] Senator Alexander Wiley (R.-Wisc.) had similar reservations. He felt that the Truman Doctrine put the United States "at the crossroads" and expressed his hope that America would "take the right road," not just on the question of Greece, "but in comprehending the whole picture. . . ."[84]

Perhaps the most cogent criticism of the bill came from Senator Walter George (D.-Georgia), who shared the concerns of Lodge and Wiley. While George said that he would support the bill, he predicted that other countries would soon be making similar requests and that the United States was irrevocably committing itself to a course of action. He warned that the United States would not be able to get out of its new role "next week or next year" and that it would have to "go down to the end of the road."[85]

It is therefore apparent that the proposed aid package to Greece and Turkey was not the issue of fundamental importance. The Truman Doctrine was significant because it heralded a new role for American foreign policy. Just what the new role for the United States would entail remained unclear. Certainly, the containment of communism was a factor, but so too were questions relating to the shape and structure of future commitments, to the relatively weak military posture of the United States, and to the balance of power in Europe. And it was this last factor that, in light of subsequent events, emerged as the most enduring legacy of the Truman Doctrine. The strategic importance of the Mediterranean to western Europe, Truman's speech, and Marshall's experiences in Europe and at the Moscow Conference combined to focus American attention on the need to restore western Europe as a factor in the East-West balance of power.[86]

Yet throughout March and April 1947, it was still unclear just how the United States would respond to the series of events surrounding the Truman Doctrine. According to Dean Acheson, Joseph Jones described the general feeling of the time as follows:

> All were aware that a major turning point in history was taking place. The convergence of massive historical trends upon the moment was so real as to be almost tangible, and it was plain that in the carrefour of time all those trends were to some degree deflected.[87]

From the Truman Doctrine to the Marshall Plan

The extent to which the future course of American foreign policy remained uncertain is best illustrated by the workings of various government officials from early March 1947 until Secretary of State Marshall's return from Moscow later that April. Activity within the U.S. government was initiated by Under Secretary of State Dean Acheson on March 5, 1947 and increased in tempo after Truman's speech one week later.

As noted earlier, Acheson was intimately connected with the American response to the British notes of February 21, and now he wished to know if there were other areas "in the world which may require analogous financial, technical and military action on our part." On March 5 Acheson wrote to Secretary of War Robert Patterson and Secretary of the Navy

James Forrestal suggesting that the Greek-Turkish situation was "only a part of a much larger problem" and asking for their views on the matter.[88] In addition, he also instructed Assistant Secretary of State John Hilldring, who headed the State-War-Navy-Coordinating Committee, to initiate a study designed to determine the aid requirements of other areas throughout the world.[89]

March 5 was also the date on which Will Clayton, undersecretary of state for economic affairs, wrote the first of two memoranda setting down his views on important problems facing the United States. According to Clayton, Britain was fast losing the "reins of world leadership," and either the United States or the Soviet Union would soon pick up those reins. He felt that if the Soviets assumed world leadership there would be a war within ten years, with the odds against the United States. The only hope was for the United States to assume a leadership role, but he felt that it would not do so unless the American people were shocked into such action. Clayton was particularly concerned about the threat posed to countries throughout the world by Communist-inspired internal subversion. He pointed to the situation in Greece and Turkey and stated that if they succumbed the whole Middle East would fall, Communists would likely take over in France, and all of western Europe and North Africa would follow in France's wake. Moreover, he predicted that the Moscow Foreign Ministers Conference would not yield any constructive results on the German question.[90]

In order to resolve these disturbing problems, Clayton had specific recommendations. He felt that the United States should assume world leadership and that, after his return from Moscow, Marshall should join with Truman to provide the necessary shocks to public opinion. In addition the United States should begin financial, administrative, and technical assistance to "gravely threatened countries." Furthermore, Clayton felt that Congress should create a "Council of National Defense" and should appropriate to the council $5 billion for foreign assistance programs designed to protect the vital interests of the United States.[91]

What is interesting about Clayton's memorandum is that it called for strong and positive action on the part of the U.S. government in response to a pattern of deteriorating relations with the Soviet Union. As would be the case with the Truman Doctrine, Clayton envisaged that congressional action would be necessary to appropriate the necessary funds to inaugurate his program. The memorandum was also similar to the logic of the Truman Doctrine in that it linked together Greece and Turkey, the Middle East, and the deteriorating situation in Europe. This last point supports the view that the major thrust of American policies in that era was aimed at restoring the balance of power by rehabilitating western Europe. However, the initial report of the State-War-Navy-Coordinating Committee failed to come to grips with the magnitude of the problems facing western Europe and lacked the precision of Clayton's document.

The study of the Coordinating Committee received its impetus from Acheson's March 5 inquiries, and shortly thereafter a subcommittee was formed to "give immediate attention to the problems incident to possible requests which may be made to the United States by foreign governments for substantial economic, financial, or technical assistance, or for military equipment." Moreover, the subcommittee was asked to determine "the relevant considerations of United States national security and interest which should govern the decision in the case of each country. . . ."[92]

When the subcommittee's work was completed on April 21, 1947, the authors took pains to emphasize that the report was based on "hasty analysis" of the "information presently at hand" and was "highly tentative in nature."[93] According to John Gimbel, the Coordinating Committee document represented "a hodgepodge of observations, recommendations, suggestions, and conclusions that the Committee itself felt to be lacking in thorough analysis."[94] While the report did recommend the immediate extension of assistance to Italy and France "for political and not economic reasons,"[95] it is apparent that the Coordinating Committee understood neither the extent to which Europe had been economically devastated during the war nor the ramifications of that devastation on European and American security. In addition the report did not come to grips with the importance of the German question to the general European situation and did not discuss any future role for Germany in U.S. assistance programs. As a result the original report made only "modest" contributions to the European Recovery Program.[96] However, Secretary of State Marshall's return from Moscow at the end of April 1947 did help to focus American attention on the problems of Germany and Europe.

The failure of the Moscow Conference to achieve four power agreement on Germany had immediate consequences for American foreign policy. While in Moscow, Marshall experienced firsthand the difficulties in dealing with the Soviets on the reparations issue, became aware of the economic and political difficulties facing the countries of western Europe, and after his talks with the French, realized the importance of Germany to European recovery and security.[97] Because of the allies' inability to agree on centralized agencies, on the status of a provisional German government, or on the strength of the German economy, the United States decided to move ahead on those questions in Bizonia. Accordingly, before Marshall and Bevin returned to their respective capitals, they instructed Clay and British zone commander General Brian Robertson to raise the level of industry in the bizonal area and to undertake reforms designed to centralize Bizonia's administrative structure.[98] Of course, this meant that the United States was accepting indefinitely the division of Germany and the presence of American occupation troops on German soil.[99]

Immediately following his return from Moscow, Marshall made a radio address to the country on the implications of the situation in Germany and Europe. He noted the inability of the four powers to resolve their differences on Germany and then linked that failure to the recovery and security of western Europe. Apparently, Marshall was aware of the need to restore west German industrial strength in order to ensure the economic recovery of Europe and was sensitive to the fears such a move would create among Germany's recent enemies.

Marshall told the nation that the German negotiations involved questions of European peace and prosperity and of world security. He reported that, although his mission had been to consider a long-term German peace treaty, there were immediate concerns facing "the impoverished and suffering people of Europe who are crying for help, for coal, for food, and for most of the necessities of life, and the majority of whom are bitterly disposed towards the Germany that brought about this disastrous situation." He said that these immediate questions were of vital importance to the people of the United States and the United Kingdom, who could not continue to support a German occupation where "current measures were not being taken to terminate expeditiously the necessity for such appropriations."[100]

Specifically, he stated that the failure of the allies (especially the Soviets) to establish a balanced German economy "[was] the most serious check on the development of a self-supporting Germany capable of providing coal and other necessities for the neighboring states who have always been dependent on Germany for these items."[101]

He then told the American people that the rehabilitation of German industry was necessary to guarantee that the other countries of western Europe would receive coal supplies from German mines to ensure their own recovery from the war. But, he added, while German recovery was progressing, "less coal would be available in the immediate future for the neighboring allied states."[102] Although he understood that this was of great concern to the other countries of western Europe, especially to France, and that it heightened fears of German militarism, he pointed out the political dangers of prolonged economic dislocation and urged action. In Marshall's words: "The patient is sinking while the doctors deliberate. . . . New issues arise daily. Whatever action is possible to meet these pressing problems must be taken without delay."[103]

Marshall spoke to the country on April 28, and on the following day he instructed George Kennan and the newly created Policy Planning Staff of the State Department to prepare a paper on European recovery. Looking at Marshall's directions from an historical perspective, John Gimbel has argued that the secretary of state was seeking "recommendations on how to implement the decision he had already made at Moscow [the agreement with the British on Bizonia] ; on how to do so without upsetting the European economic and political system, without upsetting France."[104] Again, it is clear that Marshall was aware of the importance of Germany to the economic recovery of Europe, yet acutely sensitive to increased French demands for coal and security against a revival of German aggression.[105]

April 29, 1947 also witnessed the completion of a remarkable document on U.S. assistance programs prepared by the Joint Chiefs of Staff— JCS 1769/1.[106] The Joint Chiefs, arguing from a military-strategic viewpoint, stressed the importance of western Europe to the security of the United States and maintained that in a future "ideological war" the United States would have to utilize the resources of the countries of the "Old World," which were "potentially powerful and also potential allies of the United States."[107] The Joint Chiefs pointed out the fact that two world wars had demonstrated the interdependence of the United States and western Europe in case of war with central or eastern European powers, and they maintained that the western countries were "in mortal peril" if they did not unite their forces.[108] By linking U.S. security to that of western Europe, the Joint Chiefs emphasized the growing concept of *Atlantic* security.

The Joint Chiefs' military-strategic viewpoint also helps to explain their assignment of high priority to the recovery of Germany and their criticism of the earlier Coordinating Committee report's failure to include

Germany and Japan on its assistance list.[109] Arguing that "the decisive diplomatic conflict between . . . Russia and . . . the West is taking place in Germany" and that western Europe could not hope to defend itself successfully against the Soviet Union without German participation, the Joint Chiefs' paper called for a "drastic change" in the western economic policies for Germany.[110] In calling for a revision of economic policies toward Germany, the Chiefs linked German economic recovery to that of France, whose security was "inseparable from the combined security of the United States, Canada, and Great Britain." According to the Joint Chiefs: "The economic revival of Germany is therefore of primary importance from the viewpoint of United States security."[111]

Finally, the Joint Chiefs addressed an issue of particular concern to the army: the high cost of the occupation. They cited Herbert Hoover's report that the estimated cost of the U.S. and British occupation would reach $950 million by July 1948 and urged the economic recovery of Germany in order to relieve that burden.[112]

Although the Joint Chiefs' emphasis on the Soviet military threat was at variance with the predominant perception that the main threat to Europe was political and not military, their linking of U.S. security to that of western Europe and their calls for a revision of German policy would soon become preeminent themes in American foreign policy.

Questions concerning European economic recovery and west Germany's role in that recovery did begin to receive increased attention when Dean Acheson, substituting for President Truman, delivered an important foreign policy address to the Delta Council in Cleveland, Mississippi on May 7, 1947. In his speech Acheson maintained that the potentially disastrous situation in Europe (and Asia) was due in large part to the failure of German (and Japanese) postwar recovery, which he linked specifically to the "lack of a peace settlement." The under secretary therefore called for the United States "to push ahead with the reconstruction of those two great workshops of Europe and Asia—Germany and Japan— upon which ultimate recovery of the two continents so largely depends."[113]

Acheson then drew on Marshall's April 28 speech, stating that European recovery remained "a fundamental objective" of American foreign policy, that rehabilitation of the European economies could not take place until "the various parts . . . are working together as a harmonious whole," and that the United States had to move ahead quickly—even without four power agreement—"to effect a larger measure of European, including German, recovery."[114] In his conclusion Acheson said that the U.S. government would be seeking congressional authorizations for "executive powers to deal with the situation in Europe" and linked the recovery of the continent to the security of the United States.[115] However, it remained for the Policy Planning Staff to work out a method whereby German recovery would be integrated into a more general plan for European recovery.

The Policy Planning Staff began its work on May 7, 1947, and on May 16 Kennan reported to Acheson outlining the preliminary work of the group. Kennan's memorandum stated that while the work of the Coordinating Committee was directed toward an analysis of "possible American assistance in all areas," the Policy Planning Staff confined itself to western Europe because "the character and outcome of the action we are going to take with relation to western Europe will have overwhelming implications for policy elsewhere."[116]

When the Policy Planning Staff's report was completed on May 23, it divided Europe's problems into short- and long-term questions, proposing solutions that emphasized the importance of including German recovery in a more comprehensive European recovery project. In attacking the short-term problems the staff attached "great importance" to identifying certain bottlenecks in western Europe's economic pattern and then to applying "the full weight of this Government on the breaking of those bottlenecks. . . ." The Policy Planning Staff then stated that "[t]he production of coal in the Rhine Valley and its movement to the places of consumption in Europe has suggested itself as the most suitable object of such action."[117]

By emphasizing the importance of the Rhine Valley's production and subsequent export of coal, the report clearly placed German recovery in the wider context of European recovery and established Germany—in the words of a second Policy Planning Staff report dated June 2, 1947— as "[the] most important element in [the] program."[118]

Moreover, the long-term solution proposed by the staff stated that the European countries themselves should draw up any recovery program. The motivation for this seems to be twofold: first, such a plan would help the administration to avoid congressional criticism that it was planning to commit additional American resources to a recovery program for

Europe;[119] second, it was clear that, by allowing Germany's former
enemies to design the recovery project, German recovery would not be
allowed to outstrip that of the rest of western Europe.[120]

The initial report of the Policy Planning Staff urged that the implications of the Truman Doctrine should be clarified before undertaking any
new programs. The Planning Staff warned against implications about the
association of American foreign policy with a "defensive reaction to communist pressure" or with the concept of a "blank check" for "economic
and military aid to any area in the world where the communists show
signs of being successful."[121] The Planning Staff argued that the United
States could correct this view in its European aid program by directing
its assistance "not to the combatting of communism as such but to the
restoration of the economic health and vigor of European society."[122]

On May 29, 1947, Secretary Marshall accepted an invitation to address
the commencement exercises at Harvard University on June 5. The last
major input to his speech was Will Clayton's second memorandum, which
was written in late May shortly after his return from a fact-finding mission
to Europe. Clayton opened his memorandum by stating that the United
States had "grossly underestimated the destruction to the European economy by the war."[123] He then pinpointed the central problem for the
United States: the political situation merely reflected the deteriorating
economic situation in Europe. Clayton stressed that without immediate
and substantial American aid, the economic, political, and social fabric
of Europe would disintegrate.[124] He pointed out the disastrous effect
this would have on the American economy and called for the extension
of $6 to $7 billion of aid per year to Europe for a period of three years.
He also felt that the Europeans should undertake some type of federation in order to facilitate recovery but stressed the fact—and thus differed
completely with Kennan and the Policy Planning Staff—that "the United
States must run this show."[125]

When Marshall spoke on June 5 he incorporated elements from all the
information available and indicated the general direction in which he
wished to move; yet he offered no specific solution to the problems faced
by western Europe. Although he noted that recovery had "been seriously
retarded" by the failure to conclude peace treaties with Germany and
Austria, he made no mention of the role Germany would play in the
general program for European recovery. While he spoke of the link between the European and American economic systems and indicated that

the United States would have a large role in aiding European recovery, he emphasized that the initiative "must come from Europe." In moving away from the implications of the Truman Doctrine, he maintained that U.S. policy was "directed not against any country or doctrine, but against hunger, poverty, deprivation and chaos." Yet he warned that "governments, political parties, or groups which seek to perpetuate human misery in order to profit therefrom politically or otherwise will encounter the opposition of the United States." Moreover, he expressed the seriousness of the U.S. government's interest in European recovery by stating that American assistance should "not be on a piecemeal basis," but "should provide a cure rather than a mere palliative."[126]

In essence, all that emerged from the generalities of Marshall's speech was that American foreign policy was going to give first priority to the recovery of western Europe as the area of the world most vital to the interests of the United States. As the program for European reconstruction was being developed and formalized during the next few months, it became increasingly clear that if the United States wished the program to be successful, America would have to involve itself progressively in European affairs, not just in the context of the cold war or simply in economic matters, but also in the more traditional and complicated European political system. Specifically, in order to help restore Europe, the United States would have to consider becoming involved in the European balance of power. Curiously enough, a formula that would aid the United States in that involvement was developed in Brazil during the summer of 1947: the Inter-American Treaty of Reciprocal Assistance—the Rio Pact.

The Inter-American Treaty

The Inter-American Treaty of Reciprocal Assistance was developed as an outgrowth of the American experience during World War II when it became evident that the inviolability of the Western Hemisphere could no longer be assured. This reawakened sense of hemispheric insecurity led to the first legal endorsement of the Monroe Doctrine with the Act of Havana in July 1940[127] and a further formalization of regional arrangements through the Act of Chapultepec in March 1945. Moreover, the Act of Chapultepec looked forward to increased institutionalization of hemispheric defense through the conclusion of a multilateral treaty recognizing the signatories as a "regional arrangement" and through the establishment of procedures whereby "such threats or acts [of aggression] may be met by the use of all or some of the signatories of said treaty of any one or more of the following measures . . . [including] the use of armed force to prevent or repel aggression."[128]

On August 15, 1947, the Inter-American Conference for the Maintenance of Continental Peace and Security convened in Rio de Janeiro, Brazil, to develop the treaty proposed in the Act of Chapultepec. The resulting Inter-American Treaty of Reciprocal Assistance was signed on September 2, 1947. The Rio Pact contained many provisions that were later incorporated into the North Atlantic Treaty and may therefore be viewed as a model for the Atlantic Alliance. However, the Rio Treaty contained no provision for military assistance during peacetime, and when such an article was included in the North Atlantic Treaty, it proved to be a major stumbling block for the administration during the Senate debates in the summer of 1949.

Article 3 of the Rio Pact dealt with the duties of each of the American states in the event of an act of armed aggression. Under the provisions of this article, each American state would regard an armed attack against another American state as "an attack against all American states, and consequently . . . to assist in meeting the attack in the exercise of the inherent right of individual and collective self defense recognized by Article 51 of the Charter of the United Nations." Paragraph 2 of this article provided a caveat for the signatories by stating that "each of the Contracting Parties may determine the immediate measures which it may individually take in fulfillment of the obligations contained in the preceding paragraph and in accordance with the principle of continental solidarity."[129] In this sense the automatic use of armed force by a signatory to help repel an attack on another signatory was not required, as each country was free to determine the nature of its individual response. Moreover, this article did not distinguish between attacks made by parties to the treaty or by nonparties. The obligation remained the same in both cases.[130]

Article 4 delimited the area to be covered by the treaty. The concept of a "well defined geographic zone within which the treaty would be operative" was considered to be an "important new idea" incorporated to help the Latin American parties "understand better the extent of their obligations." This article was included at the insistence of several Latin American countries that were supported by Senator Arthur Vandenberg, who in his capacity as chairman of the Senate Foreign Relations Committee, served on the U.S. delegation to Rio and felt that "it would not be just to expect Latin American states automatically to become involved if United States forces should become engaged *anywhere* in the world."[131] This was, of course, an implicit recognition of the fact that the security interests of the United States transcended the Western Hemisphere, while those of the other signatories would be more local.

In hearings before the Senate Foreign Relations Committee in December 1947, Assistant Secretary of State Norman Armour defined the area covered in the treaty as "the American continents and Greenland, adjacent waters and the Polar regions to the north and south of the Americas."[132] Armour's definition did not include Iceland, and Senator Alexander Wiley, in an executive session of the Senate Foreign Relations Committee on December 4, 1947, questioned its exclusion. Vandenberg answered Wiley:

> We would have loved to have Iceland included, but it could not be included because the answer was given to us, whenever we talked about Iceland, that it did collide with the theory of the United Nations regional chapter, because it went beyond what could be justified as a region.
>
> Therefore we have a line which does not include Iceland because we could not get a line that included Iceland.[133]

Vandenberg's answer to Wiley is important because of its recognition that an area considered to be of strategic importance to the United States was not covered by the provisions of article 3 of the Rio Pact in that it violated the principle of "regionalism" set down in the UN Charter. However, article 6 of the Inter-American Treaty was included to deal with situations that were not armed attacks and that did not necessarily take place within the security zone defined in article 4. In this sense the treaty recognized the expanding concept of American security.[134]

By providing for immediate consultations in case the security of a signatory was threatened by events outside the security zone, article 6 became one of the most important articles of the treaty. Its purpose was to avoid a repetition of the problems of World War II by solidifying hemispheric unity in order to facilitate U.S. participation in future European conflicts.

This point was brought out most clearly in the December 4 meeting of the Foreign Relations Committee when Senators Lodge and Tom Connally (D.-Texas) discussed the implications of the treaty with the administration's military witness, General Matthew Ridgway. The three men agreed that the main purposes of the treaty were to combat internal subversion in Latin American countries and to reduce the time necessary for the United States to mobilize hemispheric resources in case it was drawn into a European conflict. In fact Ridgway stated that article 6 could apply to "any fact or situation anywhere in the world."[135]

Vandenberg considered the Rio Treaty a stepping-stone to a wider concept of security and, in a letter to Senator Robert Taft (R-Ohio) on December 2, 1947, expressed the view that the United States needed "to sew up this defense pact as a further and highly significant and impressive notification to potential communist aggressors. . . . Those who are responsible for our national defense consider the Treaty to be of vital security value."[136]

The fact that the Inter-American Treaty could serve to notify potential aggressors of hemispheric solidarity in the face of foreign attack was not lost on the committee members, and considerable discussion was devoted to the implications of extending the "red line," which delimited the areas specified in article 4 to other areas of the world. While this raised questions concerning the geographic constitution of a region and the procedure for securing agreements with the countries falling within the extended security zone, it is clear that those present were thinking of an expanded concept of American security, one that would likely embrace western Europe.[137]

In support of this expanded concept of American security, Senator Vandenberg mentioned the work of Hamilton Fish Armstrong, editor of *Foreign Affairs,* who hoped to use article 51 and chapter VIII of the UN Charter to create regional arrangements similar to the one under discussion in the committee. While Vandenberg said that such an approach was "novel" and "revolutionary," he reiterated that considerable thought was being given to Fish's formula.[138] Of course, this formula would later serve as a justification for the North Atlantic Treaty.

It is apparent, then, that the Inter-American Treaty embraced only
one of the guiding principles of the Monroe Doctrine, namely, prohibiting
European intervention in the Western Hemisphere. On the other hand,
it rejected the corollary to that provision—that is, the U.S. promise not to
get involved in Old World affairs—and was actually designed to facilitate
U.S. participation in European affairs with the backing of its hemispheric
neighbors. Moreover, the Inter-American Treaty would have an important
impact on both the Brussels and North Atlantic treaties.

Conclusion

It is clear that, even though the German question was of critical importance to postwar relations among the victorious allies, the United
States did not have a coherent policy for Germany at the end of the war.
Initially, the United States hoped to administer Germany as an "economic unit" in conjunction with the British, French, and Soviets. However, French obstructionism and a growing sense of confrontation
between East and West soon made four power agreement impossible.

The absence of such accord quickly made the efficient administration
of the American zone an impossibility, and the spring and summer of
1946 witnessed American moves toward combining the U.S. and British
zones in order to ease occupation burdens. In addition by late 1946 it
was becoming evident that the industrial resources of western Germany
would have to be utilized to stimulate the economic recovery of western
Europe and to stave off Communist-inspired political turmoil.

Although 1946 did see American officials attempt to articulate a new
U.S. foreign policy in response to the collapse of western Europe and
deteriorating relations with the Soviet Union, it was not until the Truman
Doctrine of March 1947 that the new direction began to take shape.
Despite its universal and ideological overtones, the Truman Doctrine
must be viewed in the more limited context of European security and
as recognition of the strategic importance of the Near East to western
Europe. In this sense the Truman administration was clearly attempting
to help stabilize the situation on the continent by providing aid to Greece
and Turkey.

However, it was not until the failure of the Moscow Foreign Ministers
Conference on Germany that U.S. policies began to focus directly on the

problems of western Europe. Once it became obvious that four power agreement on Germany was unlikely, the U.S. government began to concentrate directly on the problems of western European recovery and on the need to include western Germany's industrial base in any recovery program.

Of course, any American plans to revitalize Germany's industry raised French fears of German domination. The Marshall Plan was designed to counter these fears by including German economic recovery in a larger program for general European recovery, but French fears persisted. Only after they had received adequate security guarantees from the United States did the French agree to merge their zone with the British-American zone and to support American policies for Germany and Europe. Interestingly, the outlines of the formula that would eventually tie the United States to western Europe and provide France the guarantees it desired were developed in Rio de Janerio during the summer of 1947 and were included in the Inter-American Treaty of Reciprocal Assistance. Ironically, the Rio Pact was supposed to be a reaffirmation of the Monroe Doctrine, which had proclaimed the mutual exclusiveness of political affairs in the Old and New Worlds.

Notes

1. U.S., Department of State, *Foreign Relations of the United States,* 1946, vol. 6, Eastern Europe; The Soviet Union, pp. 696-709; Kennan to Byrnes. Hereafter cited as *FRUS,* 1946, vol. 6.

2. The text of Clifford's memorandum appears in Arthur Krock, *Memoirs: Sixty Years on the Firing Line* (New York: Funk & Wagnalls, 1968), pp. 419-82.

3. Ibid., p. 481.

4. Ibid., p. 479.

5. Walter Millis, ed., *The Forrestal Diaries* (New York: The Viking Press, 1951), p. 210, n. 7.

6. John Lewis Gaddis, *The United States and the Origins of the Cold War, 1941-1947* (New York: Columbia University Press, 1972), pp. 95-97.

7. John Backer, *The Decision to Divide Germany* (Durham, N.C.: Duke University Press, 1978); Gaddis, *The United States and the Origins of the Cold War,* pp. 95-132; John Gimbel, *The Origins of the Marshall Plan* (Stanford, Calif.: Stanford University Press, 1976); Paul Y. Hammond, "Directives for the Occupation of Germany: The Washington Controversy," in Harold Stein, ed., *American Civil Military Decisions* (Birmingham: University of Alabama Press, 1963), pp. 313-464.

8. Backer, *The Decision to Divide Germany*, pp. 17-27; Gaddis, *The United States and the Origins of the Cold War*, p. 96.

9. Backer, *The Decision to Divide Germany*, p. 125; Gaddis, *The United States and the Origins of the Cold War*, pp. 96, 117-25, especially p. 120.

10. Gaddis, *The United States and the Origins of the Cold War*, pp. 96-97; Gimbel, *The Origins of the Marshall Plan*, p. 25; Hammond, "Directives for the Occupation of Germany," pp. 318-41.

11. Hammond, "Directives for the Occupation of Germany," p. 428.

12. Gaddis, *The United States and the Origins of the Cold War*, pp. 8-10.

13. Backer, *The Decision to Divide Germany*, pp. 13-14.

14. Ibid., pp. 17-27.

15. Gaddis, *The United States and the Origins of the Cold War*, p. 128.

16. Ibid., pp. 7, 102.

17. Hammond, "Directives for the Occupation of Germany," p. 428.

18. Ibid.; Backer, *The Decision to Divide Germany*, p. 16.

19. Gaddis, *The United States and the Origins of the Cold War*, pp. 240-41; U.S., Department of State, *Foreign Relations of the United States*, Conference of Berlin, vol. 2, 1945, p. 1506. Hereafter cited as *FRUS*, Conference of Berlin, vol. 2, 1945.

20. *FRUS*, Conference of Berlin, vol. 2, 1945, p. 1504.

21. Backer, *The Decision to Divide Germany*, pp. 46-60, 91-93.

22. Ibid., p. 92; Gaddis, *The United States and the Origins of the Cold War*, p. 241.

23. *FRUS*, Conference of Berlin, vol. 2, 1945, p. 822; Truman to Stimson.

24. Backer, *The Decision to Divide Germany*, p. 138.

25. Edgar Furniss, *France: Troubled Ally* (New York: Harper & Row, 1960), pp. 8-10.

26. Gimbel, *The Origins of the Marshall Plan*, pp. 35-49.

27. Backer, *The Decision to Divide Germany*, p. 139.

28. Gaddis, *The United States and the Origins of the Cold War*, pp. 327-28.

29. Backer, *The Decision to Divide Germany*, pp. 134-35.

30. Gimbel, *The Origins of the Marshall Plan*, p. 38.

31. *FRUS*, Conference of Berlin, vol. 2, 1945, p. 1029; Truman to Eisenhower.

32. Gimbel, *The Origins of the Marshall Plan*, pp. 155-58; U.S., Department of State, *Foreign Relations of the United States*, 1947, vol. 2, Council of Foreign Ministers, pp. 190-95. Hereafter cited as *FRUS*, 1947, vol. 2.

33. Backer, *The Decision to Divide Germany*, pp. 138-39; Gimbel, *The Origins of the Marshall Plan*, pp. 128-40; Gaddis, *The United States and the Origins of the Cold War*, p. 329.

34. Backer, *The Decision to Divide Germany*, pp. ix, 174-76.

35. U.S., Department of State, *Foreign Relations of the United States*, Conferences of Cairo and Tehran, 1943, pp. 600-03.

36. U.S., Department of State, *Foreign Relations of the United States*, 1946, vol. 5, British Commonwealth; Western and Central Europe, p. 519; Kennan to Marshall.

37. Ibid., p. 517; Gaddis, *The United States and the Origins of the Cold War*, pp. 327-28.

38. Walter LaFeber, *America, Russia and the Cold War 1945-1975* (New York: John Wiley and Sons, 1976), p. 39.

39. Backer, *The Decision to Divide Germany*, p. 153.

40. LaFeber, *America, Russia and the Cold War 1945-1975*, p. 39.

41. Edgar McInnis, Richard Hiscocks, Robert Spencer, *The Shaping of Post-war Germany* (New York: Frederick A. Praeger, 1960), p. 67.

42. Backer, *The Decision to Divide Germany*, pp. 107-08.

43. Gaddis, *The United States and the Origins of the Cold War*, pp. 329-30.

44. Ibid.

45. U.S., Department of State, *Foreign Relations of the United States*, 1946, vol. 2, Council of Foreign Ministers, pp. 160-73. Hereafter cited as *FRUS*, 1946, vol. 2.

46. Gaddis, *The United States and the Origins of the Cold War*, p. 329.

47. Backer, *The Decision to Divide Germany*, p. 141.

48. Ibid., p. 142.

49. Gaddis, *The United States and the Origins of the Cold War*, p. 330.

50. U.S., Department of State, *Foreign Relations of the United States*, 1947, vol. 2, Council of Foreign Ministers; Germany and Austria, p. 225. Hereafter cited as *FRUS*, 1947, vol. 2.

51. Robert Kaiser, *Cold Winter, Cold War* (New York: Stein and Day, 1974), p. 26.

52. Hugh Dalton, *Memoirs*, vol. 3, *High Tide and After* (London: Frederick Mueller Limited, 1962), pp. 112-13.

53. Gimbel, *The Origins of the Marshall Plan*, pp. 107-09.

54. Ibid.

55. U.S., Department of State, *Bulletin*, September 15, 1946, pp. 496-501.

56. Backer, *The Decision to Divide Germany*, p. 145.

57. Gimbel, *The Origins of the Marshall Plan*, pp. 180-83.

58. Marshall replaced Byrnes on January 21, 1947.

59. Backer, *The Decision to Divide Germany*, pp. 155-56, 164.

60. Ibid., pp. 165-70.

61. *FRUS*, 1947, vol. 2, pp. 190-95; Backer, *The Decision to Divide Germany*, p. 164.

62. Joseph Jones, *The Fifteen Weeks* (New York: The Viking Press, 1955), pp. 4-6; U.S., Department of State, *Foreign Relations of the United States*, 1947, vol. 5, The Near East and Africa, pp. 32-37.

63. David McLellan, *Dean Acheson: The State Department Years* (New York: Dodd, Mead, & Co., 1976), p. 115.

64. U.S., Department of State, *Foreign Relations of the United States*, 1946, vol. 7, The Near East; Africa, p. 913.

65. Jones, *The Fifteen Weeks*, p. 9.

66. McLellan, *Dean Acheson: The State Department Years*, pp. 117-19.

67. Ibid.

68. Ibid.

69. Robert Art, "America's Foreign Policy: In Historical Perspective," in Roy C. Macridis, ed., *Foreign Policy in World Politics* (Englewood Cliffs, N.J.: Prentice Hall, Inc., 1976), pp. 339-84, especially p. 351.

70. McLellan, *Dean Acheson: The State Department Years,* p. 117.

71. U.S., President, *Public Papers of the Presidents of the United States* (Washington, D.C.: *Office of the Federal Register,* National Archives and Records Service, 1953-   ), Harry S. Truman, 1947, pp. 176-80. Hereafter cited as *Public Papers of the Presidents, Harry S. Truman,* 1947.

72. Dean Acheson, *Present at the Creation* (New York: W. W. Norton & Co., 1969), p. 224.

73. Ibid., p. 223; U.S., Congress, Senate, Committee on Foreign Relations, *Legislative Origins of the Truman Doctrine,* Hearings held in Executive Session Before the Committee on Foreign Relations, United States Senate, 80th Congress, 1st session, on S. 938, 1947. Historical Series, 1973, p. 109. Hereafter cited as *Legislative Origins of the Truman Doctrine.*

74. *Legislative Origins of the Truman Doctrine,* pp. 50-53.

75. George F. Kennan, *Memoirs,* 2 vols. (Boston: Little, Brown and Co., (1967-1971), vol. 1, p. 321.

76. Charles Bohlen, *The Transformation of American Foreign Policy* (New York: W. W. Norton & Co., 1969), pp. 86-87.

77. Kennan, *Memoirs,* vol. 1, p. 321.

78. *Legislative Origins of the Truman Doctrine,* pp. 220-21; Report of the Senate Foreign Relations Committee on S. 938.

79. John Lewis Gaddis, "Was the Truman Doctrine a Turning Point?" *Foreign Affairs* 52, 2 (January 1974): 386-402, especially p. 391.

80. Art, "America's Foreign Policy: In Historical Perspective," p. 351.

81. *Public Papers of the Presidents, Harry S. Truman,* 1947, p. 179.

82. Kennan, *Memoirs,* vol. 1, p. 321.

83. *Legislative Origins of the Truman Doctrine,* p. 142.

84. Ibid., p. 144.

85. Ibid., p. 198.

86. Backer, *The Decision to Divide Germany,* p. 164.

87. Acheson, *Present at the Creation,* p. 220.

88. *FRUS,* 1947, vol. 5, pp. 94-95; Acheson to Patterson.

89. Acheson, *Present at the Creation,* p. 222.

90. For text see Ellen C. Garwood, *Will Clayton: A Short Biography* (Austin: University of Texas Press, 1958), pp. 115-18.

91. Ibid.

92. U.S., Department of State, *Foreign Relations of the United States,* 1947, vol. 3, The British Commonwealth; Europe, p. 198; Memorandum by Hilldring. Hereafter cited as *FRUS,* 1947, vol. 3.

93. Ibid., p. 204.

94. Gimbel, *The Origins of the Marshall Plan,* p. 10.

95. *FRUS,* 1947, vol. 3, p. 206.

96. Gimbel, *The Origins of the Marshall Plan*, p. 10.
97. Backer, *The Decision to Divide Germany*, pp. 164-70.
98. Ibid., p. 170.
99. Ibid.
100. U.S., Department of State, *Bulletin*, May 11, 1947, p. 920.
101. Ibid., p. 921.
102. Ibid., p. 919.
103. Ibid., p. 924.
104. Gimbel, *The Origins of the Marshall Plan*, p. 196.
105. Ibid., pp. 197-98.
106. U.S., Department of State, *Foreign Relations of the United States*, 1947, vol. 1, General; United Nations, pp. 734-36; Memorandum by the Joint Chiefs of Staff, enclosure dated April 29, 1947. Hereafter cited as *FRUS*, 1947, vol. 1.
107. Ibid., p. 739.
108. Ibid., pp. 739-40.
109. Ibid., p. 736.
110. Ibid., pp. 740-41.
111. Ibid.
112. Ibid., p. 741.
113. U.S., Department of State, *Bulletin*, May 18, 1947, pp. 991-94.
114. Ibid.
115. Ibid.
116. *FRUS*, 1947, vol. 3, pp. 220-24; Kennan to Acheson.
117. Ibid., pp. 225-26.
118. Gimbel, *The Origins of the Marshall Plan*, p. 203.
119. Ibid., p. 200.
120. Ibid., pp. 199-200.
121. *FRUS*, 1947, vol. 3, p. 224; Kennan to Acheson.
122. Ibid., p. 225.
123. Ibid., p. 231.
124. Ibid.
125. Ibid., pp. 231-32.
126. For the text of Marshall's speech, see ibid., pp. 239-41.
127. Pan American Union, *Report of the 2nd Meeting of the Ministers of Foreign Affairs of the American Republics, Havana.* July 21-30, 1940, p. 35.
128. U.S., Department of State, *Act of Chapultepec*. Treaties and Other International Acts Series 1543, Pubn. 2679 (1946), pp. 12-13.
129. U.S., Department of State, *The Inter-American Treaty of Reciprocal Assistance*. Treaties and Other International Acts Series 1838, Pubn. 3380 (1949), p. 24. Hereafter cited as *TIAS* 1838.
130. U.S., Congress, Senate, Committee on Foreign Relations, *Executive Sessions of the Senate Foreign Relations Committee*, vol. 1, 80th Congress, 1st and 2nd sessions, 1947-1948. *Historical Series*, 1976, pp. 129-31. Hereafter cited as *Executive Sessions*, vol. 1.

131. Arthur Vandenberg, Jr., ed., *The Private Papers of Senator Vandenberg* (Boston: Houghton Mifflin Co., 1952), pp. 367-68. Emphasis in original.

132. *Executive Sessions,* vol. 1, p. 128.

133. Ibid., pp. 135-36.

134. *TIAS,* no. 1838, p. 25. "Whether or not this meant that the subject matter of the consultations might not go beyond defense measures, or whether those consulting are bound in good faith to come to some agreement on those measures, was left unclear." Alfred P. Rubin, "SEATO and the American Legal Obligation Concerning Laos and Cambodia," *International and Comparative Law Quarterly* 20, 3 (July 1974): 500-18.

135. *Executive Sessions,* vol. 1, p. 142.

136. Vandenberg, ed., *The Private Papers of Senator Vandenberg,* p. 371.

137. *Executive Sessions,* vol. 1, p. 142.

138. Ibid.

TWO

A European Initiative: The Brussels Pact

Introduction

Although the immediate reaction to Secretary Marshall's call for a European initiative in the formulation of a recovery plan was favorable, the uncertainties of the Harvard speech led to serious disagreements that threatened to scuttle any cooperative effort. Moreover, even though some of those disagreements arose out of ideological, cold war issues, the biggest threat to the success of the Marshall Plan came from issues surrounding the German problem.

Because Marshall attempted to avoid some of the harsher ideological implications of the Truman Doctrine in his Harvard speech, participation in a European recovery program was open to any European country, including the Soviet Union. Even though British Foreign Secretary Ernest Bevin and French Foreign Minister Georges Bidault were the first and most enthusiastic respondents to Marshall's speech, they suspended their initial Paris meetings in order to invite Soviet participation. On June 23, 1947, the talks were resumed, with Foreign Minister V. M. Molotov representing the Soviet Union. However, these tripartite talks soon broke down because the Soviet delegation felt that the proposals being developed were designed to promote intervention into the internal affairs of the Soviet Union and other countries of eastern Europe.[1]

The Bevin-Bidault-Molotov talks ended on July 2, 1947, and the following day Bevin and Bidault invited twenty-two other European countries to send delegations to Paris to begin consultations on a European reaction to Marshall's call. Again, the invitations were made without ideological considerations, and of the countries that indicated a desire to participate, two, Poland and Czechoslovakia, were eastern European. However, both were soon forced to withdraw under pressure from the Soviet Union.[2] Coupled with the Soviet walkout, the Polish and Czech withdrawals limited the scope and focus of the Marshall Plan to the countries of western Europe, Scandinavia, Austria, and western Germany. However, because it was still unclear just how Germany would fit into European recovery, the German question again arose as an issue between the French and the British and Americans, and it presented a problem that threatened the whole basis of the Marshall Plan.

Trouble between the French and Americans began in late July when Foreign Minister Bidault received information about the secret level of industry agreement for Bizonia that Clay and Robertson had been working on since late April. Because the French had not been consulted, and due to his precarious political situation at home, Bidault protested strongly to the British and Americans and eventually threatened to resign unless French views were taken into account. The problem was not resolved until Marshall and Bevin, fearful lest the French government fall to extremists of the Right or Left, assured Bidault that German recovery would only be a part of a larger program for European recovery and that the announcement of the level of industry agreements would be withheld until French views could be heard. These assurances temporarily satisfied Bidault, but with the announcement of bizonal administrative reforms in January 1948, French fears intensified once again.

The administrative reform announcement came following the failure of the Four Power London Foreign Ministers Conference (November-December 1947) and immediately brought into sharp focus questions concerning France's role as an occupying power, Germany's role in Europe, and the U.S. role in an evolving "Atlantic" relationship. The winter and spring of 1948 witnessed the initial steps taken to resolve those issues, steps that included the signing of the Brussels Treaty in March, the London Six Power Conference on Germany, and the Vandenberg Resolution in the United States, the latter promising American "association" with European security efforts. Significantly, the fact that those initial, tentative steps were taken in the shadow of an intensifying cold war—highlighted by the Prague coup in February—facilitated accommodation between the western powers on general European security issues.

Level of Industry and Administrative Reforms

Following the withdrawal of the Czechs and Poles, the remaining European countries that wanted to participate in the Marshall Plan proceeded to create the interim Committee on European Economic Cooperation (CEEC), the purpose of which was to analyze the resources, capabilities, expectations, and needs of the participating countries and to formulate the guiding principles for a recovery program.[3]

Across the Atlantic, the U.S. government, working throughout the summer, set up committees designed to lay the groundwork for U.S. participation in European recovery and to coordinate its efforts with those of the Europeans.[4] However, some of the most important work was being undertaken in Germany by the American and British zonal commanders, Generals Clay and Robertson.

On July 12, 1947, Clay reported to the State Department that the American and British occupation authorities—in response to their April instructions—had agreed to a revised level of industry for Bizonia designed to make that area self-supporting. In order to accomplish that goal steel production would be raised to 10.7 million tons per year.[5] The zonal commanders also informed Washington and London that they planned to release the details of their plan on July 16 in Berlin. However, on July 11 Lincoln Caffery, ambassador to France, had reported to the State Department on a meeting between Will Clayton and French Foreign Minister Bidault; Caffery's report caused Marshall to veto Clay's announcement.

The July 11 meeting between Clayton and Bidault exposed French apprehensions over the Clay-Robertson talks. Although Bidault did not know the results of those discussions, the French government was aware that the two men were discussing the level of industry in the bizonal area, and Bidault warned Clayton that if the British and Americans planned to increase steel production substantially in Bizonia and turn the Ruhr mines over to German trusteeship, the French government would be in a very difficult position.[6] Bidault hoped that French steel production would take precedence over the restoration of the Ruhr mines to German authority, and while he agreed that German economic recovery was an important "element" in general European recovery, he felt it should not be the first priority.[7] Bidault then warned against any public announcement of the revised level of industry quotas on the grounds that if the French people were led to believe that reparations had been abandoned and that the German economic potential was to be raised, the work being done in Paris on the Marshall Plan would be "doomed to failure." After discussing the interview with Bidault, Caffery and Clayton concluded that "care should be taken to avoid any public statement at this juncture to reparations, level of industry, etc., which would react unfavorably on the

Paris Conference or strengthen the Communists in their efforts to discredit its efforts and those of the French Government."[8]

Special heed was paid to Clayton and Caffery's advice because of the precarious, yet important position of Bidault and Socialist Prime Minister Paul Ramadier. The chief political problem faced by Bidault and Ramadier was the fact that they occupied the relatively weak middle ground between Charles de Gaulle's right-wing *Rassamblement du Peuple Français* (formed in April 1947) and an increasingly militant Communist party, which had been forced out of the French government in May 1947. Ramadier's uneasy government was under constant pressure from both groups, and American diplomats warned that, should the governing coalition collapse, France would be divided "into two hostile extremist camps—the Communists on one side and de Gaulle on the other—with the inevitable struggle to the finish between them."[9] Ambassador Caffery cabled his analysis of the situation in France to Secretary Marshall on May 12 and explained the importance of the French position to American foreign policy.

According to Caffery there were "too many unknown factors" for him accurately to predict the outcome of a showdown between the Communists and de Gaulle. In either event there would be "far reaching and dangerous repercussions" that, from the U.S. point of view, "could not lead to a happy conclusion." If the Communists won, the Middle East, the Mediterranean, Africa, and western Europe would be open to Soviet penetration, and the American occupation of Germany would be endangered, if not rendered untenable. On the other hand if de Gaulle won, "France would be headed into a new and unknown adventure . . . which would make the practice in France of democracy as we understand it difficult if not impossible for some time to come."[10]

The desire not to rock the political boat in France caused the State Department to pay special attention to Clayton and Caffery's recommendations of July 11 and—in concert with the British—to instruct Clay and Robertson not to make public the details of their level of industry reforms.[11] However, on July 16 the British, responding to a request from Bidault, informed the French government of the measures being contemplated in the bizonal area. Bidault met with Ambassador Caffery and W. Averell Harriman shortly after he received preliminary reports on the details of the Clay-Robertson plan, and when the two Americans entered his office, they found him in a "hysterical condition."[12]

Bidault complained to Caffery and Harriman that the Anglo-American decision had been taken behind his back and that French views had not been sought.[13] Later, in a personal note to Marshall, the foreign minister complained that he had burned his bridges with the Soviet Union during the meetings with Molotov and had been placed in an "unacceptable and untenable" situation by the British and Americans. He informed the secretary of state that if the United States and the United Kingdom continued with their plans he would have to leave the government and cautioned that a crisis on the issue of Germany would "re-open the question of France's internal equilibrium" and might result in a reversal of the French decision to join with the United States in the Marshall Plan.[14] Marshall received an additional perspective on French views when Caffery reported on a meeting with Maurice Schumann and other French cabinet ministers.

According to Caffery's report, French officials expressed concern about Communist propaganda against their government. Specifically, the French moderates complained that the Communists were having their greatest successes by charging that the United States was protecting its vested economic interests by rehabilitating Germany rather than France. The Communists were able to point to American financial assistance to the western zones, the halt of reparations shipments, and the increases in the level of German industry as evidence for their claims, and were able to charge that French security was jeopardized by U.S. policies. Although leaders of the *Mouvement Republicain Populaire* supported the policy of utilizing German industrial capacity for both German and European economic reconstruction, they repeatedly begged the Americans "that no further measures for German rehabilitation be announced until European plan under Marshall proposals be prepared, when German program can be made to dovetail with it."[15]

Given his understanding of the precarious nature of the French political situation, the fact that the French government was facing municipal elections in the fall, and the importance of France to American policy in Europe, Secretary Marshall wrote to Bidault on July 21, 1947, informing him that the United States and the United Kingdom would "suspend further announcement upon the proposal for the revised bizonal level of industry in Germany until the French Government has had a reasonable opportunity to discuss these questions with the United States and United Kingdom Governments."[16] Henri Bonnet, French ambassador to

Washington, thanked Marshall for his decision and informed the secretary of state that France would be willing to merge its occupation zone with Bizonia if the London Council of Foreign Ministers meeting scheduled for November ended in failure.[17]

When the French, British, and Americans entered into preliminary talks on the German question, it soon became apparent that each was going to stick to its respective position. The United States and Great Britain informed the French that, in the absence of a fusion of the French zone with Bizonia, they had ultimate authority in the bizonal area and would remain firm in moving ahead with the level of industry proposals worked out by Clay and Robertson. In this sense the tripartite meetings accomplished little except for the exchange of Anglo-American plans and French views; the actual question of trizonal merger was not discussed.[18] Bidault was chagrined at the course of the talks, arguing that "no French Government . . . could agree to a revised level of industry for Germany, without assurances as to French security and access by Europe to the production of the Ruhr."[19] To smooth things, the Americans indicated to Bidault that such issues as security and the Ruhr could be considered after the London meetings, and the French seemed to be reconciled to moving ahead. Therefore, both the French and the Anglo-Americans got what they wanted from the talks. Because he had obtained a British and American pledge to discuss territorial and security questions after the London meetings, Bidault received the "political leverage" necessary for him to remain in power and to prevent a domestic political crisis in France. For their part, the United States and the United Kingdom could make public the level of industry plan worked out by Clay and Robertson and could use it as the official basis for German participation in, and contribution to, the European Recovery Program.[20]

The scene then shifted back to Paris and the Committee on European Economic Cooperation, where the Americans, after considerable debate, were able to win acceptance of a broad program "designed to dovetail German rehabilitation with the general European recovery program and to present to the Congress a single foreign aid package."[21] This American-sponsored proposal was incorporated into the CEEC's report of September 22, and one month later, on October 24, President Truman asked a special session of Congress for an interim aid package designed to help Europe through the winter until Congress could consider the more long-range program.[22] The interim aid package was needed primarily due to the deteriorating political situation in France, caused in large measure by the activities of the Communist labor unions.

On July 6, 1947, Andrei Zhdanov, Politburo member and Stalin's heir apparent, called for the creation of the Cominform to strengthen the links between the Soviet Communist party and other Communist parties through out the world. The French Communist party was one of the first western European parties to respond, and when Zhdanov issued, on October 22, a call for Communist parties everywhere to work against the Marshall Plan, Communist-sponsored strikes were already taking place in France. Following Zhdanov's call and the Communist defeat in the municipal elections,[23] the French political situation reached crisis proportions. The activities of the French Communists were designed to topple the French government (similar strikes also took place in Italy) and to prevent France's participation in the Marshall Plan. However, the violent nature of the strikes, the direct link between the French Communists and the Soviets, and the promise of support from the United States, including the American labor movement, convinced many on the non-Communist Left to break with the French party, and the strikes were eventually quelled.[24] Moreover, the strikes emphasized the growing European security problems and led many on both sides of the Atlantic to believe that economic recovery could not take place in an atmosphere of political uncertainty.

The success of the promise of American aid in helping to restore order in France (and Italy) raised questions about America's future role in European security. Some planners in the State Department were concerned that the continued presence of American occupation troops in Germany and the extension of U.S. economic aid were becoming substitutes for European efforts to maintain their own security. Moreover, these planners feared that the costs of continuing those programs would severely stretch the tight U.S. economy and create a strain on resource availability. A report of the Policy Planning Staff dated November 6, 1947, listed the measures undertaken by the United States to contain Soviet expansion and complained that America had "borne almost single handed the burden of the international effort to stop the Kremlin's political advance. But this has stretched our resources dangerously far in several respects."[25] The report continued:

> In these circumstances it is clearly unwise for us to continue the attempt to carry alone, or largely single handed, the

> opposition to Soviet expansion. It is urgently necessary
> for us to restore something of the balance of power in
> Europe and Asia by strengthening local forces of indepen-
> dence and by getting them to assume part of our burden.[26]

In order to restore the balance in Europe and to shift the burden of responsibility, the Policy Planning Staff report held that it was "essential
that Germany be fitted into this picture."[27]

The importance of fitting Germany into the picture was stressed in
State Department documents preceding the London Foreign Ministers
Conference scheduled for late November and December 1947. Although
the meeting was supposed to make another attempt to achieve four power
accord on Germany, it was generally acknowledged in the West that, in
light of deteriorating relations with the Soviet Union, such a goal was unrealistic. In fact, George Kennan feared that the Soviets would "attempt
various ruses" to get the Western powers out of Germany, "which would
leave that country defenseless against communist penetration." Therefore, both Kennan and Robert Murphy, political adviser to General Clay,
advocated moving ahead with the political development of western
Germany.[28] Kennan argued further that the French and others should
be brought "to an enlightened understanding of the necessities of the
German situation; to the acknowledgement of their responsibility for
integrating western Germany into western Europe, and to a detailed
agreement with us as to how this shall be done." In order to accomplish
these goals Kennan warned that the United States would have to make
"as well as to receive concessions."[29]

The results of the London talks confirmed preconference pessimism.
The talks opened on November 25, and were punctuated by acrimonious
exchanges over reparations, with the Soviets repeating their demands for
$10 billion. The British and Americans refused to go along because such
a policy would prevent the development of a German economy capable of
sustaining western European recovery. The conference ended in impasse
on December 15, and the four powers did not schedule another meeting.
The London Conference marked the last serious attempt to achieve East-
West agreement on Germany, and its failure led to western efforts to
consolidate their position in western Germany and to inaugurate new
security arrangements.[30]

Immediately following the four power meetings, Secretary Marshall
met individually with Bidault and Bevin to discuss the issues of European-

American relations and European security. Each of the European leaders expressed his concerns over the future, and each sought to bring the United States into closer association with European security.

Marshall's conversations with Bidault on December 17, 1947 centered on the problem of merging the French zone with Bizonia. During these talks, Marshall once again encountered French concerns about their security in relation to any new German state. Moreover, the French linked a fusion agreement with the satisfactory settlement of the Ruhr and Saar questions.

Marshall opened the conversation by explaining that the failure of the Council of Foreign Ministers raised a number of important questions concerning Germany and the three western occupation zones. The first question was the relationship between the French zone on the one hand and the U.S./U.K. zones on the other. Marshall suggested that a good initial approach would be for the French to review the Anglo-American zonal fusion agreement and prepare their criticisms of the arrangement. Bidault replied that Marshall's approach seemed reasonable but implied that it would take time for the French to merge their zone with the others and that the merger process "should be an evolutionary development." According to Bidault, the fusion question was related to many others, including "the question of the Saar and the question of the Ruhr."[31]

As a step toward the merger of the French zone with the bizonal area, Secretary Marshall suggested that the French adopt procedures "within the French zone similar to those followed in the U.S./U.K. zones. This would bring the zones into greater harmony by evolutionary processes."[32] Five days later, on December 22, 1947, Ambassador Bonnet delivered a note to Marshall indicating the steps France was preparing to take toward an eventual fusion.

In his message Bonnet said that French representatives should be invited to make a "critical analysis" of American and British fusion procedures in Bizonia and that they, in turn, would "set forth their conceptions of the organization of a fused zone. . . ." However, those measures would not imply "in any way a decision relative to the fusion of the French zone." An optimistic note was added when Bonnet said that the French would "study with their American and British colleagues the measures which might eventually be put into effect in the French zone with a view to harmonizing the activity of the Allies in the western zones."[33]

The same note indicated a French willingness to begin work on currency reform within and to study methods to facilitate the free movement of persons among the three western zones.[34]

When Marshall met with Bevin on December 18, the issue of European security was a major topic. Speaking about the ideological confrontation of the cold war, Bevin wanted to see the creation of a "spiritual federation of the west." He stated that such a grouping should include the United States, Great Britain, the Dominions, and the democratic countries of western Europe. He noted that he was not advocating a formal alliance, but rather an "unwritten and informal" understanding that would be "backed by power, money and resolute action."[35] However, when he turned to the question of Germany, Bevin's attitude changed.

On the subject of Germany, Bevin told Marshall that they would have to consider the question of security, a problem that was particularly sensitive to the French. In terms of providing security against Germany, Bevin told Marshall that he had heard discussion along the lines of a three power treaty similar to the Four Power Treaty proposed by Secretary of State Byrnes in 1946. However, Bevin indicated that he was more favorably inclined "to a treaty or understanding which also brought in Benelux and Italy."[36] Even though Marshall's reply was noncommittal, it is interesting to note that, while Bevin did not regard a treaty of alliance to be of critical importance in meeting the threat to Europe posed by the Soviet Union, he was in favor of a treaty structure designed to guarantee western Europe against a possible renewal of German aggression. Moreover, Marshall and Bevin took another step in the aftermath of the Four Power London Conference that would heighten French concerns and move the western Europeans toward the conclusion of just such a treaty.

On December 18, 1947, Bevin and Marshall instructed Generals Robertson and Clay to proceed with plans for administrative reform within Bizonia, an action that led to French fears that the British and Americans were establishing the groundwork for the creation of a west German state without French input.[37] As a result of their instructions, Robertson and Clay met with German officials in Frankfurt on January 7-8, 1948, in order to discuss a new administrative structure for the bizonal area. While the occupation authorities wished to ease their responsibilities and facilitate German participation in the Marshall Plan through the creation of centralized political and economic institutions in Bizonia, they faced German apprehensions that such a move would prejudice the eventual reunification of Germany and would strengthen French reluctance to witness the establishment of centralized German agencies without governmental discussions among the *three* occupying powers.[38] The French were mollified somewhat by a second Bevin-Marshall decision to convene another London meeting on Germany.

The second London meeting began in February 1948 and included the three western occupation powers as well as Belgium, the Netherlands, and Luxembourg (Benelux). Its purpose was to discuss questions relating to the Ruhr and Saar, reparations, Germany's relationship to the Marshall Plan, the possible fusion of the French zone with the Anglo-American zone, and security issues. These meetings witnessed the beginning of the formal process whereby French concessions on Germany would be matched by progressive American involvement in European security affairs.

However, at the same time that the Clay-Robertson meetings with German officials were taking place in Frankfurt, hearings on the European Recovery Program began in the United States. These hearings brought out two important points regarding the American perception of the role of Marshall aid to Europe. First, it was apparent that U.S. decision makers were viewing with increasing alarm the existence of a vacuum of power in western Europe. In response to this perception U.S. officials evidently saw the extension of American aid as a means of redressing the European balance and of eliminating the vacuum. Second, it was also clear that American attempts to redress the European balance through the Marshall Plan were to be taken in lieu of increased U.S. defense efforts. The reconstruction of a balance of power in Europe was to be a substitute for long-term American participation in that balance.

The European Recovery Program Hearings

President Truman presented the recovery package worked out by American officials and the Committee on European Economic Cooperation to Congress on December 19, 1947, and the Senate hearings opened on January 8 with Secretary Marshall as the first witness. In his prepared statement the secretary maintained that the western Europeans could not recover from the aftershocks of the war without American assistance. He also stated that if sufficient aid were not forthcoming from the United States then Europe, the basis of Western civilization, would fall to a new form of tyranny. Marshall continued in this vein, drawing a direct link between a growing "vacuum of power" in western Europe and American security. The secretary maintained that, unless the United States furnished "effective aid to support the now visible reviving hope of Europe," the vacuum created by World War II would "be filled by the forces of which wars are made." According to Marshall, this would seriously threaten the security of the United States and force Americans to "live in an armed camp, regulated and controlled." He concluded by proclaiming that economic recovery was the basis for Europe's "political vitality" and that lasting peace required the restoration of that vitality.[39]

On January 14-15, Secretary of the Army Kenneth Royall and Secretary of Defense James Forrestal[40] testified on the military implications of the European Recovery Program. Royall spoke first and linked aid to Europe to reduced American military expenditures.

Royall explained that the army's major responsibility was national defense and that this responsibility and the costs involved increased during periods of international economic and political instability. However, he testified that under conditions of economic stability and development, "the Army's immediate responsibility becomes correspondingly lessened." He saw the "enlightened cooperative economic endeavor" of the European Recovery Program as going "a long way toward reducing the necessity for a larger national armament in the future and probably reducing our present armament. . . ." However, he cautioned that without the Marshall Plan, "the Army budget and the Army itself should be increased."[41]

Royall also emphasized the importance of German recovery for European recovery and the corresponding reduction in expenditure by the U.S. Army in Germany. He said that during the two and a half years of military occupation the army had assumed a large financial burden for food and other essential goods to prevent disease and unrest in the American zone. He pointed out that as a result the army had come to view the economic rehabilitation of Germany as increasingly important because it would contribute to German political stability and offer "the only reasonable opportunity" of reducing occupation costs. Therefore, he felt that merging German recovery with that of the other European countries was extremely important to the Department of the Army "because of the relation of Germany's economy to that of the rest of Europe."[42]

Defense Secretary Forrestal followed Royall and pointed out that there were only two great powers in the world, the Soviet Union and the United States. He further pointed out that the area that would normally constitute the balance of power between the two, that is, western Europe, was unable to do so because of "economic instability, political unrest, and consequent military ineffectiveness." Forrestal then said that the objective of the United States in providing aid to western Europe was to reconstitute the European balance "by the creation of political and economic and social equilibrium which is requisite to the maintenance of peace." Forrestal concluded his prepared statement by asserting that the United States needed "to maintain here substantial military power, but I would rate the need for the restoration in the European community as equally strong."[43]

Following his statement, Forrestal was questioned by Senator Vandenberg, who wanted to know if a failure to provide for European recovery meant a larger role for the United States in the European balance. Forrestal replied that he thought there was "a definite relation between the two. If what I have chosen to call the imbalance of Europe continues, there will be a rising necessity on our part to provide the only alternative balance to that imbalance, namely, greater military power for ourselves."[44]

While Forrestal advocated a stronger military establishment regardless of the success or failure of the European Recovery Program, his response to Vandenberg is in basic agreement with the thesis that the purpose of the Recovery Program was to restore Europe economically in order to prevent the necessity of American rearmament and participation in the European balance of power.

The extent to which this view was accepted is illustrated by the fact that only one member of the Senate Foreign Relations Committee, Bourke Hickenlooper, (R-Iowa) questioned Royall's and Forrestal's arguments that a restoration of the European balance would ease the American burden. Hickenlooper explained that he did not have much confidence in the Europeans' ability to "sustain any military strength on their own part for a long period of time," even given the "reasonable success" of U.S. assistance programs. Therefore, he envisioned U.S. financial and military obligations continuing even after western Europe had achieved economic recovery and stability. While the Iowa senator did not raise his point as an objection, he wanted to know the long-term implications of the Marshall Plan, "rather than to consider it from too altruistic a standpoint."[45]

Hickenlooper's thinking was borne out as the U.S. government began to deal with the problem of German association with the Marshall Plan and French security concerns. However, while administration officials had informed the senators of the "essential" nature of German participation in European recovery, the restoration of the European balance, and the subsequent reduction in American costs, they had been rather circumspect in dealing with the extent to which French security demands were shaping U.S. policy in Europe.[46]

The Brussels Treaty

Immediately following the Clay-Robertson meeting with German officials in Frankfurt, Secretary of State Marshall—in response to a request from the British—clarified the American position on administrative reform in Germany. Although he agreed "that the trend should be in the direction of setting up a western German administration which would be responsive to popular will and which would perform clearly defined and limited governmental functions," Marshall did not wish to see the new administrative structure "be constituted as a government for western Germany." His thinking reflected the fact that even in the wake of the four power failure at London the United States still had no concrete plans for setting up a west German government and that future steps in that direction should be "evolutionary," dependent to a certain extent on actions in the Soviet zone.[47]

Yet despite Marshall's cautious attitude, the French immediately registered their displeasure over the Anglo-American actions. On January 11 Ambassador Bonnet delivered a telegram from the French foreign ministry to Secretary of State Marshall listing the French complaints.

In their note of protest the French government charged that the Anglo-American creation of a Bizonal Economic Administration fundamentally altered Bizonia's administrative structure, meant that a German government had, in fact, been created, "and was contrary to the understanding reached between Secretary of State Marshall and Foreign Minister Bidault during their conversation in London on December 17, 1947. . . ." The French government also protested that the Anglo-American contractual arrangements with German authorities "appeared to predetermine the future political organization of Germany."[48]

The French also expressed a desire to detach the Saar and Ruhr from Germany and to incorporate them into the French economy. Of course, the French objections to bizonal administrative reform and their reference to the Ruhr and Saar questions pointed up their tremendous concern for security against Germany. In those circumstances it was essential for the United States to make concessions regarding French security in order to get French participation in merging the three western occupation zones.

On January 17, 1948, Ernest Bevin proposed that "talks on the official level between the representatives of the United States, United Kingdom and French Governments should take place in London as soon as possible and that these talks should cover the whole range of short-term and long-term German problems." The British felt that the Ruhr should be discussed in those meetings but favored settlement of the Saar question first.[49] On that same day the U.S. government informed Clay that it was "now ready to recognize *de facto* separation of the Saar from Germany and incorporation [of] its economy with that of France [subject] to agreement on related issues involved and to confirmation of this arrangement in final peace settlement."[50] However, the Department of the Army also suggested to General Clay that he "emphasize to [the] French that in view of our willingness to accommodate them on the Saar we would expect them to be cooperative in connection with new arrangements for economic [organization] in western Germany."[51]

Secretary Marshall continued efforts to move the French closer to participating in tripartite talks on the future of the western zones of Germany in a letter to the French government clarifying his interpretation of the December 17, 1947, meeting with Bidault in London. Marshall explained that the United States was willing to participate at an early date in government level, tripartite talks designed to "explore the possibilities for the development at the appropriate time of a German political organization." The secretary of state informed the French that he considered this matter one of the long-term issues he discussed with Bidault in London.[52] Marshall also told the French that the U.S. government did not intend for the bizonal reforms to "establish political institutions prejudging the constitution of a future Germany or in any way set up a western German state."[53]

Therefore, in an exchange of notes during January 1948, the United States and Great Britain granted the French desire for the separation of the Saar from Germany, assured the French that the Frankfurt proposals for bizonal reform did not form the basis for a new German government, and extended an invitation to the French to take part in governmental discussions on the future of Germany. In return for these acts the United States clearly expected the French to begin efforts to merge the French zone with Bizonia and to take a constructive part in the six power London talks beginning the third week in February. These efforts were largely successful, for, despite a final French note protesting bizonal reform (dated January 24),[54] the French raised no further serious objection to bizonal reorganization, and that task was largely completed by February 9, 1948.[55]

However, while the French received some assurance from the separation of the Saar from Germany and from the Anglo-American intention to include France in any discussions on a future west German government, the larger question of a guarantee against a possible revival of German aggression still remained.

A model guarantee favored by the French was a modified Draft Treaty on the Disarmament and Demilitarization of Germany, which Byrnes had proposed in April 1946.[56] From the French point of view a three power version of that treaty would have accommodated the East-West split and maintained security against a remilitarization of the western zones of Germany. However, the United States deemed such a plan unworkable since it would "bind only one part of Germany leaving the Eastern zone free to develop its military establishment and war potential without any restrictions except those imposed unilaterally by the Soviets as the occupying power."[57] On the other hand the U.S. government found more to recommend in a proposal by British Foreign Secretary Bevin.

Immediately after the failure of the London Foreign Ministers Conference, Bevin began work on the outlines of a plan for the creation of a "Western Union." By January 13, 1948, Lord Inverchapel, British ambassador to Washington, was able to give Marshall a summary of Bevin's thinking. The basis of his proposal was the conclusion of a draft treaty with France and the Benelux countries, the formula for which would follow the lines of the Anglo-French Treaty of Dunkirk, which was aimed specifically at the prevention of a renewal of German aggression.[58]

However, it was clear from the ambassador's summary that the proposed treaty would serve a dual purpose by offering France security against German *revanchism* and laying the groundwork for a wider Atlantic agreement directed primarily against the Soviet Union. This second purpose was emphasized by the fact that Bevin's program envisioned the eventual participation of Germany.[59]

The dual nature of the treaty was not lost on the other proposed signatories. After receiving word of the planned extension of the Dunkirk Treaty to include Belgium, the Belgian prime minister, Paul-Henri Spaak, maintained "that unless this Pact was meant as a screen behind which to consider defenses against Russia, it was meaningless because of Germany's present position." Spaak also felt "that any defense arrangement which did not include the United States would be without practical value."[60]

The initial reaction of the U.S. government was similar to that of Spaak. While in complete agreement with the general objectives of Bevin's proposal, the Truman administration considered the relationship between the Dunkirk Pact and the future role of Germany in European security to be the major problem with the plan.[61] On January 19-20 the director of the Office of European Affairs, John Hickerson, and Kennan responded to the summary of Bevin's program.

Hickerson argued that the Dunkirk Treaty set a bad precedent for a European security system but that, in his opinion, "a European Pact modeled on the Treaty of Rio de Janeiro is the best answer to the security problem for Western Europe." He also felt that, for a pact modeled on the Rio formula to succeed, "the United States would have to adhere."[62]

Kennan also was against the idea of a European treaty based on defense against Germany because of the important role that the German people would eventually play in such a pact. He also was disturbed by the military implications of the Bevin proposal and argued that political union of Europe should be achieved first. Finally, unlike Hickerson, he did not emphasize the importance of U.S. association with the Europeans, maintaining that they "should not bother their heads too much in the initial stages about our relationship to this concept. . . ."[63]

However, Hickerson's views represented a beginning in the evolution of State Department policy regarding participation in an Atlantic security treaty. It is important to note that the Rio Pact formula and the eventual inclusion of Germany were emerging as prerequisites for American involvement, and these views received further articulation on January 21, when Hickerson met with Inverchapel and presented the American viewpoint:

> It seems that any adequate regional defense system for western European countries should envisage defense measures to be taken in the event of aggression or attack from

any source, even if one member of the group should attack another member. This is the underlying strength of the recent Inter-American Defense Treaty signed last year at Rio de Janeiro. There is full agreement with Mr. Bevin that the role of Germany in the union he proposes will eventually be of prime importance. Therefore there is some question whether the adoption of a mutual assistance pact based solely on defense against Germany would facilitate eventual entry of Germany into this concept.[64]

Hickerson also spoke of American involvement with the European efforts. He told the British that if "no regional organization could be complete without the United States" and if the proposed organization "was clearly associated with the Charter of the United Nations" the United States would consider "association" with such a grouping and would give it sympathetic consideration. Because of the State Department's view that the U.S. Congress would be reluctant to approve any closer American involvement in European security affairs at that time, Hickerson also stressed that the initiative for such action must come from Europe.[65]

The U.S. government was in fact anxious for the Europeans to move ahead with the creation of a security organization in light of the growing concern about Soviet intentions in Europe. It was not that the United States feared an invasion by Soviet forces; clearly, it did not. But because of the growing divisions between East and West and the initial successes of U.S. aid in helping the western Europeans combat internal disorder, the United States did fear Soviet political moves.

Specifically, because of successful American efforts against the Communist parties in France and Italy, the Americans felt that the Soviet Union would be forced to consolidate its control in eastern Europe and "clamp down completely on Czechoslovakia," whose relative freedom threatened Soviet policies in that area.[66] Moreover, the U.S. government was concerned that, once the Russian position in eastern Europe was more secure, the Soviets would incite the French and Italian Communists to "resort to virtual civil war." Because of the subversive nature of those moves, the State Department was apprehensive that it would have "no grounds for formal protest." Therefore, the United States felt that it should "strengthen in every way local forces of resistance" as a first step in restoring a balance of power in Europe. Because of the costs involved, the United States hoped that the Europeans would take the initiative and assume a greater share of the burden.[67] Even though the Soviet threat remained largely political in nature, the need for stronger security arrangements was increasing, and the United States was clearly anxious to see the Europeans move forward in that area.

On January 22, 1948, Bevin disclosed his plan for a regional security arrangement in a speech before the House of Commons.[68] Because of the importance attached to some U.S. connection with such a European grouping, the British soon began to press the Americans for their views on the subject. In this regard the British proposed the conclusion of an Anglo-American defense agreement to pave the way for a wider commitment by the United States and to support Bevin's treaty proposal.[69] The British realized that Europe was unable to defend itself and that American participation was necessary for European security. Moreover, given the wide range of issues to be discussed, the British wished to have a joint Anglo-American position worked out before the opening of the London six power talks on Germany, scheduled to begin on February 19, 1948. Therefore, they proposed "secret, frank, and informal discussions, without commitment on either side," similar to those that had taken place a year earlier regarding the Greek situation.[70]

The United States reacted negatively to the British proposal for a bilateral alliance. The Americans felt that such an agreement would have to involve "the most careful consideration" on the part of the Truman administration, as well as the inclusion of the appropriate committees in the Senate and the House. Unfortunately, there was "insufficient time for such consideration and preparation" before the opening of the London talks. More to the point, the State Department felt that until Bevin's proposals had been developed more fully in Europe it was "unwise for the United States to inject itself into the discussions."[71]

Moreover, because the Marshall Plan was being presented to the U.S. Congress as a move to get Europe back on its feet, restore the balance of power in Europe, and reduce the long-range costs to the United States, the State Department informed the British that discussion of an American role in European security would be unwise. On February 7, 1948, Under Secretary of State Robert Lovett told Lord Inverchapel that if the Congress found out that the Truman administration was preparing to assume "new and extensive military and political commitments" in addition to the economic commitments of the Marshall Plan, "it might well adversely affect the prospects for the approval by Congress of the European Recovery Program."[72]

While there was clearly some danger that the United States would lose a certain amount of political initiative to the Europeans by stressing that they create a security organization, sensitive relations with a Congress reluctant to approve increased American commitments overseas made caution a necessity. Moreover, by stressing the Rio formula as a model for a European grouping, the Truman administration was actually paving the way for future American association with European efforts. Since the principles contained in the Inter-American Treaty had already been approved by the Senate, congressional approval for U.S. association with an organization embodying many of those same principles would be easier to come by. In addition, since the Rio formula considered an attack on one as an attack on all, and could apply to an attack from any quarter, even if one member attacked another, it could avoid the issue of designing a treaty specifically against Germany or against the Soviet Union. Therefore, it could reconcile the Dunkirk Treaty against Germany with the growing American concern about threats from the Soviet Union and the need to restore the European balance of power through integrating western Germany into western Europe.

After the failure of the London Foreign Ministers Conference in December 1947, the United States clearly was pressured by its allies to take a more active role in European security affairs. The French, while certainly aware of the Soviet threat, began to seek greater U.S. involvement in order to counteract the steps being taken to include the western zones of Germany in the European Recovery Program. The British, although acknowledging French fears regarding a revival of German aggression, felt that U.S. participation was necessary to ensure that Europe would be defended against the Soviet Union. The British call for American involvement reflected their recognition of the complex security issues facing Europe and of the fact that Britain could no longer play its traditional role of "balancer" in the face of Soviet power.

Moreover, the French continued to press for increased American involvement in security against Germany. Paris initially favored the restrictions imposed on Germany in the Byrnes Four Power Treaty and, failing to achieve them, hoped to associate the United States with an expanded Dunkirk model. They also linked the future of trizonal fusion to adequate security guarantees for France and agreement on the status of the Ruhr. Furthermore, Paris saw no reason to abandon the Dunkirk model since it did not envision eventual German participation, which, according to the French, implied the eventual creation of a west German army. Only if Britain became completely committed on the continent could France accept such a proposition.[73]

The Truman administration's position toward both the British and the French concerns was tentative. Secretary Marshall felt that the "French preoccupation with Germany as a major threat at this time seems to us outmoded and unrealistic" and argued that the "real threat to France seems to us to be another power which will undoubtedly seek to utilize [a] substantial segment of the German economy if unable to get control of [all of] Germany."[74]

The State Department also was equivocal regarding the British proposal for using the Dunkirk Treaty as a model for a wider system of European security with which the United States might eventually associate. According to a State Department policy paper, the Dunkirk Treaty model, "which might serve as the framework for a pact against Germany . . . [was] illusory unless intended as a screen for further defense measures." The paper argued that any adequate defense arrangements for western Europe should include measures that would apply in meeting acts of aggression from any potential source. Since Bevin's Western Union concept envisaged the eventual participation of Germany, the State Department felt "that adoption of a mutual assistance pact based solely on defense against that country would militate [against] its eventual entry into the concept."[75] Furthermore, the United States indicated that it would make no specific commitment regarding the form of American "association" with European security until the shape of the Western Union concept had been clarified.[76]

The London Six Power Conference on Germany and the Brussels Conference on European Security opened on February 19 and March 6, respectively. Shortly after the beginning of the talks in London, the western Europeans and the Americans were confronted with the so-called Prague coup, wherein the Beneš government in Czechoslovakia was overthrown and replaced by a pro-Soviet regime. This action, plus Soviet attempts to draw Norway into the Soviet sphere,[77] provided the impetus for the western Europeans and the United States to begin working on a mutually acceptable formula designed to formalize the status of the western zones of Germany and to provide security against both the Soviet Union and a potential renewal of German aggression.

While preliminary thinking on a western European security arrangement clearly predated the Prague coup, the Soviet actions in Czechoslovakia added urgency to those efforts. In addition, since the original
security talks were designed to coincide with the six power meeting on
the German question, the Brussels security conference was expected to
deal, for the most part, with security against Germany. However, because
of the immediacy of the Russian actions, American efforts to emphasize
the connection between security against Germany and security against the
Soviet Union assumed added importance.

On February 28, 1948, Secretary of State Marshall cabled the chairman of the U.S. delegation to the London talks, Ambassador Lewis
Douglas, in order to inform him of the State Department's position on
Germany and French security. In his message the secretary reinforced
the link between French security against Germany and the larger issue of
security against the Soviet Union. In doing so Marshall also formally linked
the presence of American occupation troops in Germany to an existing
U.S. commitment to European security.

> The French are secure against Germany as long as [the]
> occupation continues. The French are painfully aware of the
> disagreeable connotations of recent events in Czechoslovakia.
> In view of Communist integration of a third of Germany and
> the likelihood of continuing stringent economic condi-
> tions, a united Germany bereft of Western occupation force
> would be an easy prey to Communist domination. As long
> as European Communism threatens US vital interests and
> national security we could ill afford to abandon our military
> position in Germany which can now likewise serve as [a]
> morale element in a Europe disposed to depression by Czech-
> oslovak submission. The logical conclusion is that three
> power occupation may be of unforeseeable and indefinite
> duration, thus offering protracted security guarantees and
> establishing a firm community of interests.[78]

Therefore, one of the results of the Prague coup was to make more explicit the linking of French security against Germany to the wider question of European security against the Soviet Union. As long as the Soviet
threat remained acute, the United States would retain its military presence
in Germany and by doing so would offer France security against the

Germans. In order to reinforce this position Secretary Marshall suggested to Ambassador Douglas that he mention the possibility of the establishment of a military security board as an "adjunct of eventual tripartite military government administration" of Germany. [79]

The secretary of state also used the events in Czechoslovakia to pressure the French toward a fusion of its zone with that of the Anglo-Americans. Marshall explained that events in Prague lent "new urgency" to the merger of the three occupation zones and stated that such a move would serve French security interests and "facilitate the integration of [the] area concerned within general Western European recovery." The secretary hoped that an announcement expressing agreement to the principle of trizonal fusion could be made at the end of the London talks. [80]

The U.S. emphasis on the dangerous implications of the events in Prague and on linking European security against Germany with security against the Soviet Union had the desired effect of moving the French closer to agreement on the German question. However, the price was increased demands for American participation in continental security.

Two days after Marshall's message to Douglas, Ambassador Caffery was able to report that Bidault had "changed his point of view about treaties along the Dunkirk model and at this juncture is not particularly concerned about sticking to that model." Caffery went on to report that what really interested Bidault was "a concrete military alliance (against Soviet attack) with definite promises to do definite things under certain circumstances." With regard to Germany, Caffery reported that Bidault did desire "explicit mention of Germany in some way purely for domestic political reasons." [81] Shortly thereafter, on March 4, 1948, Bidault praised American efforts to promote the economic recovery of Europe through the Marshall Plan, maintained that the time had arrived to take similar steps with security, and proposed that the United States, Great Britain, and France enter into "political consultation." [82] Clearly, the French were facing two threats to their security—one from the Soviet Union and one from the potential of a revived Germany—and it is unclear which threat was uppermost in their minds. However, it is certain that the United States felt that the Soviet Union was the greater threat to European security. The French hoped that by acknowledging the American view they could demand greater U.S. participation in European security efforts, participation that they hoped also would embrace the German question. [83]

The fact that the French continued to view the German question as a
matter of primary importance is evident from the dispatches being received from Ambassador Douglas at the London talks. On the same day
that Caffery reported Bidault's acceptance of the American concept of a
security treaty, Douglas claimed that, although the French were conscious
of the dangers posed by the Soviet Union, it was very difficult for them
"to look over their next door neighbor and at the larger problem." Moreover, he observed "that the instructions of the French delegation at the
present London talks are based on specific conditions attaching to Germany."[84] The ambassador then recommended a solution:

> The question, therefore, is to absorb the French demand for
> security by some specific provision relieving this pressure
> which is exercised on every other political and economic
> question. If the French can be satisfied with some general
> guarantee of their security, they would be free of their
> present determination to inject security into all other
> items. . . .[85]

Douglas also felt that the thinking of the State Department regarding
the creation of a military security board, and a public announcement that
the United States would consult with the French and British in case of a
threatened renewal of aggression by Germany, would help to satisfy
some of the French concerns. Moreover, he reported that the French had
reacted enthusiastically to Marshall's linking of the retention of occupation troops in Germany with the continued presence of a Soviet threat.
Douglas felt that if the Truman administration could give some further
assurance regarding the presence of occupation troops, it would help to
satisfy the French.[86]

The State Department responded immediately, giving its approval for
a public announcement regarding tripartite consultations and the creation
of a military security board. Washington also informed Douglas that he
could communicate to the French privately that the retention of American
occupation troops in Germany would be "the logical conclusion to be
drawn from present events." However, the State Department made it
known to Douglas that the American agreements regarding security
"would be conditioned by French acceptance of a reasonable basis of the
main aspects of our program to further the effective coordination of

western Germany. . . ."[87] Because the London Conference was to go into recess in two days, Marshall added that Douglas should not try to finalize the above arrangements at that time, but that the ambassador might find it useful to present them as confidential suggestions "which may facilitate subsequent discussions."[88]

Douglas communicated those views to the French on March 5, and on the following day he was able to report to Marshall that the French had "expressed the view that if these ideas could be put into effect, they would go far toward providing satisfaction."[89]

On March 6, 1948, the London Conference went into recess, and the United States, France, and the United Kingdom issued a communiqué indicating that, while security questions would be discussed again when the meetings resumed in April, substantial agreement had been reached among the three occupying countries regarding the full association of the western zones of Germany in the European Recovery Program.[90]

On the same day that the London Conference recessed, the five power talks on European security began in Brussels. Five days later, on March 11, the United States was brought a large step closer to formal involvement in European security on receipt of an *aide-mémoire* from the British embassy in Washington. In that message the British indicated that the Norwegian government was under pressure from the Soviet Union to negotiate a bilateral security pact. The British reported that, although the Norwegians were opposed to such a pact, they were concerned about the support they would receive from the western powers when they refused the Soviet offer.[91]

Foreign Minister Bevin interpreted the Soviet move as posing two serious threats: one to the strategically important Atlantic area; the other to his efforts to build a Western Union. In order to meet those threats Bevin proposed the establishment of three security systems:

(i)   The United Kingdom-France-Benelux system with United States backing;
(ii) A scheme of Atlantic security, with which the United States would be even more closely concerned;
(iii) A Mediterranean security system, which would particularly affect Italy.[92]

Regarding the second system, Bevin felt that the British and American governments should begin immediate studies designed to facilitate the development of an Atlantic security system in order to "inspire the necessary confidence to consolidate the West against Soviet infiltration and at the same time inspire the Soviet Government with enough respect for the West to remove temptation from them and insure a long period of peace."[93]

The response from the United States was immediate and favorable. On March 12, 1948, in a note to Bevin, Marshall told the British that the United States was "prepared to proceed at once in the joining of discussions on the establishment of an Atlantic security system" and that he looked forward to the early arrival of British officials.[94] Later that afternoon Marshall asked Ambassador Caffery to deliver a similar letter to Bidault informing him that the United States fully appreciated "the dangers facing France and the other free countries of Euorpe." He went on to say that he hoped France, Britain, and the Benelux countries would agree on a comprehensive security system as a "prerequisite to any wider arrangement in which other countries including the United States might play a part."[95]

Five days later the Brussels meeting ended with the signing of a Treaty of Economic, Social and Cultural Collaboration and Collective Self-Defense. The preamble stated that the signatories would seek the association of other states with similar ideals, and it also included provisions regarding a possible renewal of aggression by Germany (as did article 7). However, in order to conform to the model established by the Inter-American Treaty, the provisions of article 4 (which required an "automatic" military response to an act of aggression against a signatory) did not mention Germany and were not limited to an attack by a non-signatory against a signatory; rather, they would also apply if one signatory attacked another. The open-ended nature of article 4 envisaged the eventual participation of Germany in the pact and in that sense was prerequisite for eventual American association with the European efforts.[96]

Concurrently with the signing of the treaty, President Truman addressed the Congress on the European situation. Citing the efforts of the five European states in Brussels, Truman indicated the future course of American policy:

> I am confident that the United States will, by appropriate
> means, extend to the free nations the support which the
> situation requires. I am sure that the determination of the
> free countries of Europe to protect themselves will be

matched by an equal determination on our part to help
them protect themselves.[97]

Shortly thereafter, Robert Lovett of the State Department and Senator
Vandenberg began discussions with a view toward achieving a formula
whereby the United States would associate itself with European security.

Conclusion

The failure of the London Foreign Ministers Conference in December
1947 did much to draw the United States closer to a long-term commitment to European security. The inability to achieve a four power resolution of the German question led to intensified American efforts aimed
at consolidating the western occupation zones and integrating western
Germany into the European Recovery Program. The American policy
of including western Germany was designed to help re-create the European balance of power, to forestall increased American military spending, and to prevent a major U.S. commitment to participate in European
security. However, from the French point of view, American efforts to
create a European balance against the Soviet Union by including western
Germany in the Marshall Plan threatened to create an imbalance of
power. That perception led the French to hedge on merging their occupation zone with the Anglo-American zone and to seek security guarantees
by drawing the United States into closer association with European
security affairs. In order to accomplish this latter goal the French hoped
to negotiate a treaty of guarantee along the lines of the Four Power
Treaty on Disarmament and Demilitarization proposed by Secretary
of State Byrnes in 1946.

Because of the importance of including western Germany in the European Recovery Program, the United States began taking steps to accommodate French fears. By the third week in January the United States
had agreed to include the French in governmental talks concerning the
future of Germany and also had agreed to the separation of the Saar
from Germany and its inclusion in the French economy (the status of the
Ruhr would be discussed at the governmental talks in London). However,
the United States felt that in view of the split between the western occupation powers and the Soviet Union on the German question a treaty of
guarantee along the lines of the Byrnes proposal would be unworkable
because of its inability to include the Soviet zone in its provisions.

An alternative to the Byrnes formula was proposed by British Foreign Minister Ernest Bevin on January 22, 1948. He envisioned a treaty between Britain, France, and the Benelux countries based on the Dunkirk Treaty model and aimed specifically against a renewal of German aggression. Moreover, he saw the eventual association of the United States with such a treaty.

But this formula was also unacceptable to the United States. Because of its perception that the major threat to European security came from the Soviet Union, the United States hoped that the Europeans would negotiate a treaty that would lay the groundwork for a system of security against the Russians, a system in which Germany would eventually participate and with which the United States would associate. From the U.S. point of view it was senseless to base such a wider system of security on a specifically anti-German platform. Instead, the United States favored a treaty based on the Rio Pact formula, which provided security against attack from both members and nonmembers of the treaty.

The Prague coup of February 24, 1948, speeded the western powers in reaching accommodation on the treaty issue. For its part, the United States linked the presence of American occupation troops in Germany to guarantees against both Soviet and German aggression and agreed to participate in a military security board designed to prevent German rearmament. Given those assurances, the French agreed to participate with the British and Americans in including western Germany in the European Recovery Program and dropped their demand for a European treaty based on the Dunkirk model. As a result of the mutual concessions, the Brussels meeting produced a treaty based on the Rio formula, and the United States soon promised to associate itself with the European efforts.

Therefore, the United States decided to take part in European security efforts in response to a complex set of issues embracing both the cold war and the German question. The convergence of those issues allowed the United States and the Europeans to accommodate each other and to move closer to agreement on the status of the western zones of Germany and on the eventual association of the United States with European security. However, both final agreement on Germany and the form that the American association would take were still matters for negotiation; it was not until the first week of April 1949 that negotiations produced the Occupation Statute for Germany and the North Atlantic Treaty.

It is clear that by spring 1948 American efforts in Europe were moving in two directions. On the one hand the United States hoped to include western Germany in the European Recovery Program, re-create a balance of power in Europe to offset the Soviet Union, reduce the drain on American resources, and prevent a long-term U.S. commitment to European security. On the other hand the participation of western Germany in the recovery program and the moves to consolidate the western occupation zones raised security questions in western Europe that were in fact drawing the United States closer to making the very commitments it sought to avoid.

Notes

1. Harry Bayard Price, *The Marshall Plan and Its Meaning* (Ithaca, N.Y.: Cornell University Press, 1955), p. 27.

2. *FRUS*, 1947, vol. 3, pp. 319-20; Steinhardt to Marshall; ibid., pp. 320-22; Griffis to Marshall.

3. Price, *The Marshall Plan and Its Meaning*, p. 37.

4. In the United States three committees—headed by W. Averell Harriman, Interior Secretary Julius A. Krug, and Edwin G. Nourse of the Council of Economic Advisers—coordinated U.S. resource availability with European needs.

5. *FRUS*, 1947, vol. 2, pp. 988-90; Murphy to Marshall; see also Gimbel, *The Origins of the Marshall Plan*, pp. 225-26.

6. Gimbel, *The Origins of the Marshall Plan*, pp. 208-09, chap. 16.

7. *FRUS*, 1947, vol. 2, pp. 984-85; Caffery to Marshall.

8. Ibid., p. 986.

9. *FRUS*, 1947, vol. 3, p. 711; Caffery to Marshall.

10. Ibid.

11. *FRUS*, 1947, vol. 2, pp. 987-88; Marshall to Caffery.

12. Ibid., p. 997, n. 29; Caffery to Marshall; see also Gimbel, *The Origins of the Marshall Plan*, p. 230.

13. *FRUS*, 1947, vol. 2, p. 991, n. 19; Caffery to Marshall.

14. Ibid., p. 992; Bidault to Marshall.

15. *FRUS*, 1947, vol. 3, pp. 722-23; Caffery to Marshall.

16. *FRUS*, 1947, vol. 2, pp. 1003-04; Marshall to Bidault.

17. Ibid., Memorandum of Conversation by Marshall.

18. Gimbel, *The Origins of the Marshall Plan*, p. 252.

19. *FRUS*, 1947, vol. 2, pp. 1041-42; Caffery to Marshall. The French wanted to internationalize the Ruhr in order to facilitate French access to the area and to increase the steel production of French industry.

20. Gimbel, *The Origins of the Marshall Plan*, p. 253.

21. Ibid., p. 258.

22. Ibid., pp. 247-66; see also *FRUS*, 1947, vol. 2, pp. 397-405; Kennan Memorandum.

23. *FRUS*, 1947, vol. 3, pp. 783-84; Lovett to Caffery.

24. Walter Laqueur. *The Rebirth of Europe* (New York: Holt, Rinehart and

Winston, 1970), pp. 118-19. For the assistance offered by the American labor movement, see Roy Godson, *American Labor and European Politics: The AFL as a Transnational Force* (New York: Crane, Russak, 1976).

25. *FRUS,* 1947, vol. 1, p. 772; Report of the Policy Planning Staff.

26. Ibid.

27. Ibid., pp. 774-75.

28. Ibid.; see also Daniel Yergin, *Shattered Peace* (Boston: Houghton Mifflin
Company, 1977), p. 330.

29. *FRUS,* 1947, vol. 1, p. 772; Report of the Policy Planning Staff.

30. Yergin, *Shattered Peace,* pp. 330-31.

31. *FRUS,* 1947, vol. 2, pp. 813-14; Memorandum of Conversation by Douglas.

32. Ibid., p. 814.

33. Ibid., pp. 829-39; Bonnet to Marshall.

34. Ibid.

35. Ibid., pp. 815-16; British Memorandum of Conversation.

36. Ibid., p. 816.

37. John Gimbel, *The American Occupation of Germany* (Stanford, Calif.:
Stanford University Press, 1968), pp. 194-98.

38. Ibid.

39. U.S., Congress, Senate, Committee on Foreign Relations, *European Recovery
Program, Hearings Before the Committee on Foreign Relations, United States Senate,*
80th Congress, 2nd session, 1948, 1:2. Hereafter cited as *European Recovery Program
Hearings.*

40. The National Defense Establishment had been created by the National
Security Act of 1947, which also created the National Security Council, provided
a formal charter for the Joint Chiefs of Staff, and established the Central Intelligence
Agency. Forrestal was named the first Secretary of Defense. Warner R. Schilling,
Paul Y. Hammond, and Glenn H. Snyder, *Strategy, Politics and Defense Budgets*
(New York: Columbia University Press, 1962), p. 10, n. 7.

41. *European Recovery Program Hearings,* p. 444.

42. Ibid., p. 470.

43. Ibid., p. 478.

44. Ibid.

45. Ibid., p. 490.

46. Ibid., pp. 11-12; see also Gimbel, *The Origins of the Marshall Plan,* p. 266.

47. U.S., Department of State, *Foreign Relations of the United States,* 1948,
vol. 2, Germany and Austria, p. 25; Marshall to Inverchapel. Hereafter cited as
FRUS, 1948, vol. 2.

48. Ibid., p. 34, n. 2; for an American interpretation of the December 17 meeting, see ibid., pp. 27-28; Wallner to Bonbright.

49. Ibid., p. 26; Inverchapel to Marshall.

50. Ibid., p. 32; The Department of the Army to Clay. After tripartite discussions
on the Saar, the following statement was released: "I have the honor to inform you
that the Governments of the United States, Great Britain and France have agreed
to consider henceforth the coal production of the Saar and France as a common
resource." Ibid., p. 55.

51. Ibid., p. 32; The Department of the Army to Clay.

52. Ibid., p. 35; Marshall to Bonnet.

53. Ibid., p. 34. Marshall told the French he regretted that they had not been kept informed of the Frankfurt discussions.

54. For a summary of the French objections, see ibid., pp. 53-54; Marshall to Bonnet.

55. Ibid., pp. 59-60; Editorial Note; see also Gimbel, *The American Occupation of Germany*, pp. 198-99.

56. For text, see *FRUS*, 1946, vol. 2, pp. 190-93.

57. *FRUS*, 1948, vol. 2, pp. 61-62; State Department Policy Paper.

58. U.S., Department of State, *Foreign Relations of the United States*, 1948, vol. 3, Western Europe, p. 4; Inverchapel to Marshall. Hereafter cited as *FRUS*, 1948, vol. 3. The Dunkirk Treaty was signed on March 4, 1947. For the text, see Great Britain, Parliament, *Parliamentary Papers*, 1947-1948, Cmnd. 7217, Treaty of Alliance and Mutual Assistance Between His Majesty in Respect of the United Kingdom and Northern Ireland and the President of the French Republic, March 4, 1947.

59. *FRUS*, 1947, vol. 3, pp. 4-5; Inverchapel to Marshall.

60. Ibid., pp. 6-7; Hickerson to Marshall.

61. The United States had raised similar objections to the Dunkirk Treaty soon after it was signed. See *FRUS*, 1947, vol. 2, p. 194; minutes of a Conversation between Marshall and the president of France (Auriol).

62. *FRUS*, 1948, vol. 3, p. 7; Hickerson to Marshall.

63. Ibid., pp. 7-8; Kennan to Marshall.

64. Ibid., Memorandum of Conversation by Hickerson.

65. Ibid., p. 11.

66. *FRUS*, 1947, vol. 1, p. 771; Report by the Policy Planning Staff.

67. Ibid.

68. Great Britain, Parliament, *Parliamentary Debates* (Commons), 5th series, vol. 446 (1947-48): 883ff.

69. *FRUS*, 1948, vol. 3, p. 13; Memorandum of Conversation by Lovett.

70. Ibid., pp. 14-15; Inverchapel to Lovett.

71. Ibid., p. 17; Lovett to Inverchapel.

72. Ibid., p. 22; Memorandum of Conversation by Hickerson.

73. *FRUS*, 1948, vol. 2, pp. 63-64; Memorandum of Conversation by Achilles.

74. Ibid., p. 71; Marshall to Caffery.

75. Ibid., p. 63; Department of State Policy Paper. The Benelux countries also were opposed to the idea of a European security treaty based solely on the Dunkirk model and were more inclined to accept the Rio formula; see *FRUS*, 1948, vol. 3, pp. 26-29; Caffery to Marshall.

76. *FRUS*, 1948, vol. 2, p. 63.

77. *FRUS*, 1948, vol. 3, pp. 48-49; Bay to Marshall.

78. *FRUS*, 1948, vol. 2, p. 101; Marshall to Douglas.

79. Ibid.

80. Ibid., p. 102.

81. *FRUS,* 1948, vol. 3, pp. 34-35; Caffery to Marshall.

82. Ibid., p. 38; Editorial Note.

83. Hunter, *Security in Europe,* pp. 27-31.

84. *FRUS,* 1948, vol. 2, pp. 110-11; Douglas to Marshall.

85. Ibid.

86. Ibid., p. 111.

87. Ibid., pp. 122-23; Marshall to Douglas.

88. Ibid., p. 123.

89. Ibid., pp. 138-39; Douglas to Marshall.

90. Ibid., pp. 142-43; Communiqué Issued at the Recess of the London Conference on Germany.

91. *FRUS,* 1948, vol. 3, pp. 46-48; the British Embassy to the Department of State.

92. Ibid., p. 47.

93. Ibid., p. 48.

94. Ibid.; Marshall to Inverchapel.

95. Ibid., p. 50; Marshall to Caffery.

96. For text of the Brussels Pact, see United Nations, Treaty Series, *Treaties and International Agreements Registered or Filed and Reported with the Secretariat of the United Nations,* vol. 19 (1948), no. 304, "Treaty for collaboration in economic, social and cultural matters and for collective self defense [The Brussels Treaty]," 17 March 1948, p. 51. Article 4 mentioned article 51 of the UN Charter and article 7 provided for consultation in case of a threat to the peace "in whatever area the threat should arise."

97. U.S., President, *Public Papers of the Presidents of the United States* (Washington, D.C.: *Office of the Federal Register,* National Archives and Records Service, 1953-   ), Harry S. Truman, 1948, p. 184. Hereafter cited as *Public Papers of the Presidents, Harry S. Truman, 1948.* In his speech Truman also called for a program of "universal military training."

THREE

Formulating the Treaty

Introduction

Shortly after Truman's March 17 speech to Congress pledging United States support for European defense, American and European officials began to search for a method whereby the U.S. government would associate itself with the security arrangements of the Brussels Pact. As soon as that process began two lines of thinking emerged within the State Department regarding the form such an association should take. The first position, taken by George Kennan and the Policy Planning Staff, was that the United States should further European efforts through a unilateral guarantee in the form of a presidential declaration similar to the Monroe Doctrine. Kennan's rationale was to allow the United States the maximum amount of freedom in determining its involvement in European security and to avoid entanglement in a permanent military alliance. However, a second group of State Department officials, who had regular contacts with their European counterparts and U.S. congressional leaders, adopted an opposite point of view. These men, including Robert Lovett and John Hickerson, felt that the most effective form of association would embrace the concept of reciprocal obligations.

The perception that a treaty formula was needed stemmed from two sources: the knowledge that any American involvement—including a presidential declaration—would require congressional backing; and the fact that the Europeans, especially the French, were pressing for precise, formal guarantees from the United States. But the Congress and the Europeans viewed the treaty formula from different perspectives. The congressional attitude was that a treaty, by conforming to the formulas of the Monroe Doctrine and Rio Pact, would actually limit the American commitment by allowing each party to determine for itself whether an act of aggression had occurred and what its response would be. On the other hand the Europeans considered a treaty formula the best method of entangling the United States in European security. Of special importance was the continuing French desire for formal security guarantees from the United States before they would consent to a fusion of the French zone with the Anglo-American Bizonia. Of course, these calls for binding guarantees from the United States were intensified by the memory of the interwar period, when the Senate had rejected U.S. participation in the League of Nations and America withdrew into political isolation. The French felt that they had been abandoned by the United States in the face of the ever-present rivalry with Germany and the growing specter of bolshevism, and they were anxious not to repeat the same experience after World War II.

Yet even when it was decided to proceed with the development of a treaty formula, it was apparent that the Europeans and Americans were approaching the conclusion of such a treaty from different points of view. The Europeans, of course, wanted formal, binding guarantees from the United States that an attack on Europe would bring an immediate U.S. response. On the other hand the United States wished to avoid any automatic commitment to European defense. This difference became most apparent in the discussion of article 5 of the North Atlantic Treaty, as the Europeans pressed for the strong language of the Brussels Pact while the United States held out for the relatively weaker Rio Pact-Monroe Doctrine formula.

Although the U.S. formula was eventually accepted as the basis for the North Atlantic Treaty, the Berlin blockade, initiated by Soviet authorities soon after the successful conclusion of the London Conference in June 1948, brought a new element into the security picture. The immediacy of the Soviet action led the French to lobby for military assistance in the form of arms and equipment in order to strengthen its armed forces in Germany. Coupled with the Vandenberg Resolution (June 11, 1948) requirement for reciprocal aid, the French demand for U.S. military assistance ultimately led to the inclusion of article 3 in the North Atlantic Treaty. Because this article had no precedence in either the Rio or the Brussels pacts, it was a unique provision of the Atlantic Alliance and constituted a true departure from traditional American foreign policy, a departure that eventually would entangle the United States in a permanent military alliance.

Commitment Alternatives:
A Treaty or Presidential Declaration?

As the U.S. government began to take steps leading toward an association with the countries of the Brussels Pact, there was some uncertainty as to what form that association would take; a treaty formula was by no means the only alternative. The concept of extending a unilateral guarantee to the western Europeans while encouraging them to widen the base of the Brussels Pact also received wide attention in the State Department. Among those who favored that type of association was George Kennan of the Policy Planning Staff.

In a paper written on March 19, 1948—two days after President Truman's address on the problems of European security—George Butler of the Policy Planning Staff wrote a memorandum concerning American association with the European efforts. He stated that the Planning Staff was considering three alternatives to such association: a military assistance treaty based on article 51 of the UN Charter; a regional treaty based on article 52 of the Charter; or a unilateral declaration of U.S. support for Europe. Significantly, Butler reported that the staff of the National Security Council recommended that the United States adopt the third approach, that of extending a unilateral guarantee to the Brussels Pact countries that the U.S. would consider a Soviet attack on them as an attack on itself.[1]

Shortly thereafter, on March 22, 1948, the first of the highly secret meetings between U.S., British, and Canadian officials took place in Washington. The British representatives considered the American attitude toward the Brussels Pact the first order of business, but the American officials—Ambassador Douglas and John Hickerson—could only assure the British that U.S. support was implicit in President Truman's speech and that they should "assume" such support would be forthcoming. The British wished a "firm commitment on the part of the U.S. to aid militarily in the event of any aggression in Europe," but the two Americans were noncommital because congressional support was required for such action. Moreover, the Americans were not sure whether U.S. assurances were best delivered in the form of a treaty or a presidential proclamation, and they again cited the need for congressional approval in either case.[2]

On March 23, 1948, the Policy Planning Staff issued its report on U.S. involvement with western European security. In this report the Planning

Staff suggested that the Brussels powers eventually widen the base of their membership to include Ireland, Austria, Spain, Switzerland, and Germany, while pressing for the immediate inclusion of Portugal and Scandinavia. While the report did consider the possibility of future American association with such an organization, possibly including membership, the Planning Staff felt that the United States "should not now participate as a full member in [the] Western Union but should give it assurance of armed support."[3] Moreover, that assurance was to be given in a Monroe Doctrine-type declaration stating that the United States would consider an armed attack against the members of the expanded Brussels Pact to be an armed attack on the United States with which it would deal in accordance with the inherent right of individual and collective self-defense recognized by article 51 of the UN Charter.[4]

Furthermore, the report recommended that the countries of the Brussels Pact conclude with "other selected non-Communist states" a mutual defense agreement that would come "under the Charter of the United Nations." Although the United States was not mentioned as a party to that agreement and there was no provision for self-help and mutual assistance, the outlines of the proposed mutual defense agreement included many of the principles later incorporated in the North Atlantic Treaty, including geographic membership requirements; consultations in case of threatened attack or "indirect aggression"; collective response in case of armed attack; auto-interpretation of what constituted an armed attack; and the appropriate means of response, coordination of response, and a fixed duration.[5]

Of course, the views of the Policy Planning Staff were largely the products of Kennan's own thinking. Kennan was opposed to the creation of "a full fledged reciprocal military alliance" between the United States and western Europe because he felt it would be unnecessarily provocative to the Soviet Union and because he had no faith in the sanctity of "written treaties." While he acknowledged European fears of being abandoned by the United States, he felt that American policies since the end of World War II provided sufficient evidence of the U.S. commitment to western Europe. Instead of a formal treaty arrangement, Kennan proposed the so-called dumbbell approach, which would have meant the extension of a unilateral U.S. (and possibly Canadian) guarantee to the Brussels Pact nations.[6]

Given this high level opposition, how, then, did the treaty formula come to be the accepted form of association? Writing twenty years after the fact, Kennan argues that in the month between the March 23 report of the Policy Planning Staff and an April 22 paper submitted by the State Department to the president and the National Security Council talks between Under Secretary of State Robert Lovett and Senator Arthur Vandenberg produced a shift in attitude. Moreover, Kennan suggested that the initiative for the treaty formula came from Senator Vandenberg and other congressional leaders and stated that Lovett

> went so far as to assume on the part of the Senators a greater wisdom than was actually there, and took the form of catering to senatorial opinion in instances where one might better have attempted to educate its protagonists to a more enlightened and effective view.[7]

From Kennan's point of view the Vandenberg-Lovett conversations shaped evolving American commitment to Europe in two ways: first, by requiring that there be no automatic commitment to go to war and, second, by requiring the principle of reciprocity. Kennan felt that the second point, reciprocity, was the more important because it "would inevitably involve something in the nature of a contract—a treaty, in other words—a treaty unprecedented in our history, and one requiring, of course, the most solemn and deliberate considerations and the eventual approval by the Senate."[8]

Therefore, it is possible to see that at the beginning of discussions concerning possible American association with western European defense efforts, the idea of a treaty was not considered the only method by which that association might take place. The major proponent of a nontreaty approach within the State Department, George Kennan, has described two sources outside the department that eventually led the United States into the North Atlantic Treaty. Those two sources were congressional leaders led by Senator Vandenberg and the western Europeans themselves. In analyzing the impact of these sources Kennan emphasizes the role of the congressional leaders and their influence on key State Department officials, such as Under Secretary of State Robert Lovett.[9]

However, while Vandenberg did make an important contribution by insisting that any American association be on the basis of "self help and mutual aid," he remained "cool" to the idea of a treaty and was not the prime mover behind the treaty formula. On the other hand State Department officials, including Lovett, had accepted the idea of a treaty-based formula prior to Vandenberg's official appearance on the scene. The State Department's willingness to move ahead with a treaty was based on contacts with European officials who emphasized the need for binding U.S. commitments that would encompass security issues extending beyond the Soviet-American rivalry. In this regard it is clear that the State Department's acceptance of a treaty formula was strongly influenced by French concerns about the future of Germany and the reopening of the London Conference, which was scheduled for April 20, 1948.

The self-help and mutual aid provision emphasized by Vandenberg would be a unique feature of the North Atlantic Treaty. Its purpose was to reassure reluctant senators that the Europeans would take an active part in strengthening their own defenses and in assisting the United States whenever and wherever possible. Of course, the inclusion of this provision was designed to assure them that the United States would not be footing the entire bill for western defense. Also implicit in this provision was the belief that once adequate defense levels had been achieved cutbacks in potential American efforts could be expected. Yet despite the fact that this provision was originally intended to prevent a costly American commitment to European security, its inclusion in the North Atlantic Treaty formally committed the United States—under the mutual aid clause—to provide continuous military assistance to western Europe and ultimately led to the very entanglement it sought to avoid. However, it was other issues, more closely related to general European security and the reopening of the London Conference, that first moved the United States in the direction of the North Atlantic Treaty.

On March 23, 1947—the same date as the initial report by the Planning Staff—the second meeting of U.S., Canadian, and British representatives took place in Washington. Various methods for American association were discussed, and the conclusion reached was that the western powers faced two choices: a presidential guarantee, such as that favored by Kennan, or the conclusion of a mutual defense agreement to which the United States and Canada would adhere. The advantages of the alternatives were discussed as follows:

> The point was raised that while the US might in an emergency situation extend assurances of armed support against aggression on the basis of a declaration of intent, sooner or

later the US would have to require reciprocal guarantees
from others. Were reciprocal guarantees offered, the result
would, in effect, be a mutual defense agreement. The objective, therefore, should from the outset include a pact of
mutual defense against aggression to which the US (and
Canada) would finally adhere.[10]

While the meeting adjourned with the understanding that none of the
parties was making any commitments, it is interesting to note that each
would prepare papers for a meeting the following day that would look
toward the development of a "Western Mutual Defense Pact."[11] Moreover, the inclusion of the statement concerning reciprocal guarantees
indicates that the State Department, independent of Senator Vandenberg,
was viewing reciprocity as a requirement in any association with the
Europeans.

The next day the United States presented an undated and untitled
paper that was designed to "give effect to the President's 17 March declaration of support for the free nations of Europe, and the recommendations
of which will require consultation with US political leaders to assure full
bi-partisan support."[12] The objective of the American paper was to
develop "a Security Pact for the North Atlantic Area. . . ." The paper
further proposed that the United States would be a member of such a
pact as would all the other countries (including Iceland and Italy) that
bordered the North Atlantic area.[13]

At the fourth meeting Ambassador Douglas made specific mention of
a treaty:

[Any] treaty article committing the parties to war in the
event of aggression should in terms of American political
realities either be on the model of the Rio pact . . . or should
be explicit in indicating that each party would determine
"municipally" for itself whether an armed attack had in fact
occurred.[14]

Douglas' suggestions were incorporated into a further draft of the
American working paper, and by April 1 the representatives of the three
countries had "generally agreed that a *treaty* should be accomplished
and as soon as possible. . . . This would have much greater political effect

than a mere declaration of intent, no matter how strongly worded for Presidential delivery."[15] It also was recommended that work be started on a mutual defense agreement emphasizing the preservation of "western civilization" and drawing on both the Rio and Brussels treaties.[16]

Therefore, while the Policy Planning Staff—operating without the benefit of European input—did not favor the conclusion of a treaty, State Department officials who participated in talks with the British and Canadians were the initial American advocates of a treaty formula. There also is evidence to suggest that British cognizance of French security requirements may have influenced their position on the conclusion of a treaty.

The British initially had favored French participation in the Washington talks with the Americans and Canadians, but the Americans—claiming that the French presence would create the possibility of security leaks—declined to extend an invitation to Paris.[17] It also was clear that not all Europeans felt that a treaty was necessary to counter the threat of Soviet aggression and that the British insistence on the treaty must have evolved from other considerations.

On April 5 the chief of the Division of Western European Affairs, Theodore Achilles, met with Paul-Henri Spaak, prime minister of Belgium. Achilles recorded that Spaak believed that the Soviet Union was assuming that any Russian aggression in Europe would lead to war with the United States "whether or not the United States entered into formal treaty relations for the defense of Western Europe. . . ." However, Spaak reported that if the United States did enter into such formal arrangements all of western Europe, particularly France, would welcome such a move.[18]

It is clear from Achilles' report that Spaak, as a European, did not view a formal treaty as an essential requirement for defense against possible Soviet attack. Rather, he merely wished to see Truman's March 17 statement given "greater precision."[19] On the other hand he noted that a treaty pledging American support for European defense would be "universally welcomed in Western Europe, particularly in France. . . ." The reason why the French were more anxious than the other Europeans to have a treaty was explained four days later, when Ernest Bevin wrote to Washington about French security and Germany.

According to Bevin, a defense agreement that gave solid evidence of American backing for European efforts and that led to a "sound Atlantic Security System" would have a profound effect on France in dealing with the question of Germany. The British prime minister pointed out that the French had been anxious for a four power treaty of guarantee against a resurgent Germany, and were hoping for new arrangements to ease their fears. Bevin argued that "if the new defence system is so framed that it related to any aggressor it would give all the European States such confidence that it might well be that the age-long trouble between Germany and France might tend to disappear."[20]

Bevin also noted a continued wariness on the part of Europeans about the domestic political situation in the United States and clearly drew upon memories of the interwar years when he said that American support in the form of a presidential declaration would be "inadequate." Bevin believed that such a declaration, without the backing of the Senate, would make Europeans doubt that any reciprocal obligation had been assumed. While the European leaders would "be under a moral obligation not to leave the United States in the lurch," they would be forced to answer domestic critics by saying that a declaration by the president did not bind the Brussels powers to come to the aid of the United States. Bevin argued that in such a case European leaders would be "left in a very un-satisfactory position and might arouse resentment in America."[21]

Two days later Senator Vandenberg and Robert Lovett had their first recorded meeting,[22] and it is important to note that, although Lovett was already on record as agreeing "in principle" with a treaty-based asso-ciation,[23] Vandenberg—while willing to "develop a short term procedure which would back the efforts of the Western Union and other Western European countries"—was "cool" to a treaty-based formula.[24] Vandenberg's coolness of April 11 is further evidence that the idea of a pact or treaty did not come from the senator but rather from the State Department, as represented by Lovett, and in response to European pressures.

On April 13 the National Security Council received NSC 9, a revision of Policy Planning Staff paper 27/1, itself a blending of the March 23 paper developed by the Planning Staff and the working paper that came out of the U.S., British, and Canadian meetings in Washington. This re-port opposed American participation in the Brussels Pact but recommended that a relationship be established with that organization through "the conclusion of a Collective Defense Agreement for the North Atlantic Area. . . ."[25] The paper stated that the president should announce that invitations had been extended to various countries in the North Atlantic area to take part in a conference to conclude such an agreement. More-over, it recommended that the mutual defense arrangement should include a provision that each individual party consider an armed attack against other parties in the area defined by the agreement as an attack against itself and that it take the appropriate action to assist in repelling the attack in accordance with the provisions of article 51 of the UN Charter.[26]

When a revised version of this paper was shown to Senator Vandenberg on April 18, he continued to object to the extent of the obligations that the United States would have to accept in such an arrangement. More-over, he wished to include one paragraph regarding strengthening the United Nations and another stipulating that any American association with a security pact be based on "mutual aid and self help."[27] The refer-ence to the United Nations came in response to a number of resolutions before the Senate Foreign Relations Committee concerning reform of the United Nations, while the mutual aid and self-help provisions reflect Vandenberg's concern that the United States would shoulder the entire bill for European rearmament. However, it was this latter stipulation that, when included in the North Atlantic Treaty, ultimately led to the entanglement of the United States in European security.

Four days later, on April 22, Vandenberg's requests were incorporated into a revision of the April 13 paper by the Policy Planning Staff and certainly formed the basis for Kennan's observations about Vandenberg's input into the development of the North Atlantic Treaty.[28] Furthermore, the western Europeans were meeting in London to discuss "defence arrange-ments in which the United States might play a part . . ." and the pressures for American assistance were mounting.

Bevin and Bidault wrote to Marshall on April 17 stating that they realized the military talks they were preparing to hold had to take concrete steps toward reinforcing the machinery of the Brussels Pact, but they also knew that the simultaneous aid of the United States would be required in order to give more effective assistance to the defense of western Europe, "which at present cannot stand alone."[29]

On April 27, 1948, Lovett and Vandenberg met again to discuss the revised plans, and this time Secretary of State Marshall and John Foster Dulles also were present. Apparently, Vandenberg had given the proposals by the State Department—as well as his own inputs—further thought and had developed some misgivings. In general Vandenberg's reservations coincided with those of Dulles and were based primarily on the extent of the obligations the United States would assume: the proposals by the State Department would fall under the heading of a "regional pact system" under Chapter VIII of the UN Charter, while the approach favored by the two Republican leaders would concentrate on the more strictly defensive implications of article 51. Both Vandenberg and Dulles were opposed to "inviting countries to come to us with their shopping lists" and to giving "military guarantees." The two men also felt that the U.S. government, in order to avoid being provocative, should not issue an invitation for consultations with a view toward completing a regional pact but rather should encourage the Brussels Pact countries to "merely seek to become associated with sources of supply and assistance in the Western Hemisphere."[30]

At the conclusion of the meeting it was decided that the State Department would request a supporting resolution from the Senate Foreign Relations Committee; after the Senate had finished action on the resolution, the State Department would arrange for the Brussels powers to ask for consultations with the United States on the issue of international security; once the invitation was received, President Truman would announce that the United States was prepared to consider association with regional arrangements that affected American national security and that such association be on the basis of "self help and mutual aid."[31]

Writing of this meeting in 1950, Dulles maintained that most of the pressure for the conclusion of a North Atlantic Pact had come from Lovett and Marshall. In his own report of the meeting Lovett stated: "There was no disagreement as to the desirability of finding some method to indicate that we are going to stay in the picture but no one felt happy in the solution presently offered."[32]

On April 29 George Kennan reacted to the April 22 paper in the same way as had Vandenberg and Dulles; he too felt more inclined to extend military assistance and coordination than to participate in negotiations leading to a multilateral treaty. Responding to reports in the American press that the Soviets had "the capability of overrunning all of Europe and the Middle East," Kennan wrote to Marshall and Lovett that, if such was the case, "what the Western Europeans require from us is not so much a public political and military alliance . . . but rather realistic staff talks to see what can be done about their defense." According to Kennan, the presence of occupation troops in Germany was sufficient guarantee that America would be at war if the Russians attacked Europe.[33]

Kennan repeated this line of reasoning on May 7, when he wrote to Lovett stating that the United States should try to convince the Europeans not to seek any commitment more formal than that of the Senate resolution and the president's statement of March 17, "at least until there has been more time for the practical implementation of the Brussels Treaty system." Instead, argued Kennan, the Europeans and the United States should proceed with joint military talks.[34]

However, despite official misgivings, the idea of a treaty-based association was kept alive by the German situation. The London talks had reopened on April 20 and again ran into difficulties regarding the French concern for security.

By May 10 the U.S. representative, Ambassador Douglas, was asking for instructions as to what assurances he could offer the French with respect to Germany. He felt that, although the previous offer of a military security board was helpful, something more would be needed to push the French toward trizonal fusion. Douglas also felt that the London talks were not the place to offer additional assurances to the French but that the question of security against Germany "should more properly be dealt with in the overall arrangements for western European security."[35]

Soon thereafter, Douglas' concerns increased as the French representatives in London pressed for information about the status of U.S. occupation troops in Germany.[36] Since the occupation troops clearly could perform double duty as guarantees against possible Soviet aggression or German *revanchism,* their continued presence in Germany was extremely important to the French. Although the United States had only planned to keep the troops in Euorpe for approximately two years, failure to reach four power agreement on Germany meant that American forces would remain indefinitely. The first expression of that change in policy came with Byrnes's Stuttgart speech in September 1946, and was reaffirmed in Truman's March 17, 1948 address to Congress, when he said that it was "of vital importance . . . that we keep our occupation forces in Germany until the peace is secure in Europe."[37] Nevertheless, the French were troubled by the fact that there was no firm commitment by the United States linking the presence of those troops to a continued American involvement in European security. Since the permanent status of the U.S. occupation forces remained unclear, the French feared that the United States would, at some undetermined future date, withdraw those troops without taking into account European security concerns. Therefore, the French continued to drag their feet at London.

The pressures for American action to alleviate French concerns grew in mid-May. On the eleventh Douglas reported that French concerns were increasing because they felt that the United States was "growing cold" on "the general security problem." According to Douglas, French fears would "rapidly evaporate if they could get some assurance about the general security problem."[38] Douglas' reports received added confirmation a few days later with the receipt in Washington of a letter from Ernest Bevin.

On May 14, 1948, Bevin wrote to Marshall expressing his view of the situation in London. He said that what was needed to defeat the Communists in Europe and to encourage "democratic forces" was "some definite acceptance of obligations on the part of the United States." He said that the presence of U.S. occupation forces in Germany only provided "indirect assurance to Italy and Scandinavia," and was not sufficient "even to remove the perpetual uneasiness of the French." Bevin further stated that if France had a document signed jointly by the three western occupation powers, indicating firm commitments to European security, it would be less difficult for the French government to pursue joint policies in Germany with the United States and Great Britain.[39]

The link that Bevin made between the French inability to proceed with plans for trizonal fusion and a general agreement on European security, and the knowledge that American occupation troops in Germany only gave the Europeans partial assurances against Soviet attack or renewed German aggression, troubled the Truman administration. In an effort to reassure the British and French, the U.S. government decided to inform the Europeans of the progress being made on the so-called Vandenberg Resolution.

The Vandenberg Resolution and the London Agreements

On May 11, 1948, Under Secretary of State Lovett appeared before the Senate Foreign Relations Committee—meeting in executive session—with a draft of the proposed Senate resolution. While not explicitly committing the United States to a policy that sought to conclude a treaty, the proposed resolution did include the following provisions:

> Progressive development of regional and other collective arrangements for individual and collective self defense in accordance with the purposes, principles and provisions of the charter.
> Association of the United States with such regional and other collective arrangements as are based on self help and mutual aid, and affect its national security.[40]

During discussions in the committee, the extremely limited nature of the proposed resolution was emphasized, as well as the differences between European and American perceptions regarding what form the future association should take. Senator Alexander Wiley stated his belief that the Europeans were "looking for something much more" than the United States was offering in the Senate resolution, and Lovett agreed: "they were very definitely looking for some form of engagement by us. . . . Which would in effect be a guarantee." However, despite the fact that he had already come out in favor of a treaty and was in fact leading the United States in that direction in talks with the Europeans, Lovett informed the senators that the administration was "in no position to meet [the European] views as originally expressed." On May 12, 1948, Vandenberg himself expressed the noncommital nature of the resolution, but he also indicated its usefulness in dealing with the Europeans:

> I think the great gain to us on the one hand is that we have moved forward into the field of security without involving ourselves in any permanent obligations of any nature; second that by so moving we have provided a complete answer to those who are going to constantly press for greater movements in this direction, and we must have an affirmative answer. We cannot rest entirely on the negative answer.[41]

Shortly thereafter, the text of the proposed resolution was used for just the purposes Vandenberg had in mind. In order to assure the French that the United States was "not in any sense 'growing cold' on [the] general security problem," Lovett communicated the text to Ambassador Douglas in London with instructions to show it to the French. It was hoped that evidence of American willingness to associate with European security would encourage the French to be more cooperative on the German question.[42] Lovett's reassurances were momentarily successful, but on May 20 the French government handed the American embassy in Paris two notes that threatened to destroy the efforts of the London Conference.

Briefly, the French notes expressed apprehension over the course of the London Conference, which was nearing its conclusion. Chief among French concerns was the fact that the United States and Great Britain were approaching agreement on a west German political structure that created a constituent assembly, authorized the assembly to prepare a constitution, and developed an Occupation Statute.[43] The French favored more limited policies, such as currency reform, the revision of internal frontiers, and the pooling of foreign trade. They also wished ministerial-level talks on the more substantive issues of the political structure of western Germany, control of the Ruhr, and disarmament and demilitariza-tion. Accordingly, the French proposed coordinating political policy and western unity in the face of what they considered to be a growing Soviet menace. In addition, they linked western unity against the Soviet threat to similar unity on the German question, including the timing of political policy on Germany.[44]

The stated reason for the French reluctance to proceed on the German question was a fear that such moves by the western allies would "cause a dangerous Soviet reaction," and they expressed concern "over the western military weakness in Germany in the face of possible Soviet aggression."[45] Of course, the American and British representatives in London viewed the French concerns as merely a stall designed "to force a postponement of the establishment of the provisional government in Germany" and to obtain concessions regarding security and the Ruhr.[46] This belief was confirmed in talks between Lovett and Ambassador Bonnet in Washington on May 21, 1948. Lovett reported that on two occasions during the talks Bonnet had "intimated that French worries over Germany were not unrelated to disappointment over lack of progress on American support for the Brussels Treaty."[47]

The Truman administration responded sharply to the French hesitance by indicating that the United States and Great Britain would "go ahead with [a] provisional [government] for [the] Bizonal area on [the] proposed time schedule, without the French if necessary." Moreover, the U.S. government informed Paris that, unless the French came around, it would be impossible for the United States to undertake any commitment regarding security against Germany.[48]

However, on the same day that the United States reacted so sharply to the French, May 24, George Kennan presented a paper to Marshall that accepted the idea of a treaty formula for American association with European security.[49] In his memorandum to the secretary of state, Kennan indicated that in light of a recent speech by Canadian Foreign Minister Louis St. Laurent[50] and the Bevin message on May 14, the United States should "be very careful not to place [itself] in the position of being an obstacle to further progress toward the political union of the western democracies." Kennan also recommended that the United States "should attempt to establish all facts bearing on the effort of opening the question of a North Atlantic Security pact" in order to "keep the ball rolling and keep up the hopes of the peoples of Europe."[51]

There are a number of explanations behind Kennan's switch. First, it was becoming clear to Kennan that events were moving too fast for his opposition to prevent the conclusion of a treaty. Therefore, he may have been hoping to use his acceptance of a treaty formula to moderate the steps that would inevitably be taken toward a formalized pact. Second, Kennan continued to view the Soviet threat to the Europeans as primarily political in nature, and it is apparent that he saw the conclusion of a treaty as a means to stiffen the morale of the western Europeans and to promote their recovery efforts.[52] A third influence on Kennan's switch was the German question.

In February 1948 Kennan expressed himself on the German question. As he saw it, the problem was to integrate western Germany into a larger western European community while still providing Germany's neighbors with safeguards against German domination. While he had "no confidence in any of the old-fashioned concepts of collective security," Kennan accepted the idea that "mutual defense arrangements will no doubt be necessary to the prejudices of the other Western European peoples, whose thinking is still old fashioned and unrealistic on this subject."[53] What the direct impact of the German question was on Kennan's May memorandum is unclear, but it is important to note that his recognition of the need to give the western Europeans security against German *revanchism* did provide him with a rare justification for concluding a mutual defense pact.

In the days following Kennan's memorandum both Ambassador Caffery and Secretary Marshall sought to "keep the ball rolling" by presenting the French with a realistic picture of American intentions regarding European security and to prod them toward agreement on Germany. In this effort the implications of the Vandenberg Resolution (then pending before the full Senate)[54] assumed prime importance. Although Marshall took pains to warn the French that no further legislative action would be possible in the current session of Congress, the intent of his efforts is clear.

On May 25 Caffery told the French that Marshall was earnestly hoping that the French government could find its way clear to approve the London program for western Germany because the dangers of delay were more serious than prompt implementation. In terms of security Caffery reported that the United States desired to strengthen the ability of the Brussels Pact countries to resist aggression by associating itself with the European efforts through the Vandenberg Resolution. Moreover, Caffery stated that the United States would regard any attack on areas affecting its national security as an attack on itself and would meet such an attack by the exercise of the inherent right of self-defense recognized by article 51 of the UN Charter. Once the Senate resolution had been passed, Caffery said, the extent and form of U.S. association with the western Europeans would be developed through consultations with members of the Brussels Pact.[55]

While Caffery clearly was trying to use the U.S. promise to associate with European efforts to move the French on the German question, he suggested to the executive secretary of the French Ministry of Foreign Affairs, Jean Chauvel, that American support for Europe would diminish if the French did not cooperate on the London agreements. Caffery then said that if the French cast aside the recent progress on Germany and reverted to more limited measures, such as currency reform, "European belief in the force and unity of the Western Powers [would] suffer a severe blow . . . [and] the confidence of the American people in Western Europe would sustain an even greater shock."[56]

The assurances and pressures from the United States had the desired effect: the French soon became more cooperative. On the same day that

Caffery met with Chauvel, the French representatives in London informed Douglas that the French government had decided to proceed with the London program for Germany. However, they added, any agreements coming out of London would have to be submitted to the Assembly for debate.[57] Shortly thereafter, Caffery reported on a conversation with Bidault in which the latter had indicated his government's desire to co-operate, but at the same time he explained the problems faced in doing so.

According to Caffery, Bidault was anxious for the success of the London Conference and would go along with the Americans, but he warned Washington: "don't make it too hard for me." He told Caffery of his troubles with the Socialists, Communists, and Gaullists in the Assembly and stated that everyone would be asking him what the Americans would do if the Soviets took aggressive action in Europe. This was the crucial question for Bidault; while he knew ultimate victory would be with the United States, he had to be able to present evidence of American support to his "critics who do not want to see France overrun by the Russians."[58]

The Final Report on the Political Organization of Germany was completed on May 31, 1948, and Ambassador Douglas suggested that, in order to strengthen Bidault's position, the British and American governments approve the agreements prior to the opening of debates in the French Assembly.[59] The United States also assured the French that it would keep its occupation troops in Germany until after a formal peace settlement, and Marshall offered further encouragement by tracing the progressive American interest in European security. These assurances appeared in the Final Report, which referred to Truman's March 17 speech and the Vandenberg Resolution. Moreover, the three governments agreed to "give consideration, in such manner as developments might require, to all aspects of the situation in Germany, which may result from the announcement or the implementation" of the London accords.[60]

Although American assurances and threats helped to secure French cooperation on the London Agreements, the United States continued to receive pressure for the conclusion of a treaty. On May 28, 1948, Marshall replied to Bevin's note of May 14, in which he discussed the implications of the Vandenberg Resolution in providing assurances to Europe but also informed the British foreign secretary that no further congressional action would be possible until after the elections in November. He further expressed doubt that the world situation would deteriorate significantly prior to the beginning of 1949.[61]

Bevin replied on June 1, stating that he could not agree, that, in his opinion, the situation in Europe was likely to deteriorate if security conversations were postponed until after Congress reconvened. He pointed to the recent success of a Soviet "peace offensive" in Europe and stated that "it seems above all necessary to give the French some additional hope of a really workable Security System if they are to be induced to accept the plan for Germany."[62]

Bevin's mention of a "peace offensive" referred to the Soviet Union's use of a growing pacifist sentiment among western intellectuals as an instrument of Soviet foreign policy. The pacifist movement itself had strong roots in France, but it was shortly brought under Communist control and became, in the words of Marshall Schulman, "a more significant instrument of Soviet policy than the foreign Communist parties themselves."[63] Because of the size of its Communist and Socialist parties and the intensity of its feelings on the German question, France was most vulnerable to the Soviet peace offensive.[64] However, Bevin too was having difficulties with his own Labour party on domestic as well as on foreign policy issues. Many in the Labour party saw the defection of Yugoslavia from the Soviet camp and the presence of a large Socialist party in Germany as opportunities to create a "third force" in central Europe, standing between the United States and the Soviet Union in the cold war. Bevin often was criticized by the left-wing of the Labour party for pursuing foreign policies far too similar to Winston Churchill's anti-Sovietism and for supporting German policies that ran counter to the interests of the German Social Democrats.[65] Therefore, if he and Bidault were going to follow the American lead on the German question, they wanted concrete evidence of support from the United States.

Because the London Agreements signaled western accord on the division of Germany and hence final recognition of the split between East and West, the pressures on Bevin and (even more so) on Bidault were severe. In order to follow the American lead the European leaders would have to have concrete evidence of support from the United States. While the Vandenberg Resolution was helpful, it simply was not enough.

The importance of American assurances was nowhere more apparent than in Bidault's presentation of the London Agreements to the French Assembly. On June 4, 1948, the French representatives in London asked Douglas if Bidault could use in the Assembly debates the verbatim record of the assurances given the French by the United States on the German question. While the United States did not agree, it did approve the use of "incidental references to the text of the London accords."[66] In addition, the British and American governments approved the London Agreements prior to the debates in the French Assembly and offered a public explanation of the London Conference and the security arrangements for Germany.

In this explanation it was pointed out that the three western powers, but especially France, were aware of the need for guarantees against future aggression from Germany and stated that this need had been accentuated by the failure to reach four power agreement on the German question. The allies said that certain measures that ensured against German aggression should be taken pending a comprehensive solution to the German peace treaty. They felt that the London accords would provide ample guarantees for any foreseeable contingencies and pointed "to the evolution of a regional security system under U.N. auspices which will provide further and lasting insurance against the possibility of German military resurgence." Furthermore, it was hoped that the long-range outcome of the London meetings would be increased "cooperation among the western nations in the evolution of a policy which . . . will lead to a peaceful and fruitful association of Germany with western Europe."[67]

Therefore, when Bidault addressed his colleagues on June 11, 1948, he was able to use the "evolution of U.S. policy towards Europe as evidenced by President Truman's speech of March 17 and the adoption of the Vandenberg Resolution by the Senate Foreign Relations Committee" as justification for French agreement on the German question.[68] Bidault also mentioned that the French government was looking toward the conclusion of a treaty with the United States that would be analogous to the Brussels Pact.[69]

On the same day that Bidault addressed the French Assembly, the Vandenberg Resolution passed the Senate by a vote of 64 to 4. Regarding the action taken by the Senate, Arthur Vandenberg, Jr., the son of the senator, wrote:

> One who reads the Congressional Record of June 11,
> may well wonder whether some members of the Senate
> were fully aware of the far reaching action they were taking
> on that occasion. The language of the Vandenberg Resolu-
> tion was general—perhaps even a bit vague—and it was
> impossible to know exactly what the framers had in mind.[70]

One week later, on June 18, the French Assembly approved the London Agreements by the narrow vote of 300 to 286, and even that approval contained seven reservations, one of the most prominent of which tied the successful implementation of the London accords to a guarantee against Germany.[71] Although the Vandenberg Resolution was viewed as merely a "vague" promise of some form of association, it soon was to be used to obtain the stronger commitment sought by the Europeans.

Military Assistance and the Formulation of the North Atlantic Treaty

On June 23 Secretary of State Marshall advised Ambassador Caffery that the United States had agreed to participate in "top secret exploratory talks pursuant to the Vandenberg Resolution" with the governments of France, Great Britain, Canada, Belgium, and the Netherlands.[72] The talks were scheduled to begin on June 29 in Washington, and on June 28 the National Security Council issued a report stating the American position with respect to these talks. The paper recommended that the Vandenberg Resolution "be implemented to the fullest extent possible in so far as its provisions apply to the problems discussed in this paper." It was hoped that the United States would encourage military talks among the Brussels Pact countries "without seeking [a] U.S. commitment more formal than that given in the President's March 17 message and the Senate Resolution. . . ." Moreover, the National Security Council advocated the eventual membership of Germany in the Brussels Pact and the development of a military assistance program based on the concept of reciprocal aid.[73]

Although the language of the National Security Council paper continued to express a certain U.S. reluctance to undertake any wider commitment to European security, it also reflected a growing realization that the United States would have to do something concrete to support its allies. The statement concerning the implementation of the Vandenberg Resolution "to the fullest extent possible" gave evidence of the growing U.S. resolve that "some further political commitment was necessary at this time to bolster public confidence in Western Europe. . . ." While the United States should assume no commitments prior to obtaining full bipartisan cooperation, and in any case not before Congress reconvened in January 1949, the National Security Council felt that the United States "should discuss with the parties to the Brussels Treaty some form of association by the U.S., and if possible Canada, with them along the lines recommended in the Senate resolution."[74]

However, concomitant with a U.S. move toward accepting a formal association with European defense, events forced a reevaluation of France's security concerns. Instead of pressing the United States for a multilateral treaty protecting them against both Soviet and German aggression, the French began to call for military assistance to strengthen their armed forces. This shift in tactics was the result of two considerations. First, the conclusion of the London talks without completely satisfying security guarantees, the realization that the British and Americans would proceed with the creation of a west German state in Bizonia if the French did not agree to trizonal fusion, and the adjournment of the U.S. Congress until after the 1948 elections convinced the French that they were not going to receive any further commitment from the United States until the winter of 1949, if at all. Second, the conclusion of the London talks brought, as the French had feared, an increase in cold war tensions and provocative Soviet actions in Berlin.[75] On June 24, 1948, following weeks of harassment, the Soviet Union imposed a full blockade on Berlin, refusing to allow any overland traffic to reach the western zones of that city.

The Berlin blockade increased French apprehensions *vis-à-vis* the intentions of Soviet policies in Europe and caused a shift in their security requirements from the United States. This shift was first noted in a June 29 telegram from Bidault to Marshall. The telegram stated that, as France saw it, the western countries were faced with three threats: a potential threat from Germany, an actual threat from the Soviet Union, and an immediate threat from Russian actions in Germany. In Bidault's view, "the last two threats enumerated above are the ones which particularly concern the United States Government."[76]

Although the French felt it unlikely that the Soviets would attack the western powers, they did feel it imperative that greater coordination be devoted to purely defense matters. Toward this end, they asked to be included in the talks that regularly took place in Washington between the U.S. and British military, sought an American observer for the Brussels Pact military talks, and called for more formal cooperation between the three western occupying authorities in Germany. Furthermore, the French stated their belief that the greatest danger faced by the West was the military weakness of western Europe, and they pressed for American aid to help reconstitute European armed forces: "What the French Government desires is not a spectacular system of guarantees, but an effective and concrete system of assistance."[77]

By concentrating on the "actual" and "immediate" threats of the Soviet Union and "Soviet action in Germany," the French were addressing the two threats "which particularly concern the United States Government," while seeming to leave in abeyance the "eventual" threat of Germany, which by implication was of more concern to France.

Just as in February 1948, the French now faced two matters of great concern: Anglo-American decisions regarding the reorganization of western Germany, and hostile action by the Soviet Union. First in Prague and then in Berlin, the Soviets took aggressive actions that greatly concerned the French and led them to join with the British and Americans in meeting what they considered to be the immediate threat to European security. In the case of Berlin, where the Soviet threat was of more direct concern to the western powers, the French moderated their calls for guarantees and began pressing for a program of military assistance to meet the short-run problem. While the French desire for a treaty was clearly related to the German question, their call for military assistance drew impetus from the situation in Berlin and the Soviet threat. Yet the question of military aid also was an important one in shaping the American commitment to Europe, and it is important to note that any program of military assistance for France could not but help to increase French military strength in relation to a disarmed Germany, especially since the first French units to receive American aid would be its occupation force stationed in Germany.

As the talks on European security got under way in July 1948, the U.S. position was presented by Under Secretary Lovett, who outlined American policy as follows: first, any treaty and/or military aid program would have to be based on the Vandenberg Resolution and would have to be approved by the appropriate congressional action, which the upcoming presidential election would delay until at least January 1949. Second, any program of military assistance or any association by the United States with European defense would depend on an assessment by the Brussels powers of their military capabilities and requirements and on the prior establishment of an effective Brussels Pact defense organization. Third, because of the separation of powers inherent in the U.S. Constitution, any formal association by the United States with Europeans would have to be similar to the Rio Pact, which, unlike the Brussels Pact, did not authorize an automatic military response in case of an armed attack.[78]

Running counter to the opinion of the Americans on all points, the French argued that all democracies faced the problem of legislative approval of executive agreements, and such requirements should not prevent the progressive development of long-range defense plans.[79] The French also maintained that they and the other Brussels Pact signatories had taken definite risks in entering into that pact and that they deserved military assistance and some indication of the form of American association prior to further organizational efforts on their part.[80] Moreover, the French (as well as the other Europeans) wanted a stronger guarantee from the United States than that contained in the Rio Pact.[81] The disagreements between the French and the Americans came to a head on August 6 when the French government, in a note to the Department of State, formally indicated general dissatisfaction with the course of the Washington talks, particularly with the nature of the evolving U.S. commitment.

According to the French, they believed that once the Brussels Pact military organization was established, and military inventories taken, the United States actively would consider "association" with the Western Union and would consider supplementing the military supplies of the Brussels powers. However, in the French view discussions with the United States were leading to the conclusion of a "very loose and indefinite arrangement" called the "Atlantic Pact." This arrangement, based on the model of the Rio Pact, was very disturbing to France because its "provisions for consultations, in the absence of any precise engagements of a military character . . . would be insufficient for the European problem where the menace of Soviet aggression was very real and immediate." Moreover, the French were aware that, as long as U.S. occupation troops remained in Germany, a "political pact" was more appropriate for the future. However, they felt that the future required a "more precise and definite mutual obligation." While the French government understood the problems that the Truman administration faced with Congress, it argued that every democratic country faced similar problems and "that this should not prevent any arrangement from being precise as to the nature of the obligation and assistance which would occur in the event of hostilities."[82]

The French obviously were unhappy with the way the United States was approaching the questions of short- and long-term European security and were asking for immediate military assistance to meet the short-term threat of the Soviet Union and a precise commitment to meet the long-term problem of Germany. The French position regarding short-term assistance was repeated on August 20 by Ambassador Bonnet, who maintained "that France, although a member of the Brussels Pact, had immediate problems to meet which a long-term pact would not solve. She wanted military equipment at once and she needed some form of assurances today."[83]

The Americans and other participants in the talks reacted strongly to Bonnet's impassioned plea by arguing that the French were seeking preferential treatment in receiving arms, that American occupation troops in Germany were an adequate guarantee of French security, and that, even if France did get immediate military aid, it still would be no match for Soviet capabilities.[84]

Given the determination of the United States to proceed at its own pace and the support it received from the other participants in the talks, the French modified their position,[85] and a working paper was produced by the Washington conferees on September 9, 1948. Although it was a study in compromise, it still contained points of disagreement.

The working paper expressed doubts that the Soviets would unleash an attack on western Europe, but it did admit the possibility of a "miscalculation" that could lead to war. It acknowledged that the presence of American occupation troops in Germany gave the Europeans assurance that the United States would be drawn into such a war, but declared that "something more is needed to counteract the fear of the peoples of Western Europe that their countries [might] be overrun by the Soviet Army before help could arrive."[86] In order to provide the extra measure of assurance, it was recommended that the United States and Canada join in a North Atlantic security system that included the countries of the Brussels Pact as well as Denmark, Norway, Iceland, Portugal, and Ireland. Sweden and Italy also were mentioned as possible members, but it was agreed that any attempt to determine the ultimate relationship of Spain and western Germany to the pact would be "premature."[87]

The report then addressed the type of U.S. commitment that would be required to make European security effective. The paper erroneously stated that the Senate's approval of the Vandenberg Resolution meant that a treaty-based formula was favored by that body and followed with a discussion of the security role played by American occupation troops in Germany.[88]

The participants in the security talks clearly had mixed views on the guarantees afforded by the maintenance of U.S. occupation troops in Germany. On the one hand it was felt that the presence of those forces ensured U.S. participation in any hostilities on the continent and demonstrated U.S. involvement in European security. On the other hand the conferees did not feel that the mere presence of troops was an adequate indication of an American commitment to western Europe.

Because the long-term status of the American occupation forces remained indefinite, the Europeans, especially the French, feared that the United States would, at some undetermined time in the future, withdraw its troops without considering European security. Therefore, the Europeans did not feel that American troops by themselves provided the necessary long-term assurances of American intentions. Moreover, since many felt that the Soviet threat remained largely political, the representatives at the security talks pressed for binding arrangements that would commit the parties jointly to resist aggression, give the Europeans confidence in the long-range intentions of the United States, and bolster their sagging morale.[89]

The importance of framing a U.S. commitment that would go beyond the immediacy of the Soviet threat and embrace the German question was emphasized when the report stressed that any joint defense arrangements should meet aggression "from whatever quarter and at whatever time." Given the above concerns, the paper concluded that "[n] o alternative to a treaty appears to meet the essential requirements."[90]

While the memorandum prepared by the participants in the Washington talks sought to accommodate the Europeans on both short- and long-term security issues through the conclusion of a treaty, it was apparent that there were still serious differences between the parties. Specifically, while the Europeans hoped that the assistance given in case of an attack would be immediate and military in nature, the United States insisted that treaty implementation take place according to "constitutional processes" and that there could be no automatic U.S. commitment to war. Furthermore, the U.S. representatives informed the Europeans that the Vandenberg Resolution's provisions calling for "self help and mutual aid" meant that American assistance must supplement, not replace, European efforts.[91]

The differences between the European and American positions were nowhere more apparent than in the proposed article for mutual assistance in case of an armed attack. The Europeans desired the most binding language possible, approaching that of an automatic guarantee with specific provisions for military action. In essence they sought an article along the lines of article 4 of the Brussels Pact and proposed the following language for the North Atlantic Treaty:

> If any Party should be the object of an armed attack in the area covered by this Treaty, the other Parties will, in accordance with the provisions of Article 51 of the Charter, afford the Party so attacked all the military and other aid and assistance in their power.[92]

However, the Americans, conscious of the necessity of Senate approval, favored wording more in line with article 3 of the Rio Pact, which made no specific mention of the extension of military aid and was more in line with the concept embodied in the Monroe Doctrine. The U.S. version read:

> An armed attack by any State against a Party shall be considered as an attack against all the Parties and, consequently, each Party undertakes to assist in meeting the attack in the exercise of the inherent right of individual or collective self-defense recognized by Article 51 of the Charter.[93]

A suggested compromise formula referred to the necessity of observing constitutional processes prior to the extension of military assistance in meeting an attack. This compromise was, of course, designed to win Senate approval while continuing to assure the Europeans of a military response to aggression. The compromise read:

> Provision that each Party should agree that any act which, in its opinion, constituted an armed attack against any other Party in the area covered by the treaty be considered an attack against itself, and should consequently, in accordance with its constitutional processes, assist in repelling the attack by all military, economic and other means in its power in the exercise of the right of individual or collective self-defense recognized by Article 51 of the Charter.[94]

The rest of the proposed treaty borrowed heavily from the Brussels and Rio pacts and included limited membership based on geographic and strategic considerations, consultation to meet an armed attack or a threat to the peace outside the area defined in the treaty, development of agencies to assist in the implementation of the treaty, references to the United Nations, and provisions relating to "accession, ratification and duration."[95] However, one proposed article, that calling for "continuous and effective self help and mutual aid, to strengthen the individual and collective capacity of the parties to resist aggression," had no history in either the Rio or the Brussels pacts. Rather, it was based on the Vandenberg Resolution and reflected both the European desire for a program of military assistance from the United States and the conflicting desire of the Senate Foreign Relations Committee to avoid a unilateral U.S. obligation. Because it was a unique provision of the report, and subsequently of the North Atlantic Treaty, it constituted a real point of departure and ultimately entangled the United States in European defense.

September 1948 also witnessed the creation of the military organization of the Brussels powers, a move designed to give evidence of European organizational efforts and to speed the receipt of American military equipment. The establishment of the Brussels organizational structure had the desired effect, and on September 20, 1948, Lovett reported to Caffery that the "President has now approved transfer from US stocks in Germany to French forces of equipment adequate substantially to reequip three French divisions now in Germany."[96] Later, on October 29, 1948, the Brussels powers informed Washington that, based on the report of September 9, they were willing to begin negotiations on a North Atlantic Treaty in Washington and requested the U.S. government set a starting date for those talks.[97]

Approximately one month later George Kennan, in *Considerations Affecting the Conclusion of a North Atlantic Treaty*, set forth his opinions about the movement toward the conclusion of a treaty. In that paper Kennan, reflecting his changed view of a treaty formula, stated "that there *is* valid long-term justification for a formalization, by international agreement, of the natural defense relationship among the countries of the North Atlantic community." Kennan pointed out that such long-term formalization might "contribute to the general sense of security in the area" but that the proposed North Atlantic Pact was "not the main answer to the present Soviet effort to dominate the European continent,

and will not appreciably modify the nature or danger of Soviet policies."
Kennan also maintained that the scope of the North Atlantic Treaty should
be determined by geography alone and cautioned against including Italy
because that would lead to a "series of demands from states still farther
afield that they be similarly treated." Finally, Kennan argued that U.S.
policy should be directed not toward formalizing the division of Europe
but rather "toward the eventual peaceful withdrawal of both the United
States and the U.S.S.R. from the heart of Europe, and accordingly toward
the encouragement of the growth of a third force which can absorb and
take over the territory between the two."[98]

For the above reasons, Kennan believed that there was a long-term
need permanently to formalize the defense relationship between the
states of the North Atlantic area and that such a formalization would have
the "short term value" of increasing "the general sense of security" of the
Brussels Pact members. On the other hand he cautioned that the Soviet
threat to western Europe remained primarily political in nature and that
a military pact would be viewed as a substitute for the political and
economic measures that were already being taken to meet the Russian
challenge.[99]

Kennan's concentration on the long-term versus the short-term benefits
of the treaty is interesting because it coincided with the French views,
and his statements regarding a "general sense of security" reflect the notion that the North Atlantic Alliance would have a purpose that extended
beyond that of merely providing security against Soviet attack. Also of
interest was Kennan's desire to encourage the "growth of a third force"
in central Europe to facilitate American and Soviet withdrawal from the
area. However, the only force that could accomplish such a task would
have to be Germany alone or in some combination with other powers.
But this would increase French fears and make American disengagement
extremely difficult.

Indeed, Germany was still a sensitive issue for the western allies as
they attempted to implement the London accords. The French were becoming very concerned over Germany's rapid economic growth and the
level "which it must be allowed to reach if Germany is to become self
sustaining." The French, therefore, were hesitant to implement the
London agreements, and in order to press France the State Department
recommended that the United States take "all possible steps to allay
French fears consistent with conditions which would give Germany a
chance for economic recovery." Those steps included efforts to convince

the French that their security would be guarded by the London Agreement provisions for consultations among the western powers in the event of any threat of German *revanchism,* the establishment of a joint security board with inspection powers, the internationalization of the Ruhr, limits on German industry, and "the Brussels and North Atlantic Pacts."[100]

The view of accommodating the French in order to revive German economic growth received added official sanction following the 1948 election when President Truman won his second term in office. Immediately after the election, Truman called Dean Acheson to the White House, informed him that Secretary Marshall was retiring as of January 20, 1949, and asked Acheson to be the new secretary of state. Acheson agreed and brought with him certain ideas regarding the future of Germany, Europe, and the role that the United States would have to play in European defense.

Acheson knew that Germany was the key to the balance of power in Europe. Because the Soviets had not given up their goal of dominating Germany—at least eastern Germany—Acheson was certain that the resources of western Germany would have to be included in any Atlantic alignment in order to prevent Soviet domination of Europe. While Kennan and others wanted the United States and the Soviet Union out of the heart of Europe, Acheson was convinced that America had a long-standing interest in European security. Two world wars had demonstrated the importance of Europe to America, and Acheson knew that even if there were no Soviet threat the United States still would have an interest in preventing a renewal of hostilities between France and Germany.[101]

In order to create circumstances favorable to a revival of western Germany without threatening France, Acheson placed increased reliance on the evolving North Atlantic Treaty. The reason he demanded a strong treaty is clear when one examines his efforts to convince the French (and others) that a revived western Germany would not threaten European security.[102]

With the dual nature of the treaty in mind, the representatives of the United States and the Brussels Pact worked throughout the remainder of 1948 to finalize a draft treaty and to work out the details of membership and the area to be incorporated. It was decided to limit the membership, as far as possible, to the countries of the immediate North Atlantic area with the possible inclusion of Italy because of its vital position in the Mediterranean, and of Algeria because it still was part of the French *métropole*.[103] It also was agreed that it would be desirable to present a draft treaty to the various governments by February 1, 1949, and Lovett made an important statement regarding the special considerations that would apply when the treaty was presented to the Senate for approval.

Lovett declared that the only precedent for American participation in such a treaty was the Rio Pact, which belonged to the unique area of the Western Hemisphere. From the U.S. point of view, it would therefore be necessary for the treaty to define each member's exact obligation and to refer—in both the body and the preamble—to "constitutional processes" in order to gain congressional approval.[104]

When a draft of the treaty was completed on December 24, 1948, the proposed article dealing with mutual assistance in case of attack—article 5, the most controversial in the treaty—was a hybrid of similar articles in both the Rio and the Brussels pacts. As such it provided that if one member was subject to an armed attack in the area defined by the treaty such would be considered an attack on all members and that each of them (acting in accordance with article 51 of the UN Charter) would take "forthwith such military or other action, individually and in concert with the other Parties, as may be necessary to restore and assure the security of the North Atlantic area."[105]

Because of the automatic commitment contained in the draft article, it quickly ran into trouble with members of the Senate. On February 3 and 5, 1949, Acheson met with Senators Connally (chairman of the Foreign Relations Committee following the Democratic victory in 1948) and Vandenberg to discuss the draft treaty. Almost all of their talks centered on proposed article 5, and on February 8 Acheson summarized their objections for the European representatives to the Washington talks on the North Atlantic Treaty.

Acheson reported that the senators felt the language of article 5 implied that the United States "was rushing into some kind of automatic commitment." While he maintained that the senators did not question the advisability of the United States taking on an "international legal and moral" commitment to western Europe, they hoped "to find more neutral language than that contained in the present draft."[106]

When the Europeans heard the objections, they immediately took exception, especially the French. Ambassador Bonnet argued "that the draft text as it stood at present had only been arrived at after much thought and negotiation," that other treaties of a similar nature were far more binding, and that "a bad impression [would be created] if the wording of the Atlantic Pact were weaker than the Rio Treaty."[107]

The situation got worse shortly thereafter, when, on February 14, Senator Forrest Donnell (R.-Missouri) touched off a debate on the floor of the Senate that, in Acheson's words, "set off a land mine under our discussions."[108] Donnell's action led to a hurried meeting between Connally, Vandenberg, and Acheson, and the senators suggested a revision of the language of article 5. Connally even went so far as to question the desirability of including the statement "that an attack on one would be considered an attack on all," favoring instead "an attack on one would be regarded as a threat to the peace of all." Vandenberg thought it unnecessary to follow Connally's suggestion but felt that "the type of action should be a matter of individual determination and also that the word 'military' be omitted." Acheson stressed the importance of the treaty to the French, especially regarding the German question.

Acheson reviewed the State Department's attitude toward the treaty and pointed out to the senators its deterrent value against any potential aggressor. He particularly stressed the German question and its importance in reconciling the French "to the inevitable diminution of direct allied control over Germany and the progressive reduction of occupation troops. . . ." He also emphasized that the treaty would increase France's security against both Germany and the Soviet Union and would be of major assistance in moving the French to a "realistic consideration of the problem of Germany."[109]

However, given the concerns of the senators, further revision of article 5 was necessary, and by February 16 the State Department was able to present to President Truman four different drafts of article 5. While each varied in the degree of obligation that a signatory would assume, all embodied a commitment somewhat less than that of the December 24 draft.[110]

On February 18, 1949, Acheson appeared before the Senate Foreign Relations Committee with the revised treaty. As presented to the senators, article 5 stated that the parties would consider an attack on one in the defined area as an attack on them all and that, in exercising the inherent right of individual and collective self-defense recognized in article 51 of the UN Charter, each member would "assist the party or parties so attacked by taking forthwith, individually and in concert with the other parties, such action, including the use of armed force, as it deems necessary to restore and maintain the security of the North Atlantic area."[111]

Although this draft did not contain provisions for "constitutional processes," that phrase was incorporated in the preamble and article 11 of the North Atlantic Treaty, which stated that all the provisions of the treaty were to be "carried out by the Parties in accordance with their respective constitutional processes."[112] Moreover, the phrase "such action . . . as it deems necessary" ensured that each member would determine for itself the action it would take. For their part, the Europeans had to be content with the wording, "including the use of armed force," which was intended to reassure them of American intentions. However, much of the force behind the original commitment of article 5 had been depleted, and in the ensuing months the Europeans, notably the French, would switch their attention from the guarantee contained in article 5 to the provisions of article 3—which called for "continuous and effective self help and mutual aid"—to strengthen their armed forces and to involve the United States progressively in European security.

Conclusion

In the eleven months between March 1948 and February 1949 a number of considerations led to the formulation of the North Atlantic Treaty. Although a treaty formula was by no means the first priority for U.S association with European security—some, such as George Kennan, argued for a presidential declaration similar to that of James Monroe—it became apparent to those members of the State Department who had direct dealings with their European counterparts that the complexity of continental security issues demanded a formal American commitment. One of the chief reasons for this was the necessity to reach accommodation with France on the German question at the London Conference. Thus, by early April 1948 the State Department was actively looking toward the conclusion of a treaty with the countries of the Brussels Pact and other western European states.

However, given the need for bipartisan congressional support, the administration sought to include Senator Arthur Vandenberg and the Senate Foreign Relations Committee in the process of shaping the U.S. commitment to Europe. Although not enthusiastic about a treaty formula, Vandenberg did agree to a U.S. move toward some association with European security efforts as long as due constitutional processes were observed and any American assistance was based on the principle of reciprocity. The resultant Vandenberg Resolution (S. 239) aided the

State Department in assuring France of American support of European security and moving the French government toward accepting the London Agreements on the German question.

Partially because of the promises of the Vandenberg Resolution and partially because of American threats, the French finally accepted the principle of trizonal fusion in June 1948. Yet shortly after the London Agreements were announced, the Soviets initiated the Berlin blockade, and the immediacy of the Soviet action caused the French temporarily to abate their calls for a treaty of guarantee and to press instead for military supplies from the United States. Therefore, when treaty discussions began in Washington during July, the participants faced two issues of major importance: the question of a military supply program and that of a commitment for individual or collective response to an act of aggression against one of the parties to the treaty. It also was apparent that the French viewed the military supply program as having short-term value in bolstering European defenses in response to Soviet actions in Berlin, while they saw a formalized treaty as the long-term answer to the perennial problem of Germany.

From the outset of the discussions, it was apparent that the Europeans and the Americans were approaching those issues from different viewpoints. While the Europeans—especially the French—wanted immediate military aid in the form of equipment and supplies, the United States required that first a Brussels Pact military organization be established; while the Europeans—again especially the French—wanted an assurance of immediate military response to an act of aggression, the Americans favored retaining the maximum amount of flexibility in determining whether or not an attack had occurred and what the response would be.

It was not until September 1948 that the problems concerning military assistance and the form of guarantee had been solved to the satisfaction of the participants in the Washington talks. The creation of the Brussels Treaty Organization (Western Union) enabled the United States to transfer military supplies to French divisions in Germany, while the proposed article 5 of the North Atlantic Treaty embodied both the Monroe Doctrine formula and provisions for constitutional processes favored by the United States and promises of strong military measures desired by the Europeans. However, even that compromise language (as well as that of a December 24 draft treaty) was too strong for Senators Connally, Vandenberg, and others, and the final version—completed in

February 1949—represented almost complete acceptance of the American view. The only concession to the Europeans was the specific mention of the use of armed force as a possible method of individual or collective response to an armed attack on a signatory in the area defined by the treaty.

With the failure to achieve a strong guarantee in article 5, the Europeans began to concentrate on the provisions of article 3—which called for "continuous and effective self help and mutual aid"—in an attempt to involve the United States more firmly in European security. As French military expert General André Beaufre has written of the North Atlantic Treaty:

> Such as it is, the treaty does no more than express very
> broad and—it must be admitted—very vague principles of
> cooperation. The architecture of the Alliance, then,
> will have to be filled in gradually—in the application of
> the treaty, in its practice rather than its theory.[113]

Moreover, the nature of the relationship between practice and theory would assume great importance as the North Atlantic Treaty went before the U.S. Senate.

Notes

1. *FRUS,* 1948, vol. 3, pp. 58-59; Butler Memorandum.

2. Ibid., pp. 59-60; Minutes of the First U.S., U.K., Canadian Security Conversations.

3. Ibid., p. 62; Report of the Policy Planning Staff.

4. Ibid., p. 63.

5. Ibid., pp. 63-64.

6. Kennan, *Memoirs,* vol. 1, p. 407. Kennan saw "no real necessity" for even this approach.

7. Ibid., p. 405.

8. Ibid., p. 407.

9. Ibid.

10. *FRUS,* 1948, vol. 3, pp. 64-65; Minutes of the Second U.S., U.K., Canadian Security Conversations.

11. Ibid., p. 65.

12. Ibid., p. 66; Minutes of the Third U.S., U.K., Canadian Security Conversations

13. Ibid.

14. Ibid., p. 69; Minutes of the Fourth U.S., U.K., Canadian Security Conversations.
15. Ibid., p. 72; Minutes of the Sixth U.S., U.K., Canadian Security Conversations.
16. Ibid., p. 74.
17. Ibid., pp. 59-60; Minutes of the First U.S., U.K., Canadian Security Conversations.
18. Ibid., p. 76; Memorandum of Conversation by Achilles.
19. Ibid.
20. Ibid., pp. 79-80; Bevin Telegram, Summary.
21. Ibid., p. 80.
22. The first official Vandenberg-Lovett talks are recorded as having taken place on April 11, 1948. Ibid., pp. 82-85; Memorandum of Conversation by Lovett; see also U.S., Congress, Senate, Committee on Foreign Relations. *The Vandenberg Resolution and the North Atlantic Treaty,* Hearings Held in Executive Session before the Committee on Foreign Relations, U.S. Senate, 80th Congress, 2nd session on S. 239 and 81st Congress, 1st session on Executive L, The North Atlantic Treaty. *Historical Series,* 1973, p. 2. Hereafter cited as *The Vandenberg Resolution and the North Atlantic Treaty;* and Arthur Vandenberg, Jr., *The Private Papers of Senator Vandenberg,* p. 404. For speculation that the talks may have begun earlier, see *FRUS,* 1948, vol. 3, p. 89, n. 3.
23. *FRUS,* 1948, vol. 3, p. 71; Minutes of the Fifth U.S., U.K., Canadian Security Conversations.
24. Ibid., p. 89; Lovett Memorandum.
25. Ibid., p. 86; Souers to the National Security Council.
26. Ibid., p. 87. Other than the Brussels Pact countries, the report advocated the inclusion of Norway, Sweden, Denmark, Iceland, Italy, Eire, and Portugal. The intention of the agreement was to give the Europeans evidence of military support from the United States.
27. Ibid., p. 93; Memorandum of Conversation by Lovett.
28. Ibid., p. 101; Kennan to Souers.
29. Ibid., p. 91; Bevin and Bidault to Marshall.
30. Ibid., pp. 105-06; Memorandum of Conversation by Lovett.
31. Ibid., p. 107.
32. Ibid., p. 108; John Foster Dulles, *War or Peace?* (New York: Macmillan, 1950), p. 96. Dulles said that he, too, favored a Monroe Doctrine approach. Ibid., pp. 95-96.
33. *FRUS,* 1948, vol. 3, p. 109; Kennan to Lovett.
34. Ibid., p. 117; Kennan to Lovett.
35. *FRUS,* 1948, vol. 2, p. 231; Douglas to Marshall.
36. Ibid., p. 232; Douglas to Marshall.
37. *The Public Papers of the Presidents, Harry S. Truman,* 1948, p. 52.
38. *FRUS,* 1948, vol. 2, p. 233; Douglas to Marshall.
39. *FRUS,* 1948, vol. 3, p. 122; Substance of a Message from Bevin.
40. *The Vandenberg Resolution and the North Atlantic Treaty,* p. 2.
41. Ibid., pp. 7-8.
42. *FRUS,* 1948, vol. 2, p. 233, n. 2.

43. Ibid., p. 266, n. 2; also Gimbel, *The American Occupation of Germany,* pp. 198-200.

44. *FRUS,* 1948, vol. 2, pp. 266-68; Douglas to Marshall.

45. Ibid., p. 267.

46. Ibid., p. 268.

47. Ibid., pp. 271-72; Memorandum of Conversation by Lovett.

48. Ibid., p. 275; Marshall to Douglas.

49. *FRUS,* 1948, vol. 3, p. 128; Kennan to Marshall and Lovett.

50. In a speech before the Canadian House of Commons on April 29, 1948, St. Laurent expressed his desire for a Canadian association with the countries of the Brussels Pact based on article 52 as well as article 51 of the UN Charter.

51. *FRUS,* 1948, vol. 3, p. 128; Kennan to Marshall and Lovett.

52. Kennan, *Memoirs,* vol. 1, pp. 409-10.

53. U.S., Department of State, *Foreign Relations of the United States,* 1948, vol. 1, part 2, General; United Nations, pp. 516-17; Report of the Policy Planning Staff. Hereafter cited as *FRUS,* 1948, vol. 1, part 2.

54. The Foreign Relations Committee had given the Vandenberg Resolution its unanimous endorsement on May 19, 1948, with only Walter George reluctant to move in the direction that the resolution seemed to be leading the United States. *The Vandenberg Resolution and the North Atlantic Treaty,* p. 65.

55. *FRUS,* 1948, vol. 2, p. 277; Marshall to Caffery.

56. Ibid., p. 279; Caffery to Marshall.

57. Ibid., p. 280; Douglas to Marshall.

58. Ibid., p. 281; Caffery to Marshall.

59. Ibid., p. 308; Douglas to Marshall.

60. Ibid., p. 312; Final Report of the London Conference on Germany.

61. *FRUS,* 1948, vol. 3, p. 133; Marshall to Balfour.

62. Ibid., p. 138; Bevin Telegram.

63. Marshall Schulman, *Stalin's Foreign Policies Reappraised* (Cambridge, Mass.: Harvard University Press, 1963), p. 80.

64. Ibid., p. 100.

65. For material on the troubles Bevin was facing within the Labour party, see Michael Foot, *Aneurin Bevan: A Biography* 2 vols. (New York: Atheneum, 1974), vol. 2, pp. 229-334.

66. *FRUS,* 1948, vol. 2, p. 318; Douglas to Marshall; also n. 1.

67. U.S., Department of State, *Germany, 1947-1949; The Story in Documents,* European and British Commonwealth Series 9, Pubn., no 35556 (1959), pp. 82-83.

68. *Keesings Contemporary Archives,* 1948-1950, p. 9375.

69. Ibid. On June 3, 1948, Under Secretary Robert Lovett appeared before the Senate Foreign Relations Committee and told the senators that the French still wanted an alliance against Soviet aggression. *The Vandenberg Resolution and the North Atlantic Treaty,* p. 76.

70. Vandenberg, *The Private Papers of Senator Vandenberg,* p. 411; see also McLellan, *Dean Acheson: The State Department Years,* p. 115.

71. *Keesings Contemporary Archives,* 1948-1950, p. 9376.

72. *FRUS,* 1948, vol. 3, p. 139; Marshall to Caffery.

73. Ibid., pp. 140-41; Report of the National Security Council.

74. Ibid., p. 141.

75. Gimbel, *The American Occupation of Germany,* pp. 201-06.

76. *FRUS,* 1948, vol. 3, p. 1421; Caffery to Marshall.

77. Ibid., pp. 142-43.

78. Ibid., pp. 149-51; Minutes of the First Meeting of the Washington Exploratory Talks on Security; Kennan, *Memoirs,* vol. 1, p. 407.

79. *FRUS,* 1948, vol. 3, p. 158; Minutes of the Third Meeting of the Washington Exploratory Talks on Security.

80. Ibid., p. 172; Minutes of the Fifth Meeting of the Washington Exploratory Talks on Security.

81. Ibid., p. 212; Minutes of the Ninth Meeting of the Working Group Participating in the Washington Exploratory Talks on Security.

82. Ibid., p. 206; Memorandum of Conversation by Bohlen.

83. Ibid., Memorandum of Conversation by Lovett.

84. Ibid., pp. 218-20.

85. Ibid., p. 230; Minutes of the Sixth Meeting of the Washington Exploratory Talks on Security.

86. Ibid., p. 239; Memorandum by the Participants in the Washington Security Talks, July 6 to September 9, Submitted to Their Respective Governments for Study and Comment.

87. Ibid., pp. 239-42.

88. Ibid., p. 242.

89. Ibid.

90. Ibid.

91. Ibid., p. 244.

92. Ibid., p. 247.

93. Ibid.

94. Ibid. The proposed treaty also included provisions for consultation in case of an attack occurring on a party outside of the North Atlantic area or in case of a threat to the peace in any area of the world. Ibid., p. 248.

95. Ibid., pp. 247-48.

96. Ibid., p. 253; Lovett to Caffery; for details of the creation of the Western Union, see André Beaufre, *NATO and Europe* (New York: Vintage Books, 1966), p. 16.

97. *FRUS,* 1948, vol. 3, p. 270; Memorandum from the Ambassadors of France, the United Kingdom, Belgium, the Netherlands, and the Minister of Luxembourg, to the Department of State.

98. Ibid., pp. 284-88; Memorandum by Kennan. There also was a "Third Force" developing in Britain under the leadership of Aneurin Bevan. See Foot, *Aneurin Bevan,* vol. 2, pp. 319, 345.

99. *FRUS,* 1948, vol. 3, p. 28; Memorandum by Kennan.

100. Ibid., p. 308; Lovett to Harriman.

101. McLellan, *Dean Acheson: The State Department Years,* p. 147.

102. Ibid., pp. 147-48; also, Acheson, *Present at the Creation,* p. 338; *FRUS,*

1948, vol. 3, p. 327; Minutes of the Tenth Meeting of the Washington Exploratory Talks.

103. *FRUS*, 1948, vol. 3, pp. 339-42; Report of the International Working Group to the Ambassador's Committee.

104. Ibid., p. 317; Minutes of the Ninth Meeting of the Washington Exploratory Talks.

105. Ibid., p. 335; Report of the International Working Group to the Ambassador's Committee.

106. U.S., Department of State, *Foreign Relations of the United States*, 1949, vol. 4, p. 74; Minutes of the Twelfth Meeting of the Washington Exploratory Talks. Hereafter cited as *FRUS*, 1949, vol. 4.

107. Ibid., p. 76.

108. Acheson, *Present at the Creation*, p. 281.

109. *FRUS*, 1949, vol. 4, p. 109; Memorandum of Conversation by Acheson.

110. Ibid., pp. 113-16; Bohlen to Acheson and Webb.

111. *The Vandenberg Resolution and the North Atlantic Treaty*. This specific language did not appear in any of the drafts mentioned in note 110 but was apparently developed at the same time. See *FRUS*, 1949, vol. 4, p. 117; Memorandum of Conversation by Acheson.

112. *The Vandenberg Resolution and the North Atlantic Treaty*, p. 106.

113. Beaufre, *NATO and Europe*, p. 19.

FOUR

Approving the
Treaty

Introduction

The process whereby senatorial approval was obtained for the North
Atlantic Treaty was difficult and fraught with dangers for the Truman
administration. Two crucial issues were involved: the question of the
guarantee included in article 5 and the problem of subsequent implementation under article 3.

Throughout the period when the treaty was being presented to the
Senate, the State Department faced a very difficult problem: it had to convince western Europe that the American commitment through the North
Atlantic Treaty was a strong one, and it had to assure Congress that the
treaty did not involve the United States in an "entangling" military alliance.
The Truman administration's difficulties were complicated by the fact
that securing a two-thirds majority in the Senate would not be easy because certain groups of powerful senators were prepared to fight the treaty
"every step of the way."[1]

After the draft of the North Atlantic Treaty was presented to the Senate
Foreign Relations Committee, on February 18, 1949, the battle lines began to emerge. Basically, there were three positions. The first was held by
the bedrock isolationists of the Republican Midwest. Holders of this position, including Forrest Donnell, William Jenner (R.-Ind.), and Kenneth
Wherry (R.-Neb.), wanted the minimum possible American commitment.
Although many were vehemently anti-Communist, they were strongly
opposed to alliances and "automatic" commitments to use force. Because the treaty challenged the clearly defined constitutional distinction
between a state of war and a state of peace, much of the debate centered
on the power of the president as commander in chief and Congress's
prerogative to declare war. The isolationists' concentration on the constitutional question obscured a more important issue: the relationship
between military power and foreign policy.[2]

A second position was held by senators whose view was remarkably similar to that of George Kennan. These men felt that the North Atlantic Treaty should not contain any obligations extending beyond that of a political guarantee, and some (such as Robert Taft, R.-Ohio) were even uncomfortable with the modified provisions of article 5. However, their most serious objections centered on article 3, which, they felt, made the North Atlantic Treaty nothing more than a military alliance. Prominent members of this group were Taft, Walter George, and Arthur Vandenberg, the latter two being influential members of the Foreign Relations Committee.

Finally, some senators accepted the lead of Secretary Acheson and his concept of the North Atlantic Treaty. David McLellan argues that the supporters of the treaty "sensed its utility for getting the Europeans, particularly France and Germany, to bury their quarrels and collaborate in producing a stronger, more unified front to the Russians."[3]

In order to win approval the Truman administration had to build on the existing body of support and convince enough senators who believed in extending some form of political commitment to Europe that the obligations inherent in the North Atlantic Treaty would not entangle the United States in a permanent European alliance. This put administration spokesmen, such as Acheson, in a difficult position since they were aware of the pressures from western Europe for tangible evidence of American participation in Atlantic security. Because of the relative weakness of the Monroe Doctrine-Rio Pact formula, many Europeans regarded the implementation of the treaty through military assistance as more important than the vague promises contained in article 5. Therefore, Acheson (and others) had to avoid giving the impression to the Senate that approval of the treaty meant American participation in a full-scale military alliance, while at the same time assuring the Europeans that the American commitment was real.[4] In order to ensure the success of the administration's policies, the State Department sometimes had to use methods in dealing with Congress that bordered on outright deception.

This chapter will examine the events surrounding the signing and approval of the North Atlantic Treaty. It will be demonstrated that while the main focus of the debates in the Senate was on the question of "constitutional processes," relating specifically to the war-making powers of the president and article 5 of the treaty, the central issue was really the implementation of the treaty through article 3. This fact, in turn, raises the question of the relationship between the Military Assistance Program and the North Atlantic Treaty, and it will be argued that the administration's awareness that article 3 and the military aid question would be the main obstacle to treaty approval led it to postpone consideration of the military aid program until after the treaty had passed the Senate. By concentrating on the "legal legerdemain"[5] of article 5 the administration was able to present the treaty as being in the tradition of the Monroe Doctrine and as preserving Congress's role in foreign affairs. In doing so Acheson and other administration witnesses "succeeded in invoking the shibboleths of isolationism to win acceptance of a policy that marked a departure from isolationist traditions."[6]

Moreover, this chapter also will continue to demonstrate the intimate connection between the U.S. commitment to Europe and the German question. It was no accident that Britain, France, and the United States reached final agreement on trizonal fusion, the status of the Ruhr, and the Occupation Statute while the foreign ministers were in Washington to sign the North Atlantic Treaty. Moreover, although the agreements on Germany were finalized in April 1949, they were not formalized until after final ratification of the treaty in the fall.

Military Assistance and the North Atlantic Treaty

The early days of 1949 brought agreement between the United States and the Europeans on the proposed text of the North Atlantic Treaty but also brought an intensification of the European, especially the French, desire to receive tangible evidence of America's commitment to Europe through a program of military assistance. Because the concept of "self help and mutual aid" in article 3 was not clear in practice, the European calls for military supplies caused many U.S. officials to raise the question of coordinating a military aid package with the provisions of the North Atlantic Treaty, in order both to restore Europe militarily and to receive reciprocal benefits from the allies. This latter consideration was based on the growing American perception that the international commitments it was assuming through such programs as the North Atlantic Treaty would require increased military capabilities. Of course, such reasoning was at odds with the earlier argument that money spent to restore western Europe would lead to reduced defense spending in the United States. Yet by the summer of 1948 aid to Europe was seen as cutting into military supplies essential to the defense of the United States, and it was hoped that some way would be found to use the mutual assistance clause of article 3 to offset some of that loss. Naturally, the Europeans could not be expected to extend material assistance to the United States. However, some military experts felt that, if the Europeans could grant basing privileges to the United States outside the Western Hemisphere, it would increase America's military capabilities and help make up for some of the material drain that would eventually take place under a military assistance program.

The issue of foreign arms assistance had a considerable history prior to the North Atlantic Treaty. In December 1947 the Joint Chiefs of Staff, following the recommendation of the State-Army-Navy-Air Force Coordinating Committee (formerly the State-War-Navy Coordinating Committee), prepared enabling legislation for a "comprehensive military assistance program. . . ." This proposed legislation was included as Title IV in the Foreign Assistance Act of 1948 but was withdrawn "in order to expedite the passage of the remainder of the bill, including the Economic Cooperation Act."[7] The military aid question was raised again in the summer of 1948, when, on July 1, the National Security Council issued a paper (NSC 14/1) calling on the U.S. government to create a program of military assistance similar to that of the defunct Title IV. In justifying this program, the Council explained that U.S. military assistance would increase the material and moral strength of its allies, increase their military and political loyalty toward the United States, develop America's own armaments industry, and "increase the effectiveness of military collaboration between the United States and its allies in the event of war."[8]

Because of the prior difficulty in receiving congressional approval for arms aid, an important feature of the legislation proposed by the National Security Council in NSC 14/1 was the inclusion of provisions to "broaden the authority of the President to provide military assistance under appropriate conditions." Moreover, NSC 14/1 also maintained that western Europe should receive primary consideration for arms, again departing from the traditional policy of according Latin America first priority.[9]

President Truman approved the recommendations of NSC 14/1 on July 10, but questions soon arose regarding the relationship between arms assistance for western Europe and an increase in the U.S. defense budget. On the same day that Truman approved the National Security Council's report, Secretary of Defense James Forrestal wrote to the

Council addressing that issue. Forrestal was preparing the defense budget for fiscal 1950 and was asking for the comparatively high figure of $17.5 billion. In writing about the trade-off between arms aid to Europe and increased military spending by the United States for its own forces, Forrestal felt that perceptions of global political/strategic considerations would determine which programs should receive priority.

In his July 10 letter, Forrestal made several important points. He argued that both the size and the purposes of the military budget should be adjusted in light of the general military situation throughout the world. If the overall situation was threatening and of an immediate and military nature, Forrestal felt that the defense budget should be increased. On the other hand if the dangers were small, distant, and nonmilitary, the budget should be adjusted downward. The defense secretary felt that an analysis of the general military situation also would help determine whether the United States should strengthen its own forces or appropriate a portion of its budget to equip potential allies. Clearly, Forrestal felt that the latter course should be adopted only if the danger to the United States was relatively distant. While Forrestal knew that such decisions had to involve "political as well as military considerations," he argued that a decision on the defense budget could not be made without an appraisal of the military risks and objectives facing the United States.[10]

Forrestal's letter was, in fact, reflective of a growing dispute between the State and Defense departments over the size and purpose of the military budget. While Defense was proposing the $17.5 billion figure, State considered $14.4 billion to be more appropriate. The State Department's lower figure was based on its long-standing policy of trying to increase the security of the United States through the economic, political, and military rehabilitation of western Europe. Moreover, the disagreement between State and Defense can be traced to an even more fundamental difference regarding the nature of the obligations the United States was assuming in world affairs.

Although the State Department continued to view assistance programs and political commitments as methods of restoring the European balance, and ultimately leading to less defense spending on the part of the United States, the Defense Department saw these programs as constituting new U.S. commitments, requiring increased military capabilities, and justifying expanded defense spending. For this reason the Department of Defense felt that U.S. rearmament should precede that of western Europe and wanted the total defense budget raised to cover the costs of both military aid to Europe and defense spending in the United States.[11] Moreover, both State and Defense interpreted the events of the spring of 1948 as supporting their respective viewpoints.

The Berlin blockade and the subsequent French calls for increased military aid from the United States seemed to have a major impact on State Department thinking. Writing on August 6, 1948, Secretary of the Army Kenneth Royall maintained that the "requirements for the members of the Western Union, particularly France, have become imminent. Even though assistance programs in connection with these countries do not have final approval, it is necessary to accord them priorities with respect to other programs in order to facilitate requisite planning and to determine availabilities of equipment."[12]

Marshall replied to Royall's letter on August 23, 1948 and agreed that the "imminent submission of requirement estimates from France and other Western European nations makes it desirable" that those countries be given first priority in arms assistance programs.[13] Marshall's thinking reflected the State Department's view that the security of the United States could be best increased by devoting a portion of the U.S. defense budget to reequiping America's allies in Europe.

On the other hand the Defense Department viewed policies such as those implied in the Vandenberg Resolution as requiring increased defense spending by the United States. Writing on November 17, 1948, the Joint Chiefs of Staff reported that, although "the Vandenberg Resolution has not yet become literally a commitment, its implications are, nevertheless, very great, and can extend to United States involvement in global warfare." Accordingly, the Joint Chiefs recommended that the United States "bring our military strength to a level commensurate with the distinct possibility of global warfare."[14]

As the deadline on the budget issue approached, the gulf between the State and Defense departments widened. On October 31, 1948, Forrestal wrote to Marshall asking for the secretary of state's assessment of the trends in the world situation since the spring of 1948. If conditions had improved, could the United States reduce its military expenditure? If they had worsened, should the United States augment its current military strength? Was the situation mainly the same, requiring no change in American defense policies?[15]

Forrestal's inquiry made the rounds of the State Department, and it was not until November 8, 1948, that Marshall replied, drawing on the expertise of Lovett, Kennan, and Bohlen. In his answer Marshall indicated that despite the Berlin blockade the world situation had not undergone a radical change since the spring and that the United States should continue to pursue a policy of restoring Europe with the eventual hope of diminishing U.S. responsibilities.

Specifically, Marshall told Forrestal that, for the foreseeable future, the United States would probably be facing a world situation that would be "neither better nor worse than that which we have found in 1948 insofar as it affects the ceiling of our military establishment." Moreover, he reported that American responsibility in restraining potential Soviet aggression would remain unchanged. However, U.S. worldwide responsibilities could not be expected to diminish until western Europe had been restored to strength and stability. Accordingly, Marshall stated that U.S. policy should assist western Europe to build up its armed forces. He went on to emphasize that the United States "should not . . . proceed to build up US ground forces for the express purpose of employing them in Western Europe."[16]

Marshall's view, that the world situation had not changed enough to warrant an increase in defense spending, became accepted policy when President Truman rejected Forrestal's request for the $17.5 billion budget on December 9, 1948.[17] Apparently, the administration felt easier about presenting Congress with an aid package that could be justified as eventually reducing the American commitment to Europe than it did about asking for a defense budget based on an expanding U.S. role in world affairs, a role that involved a long-term American commitment to maintain international peace and security.

In partial response to its defeat on the budget issue the Defense Department sought to increase American access to military bases on foreign territory. Writing on December 21, 1948, the Joint Chiefs of Staff held "that the lack of needed bases and base rights can, because of its limiting effect on the capabilities of our armed forces for both offensive and defensive operations, constitute an indirect but definite and possibly very great weakening of the National Military Establishment." Referring specifically to budgetary constraints, the Joint Chiefs maintained that "negotiations for base rights can be of momentous influence with respect to budgetary dividends in terms of expenditure effectiveness, in planning, in actual war strategy, and even on both the length and the outcome of war."[18]

However, the Joint Chiefs of Staff felt that the process of negotiating for base rights would be "difficult and time consuming," and as a remedy, they suggested the use of military aid as a "bargaining chip" for the acquisition of base rights. Of course, this was in accord with the mutual aid provisions of the Vandenberg Resolution and the proposed article 3 of the North Atlantic Treaty. Regarding those provisions, the Joint Chiefs made two points: first, that it was a "logical extension" of mutual assistance for the aid recipients to make U.S. combat assistance in war emergencies "more effective" by extending base rights to the United States; second, that it was therefore appropriate to link the granting of American military assistance with U.S. base requirements in Europe.[19]

When Forrestal transmitted the views of the Joint Chiefs to the State Department, he linked even more directly arms aid, the North Atlantic Treaty, and the acquisition of base rights by the United States:

> If the purpose of the North Atlantic Pact and other arrangements under which aid may be furnished is to develop the concept of collective security, it seems to me reasonable, at least as a general proposition, to couple the granting of such aid with the securing of reciprocal advantages which the recipient of the aid may be in a position to provide.[20]

On January 17, 1949, Under Secretary of State Lovett indicated to Forrestal support for the concept of trading military assistance for base rights. Moreover, Lovett advised against the unilateral maintenance of overseas bases and favored instead the collective approach of the North Atlantic Treaty. Lovett told Forrestal that the "unilateral maintenance of military bases by this country on the territory of other countries involved considerable disadvantage from the political point of view" in that such a policy carried with it the "strong implication that the United States would undertake to defend in its entirety the territory of the country on which the base is established." However, Lovett pointed out that, if "studies indicated the advisability of the maintenance of military bases of one sort or another on the territory of any member [of the North Atlantic Treaty]," it would be advisable for the other signatories to make a collective approach to secure the base rights. Lovett concluded "that a clear connection can be established between the granting of military aid and negotiations for base rights."[21]

In this manner, the link was established between the mutual aid provisions of article 3 of the North Atlantic Treaty and a military aid program for western Europe. Yet this relationship remained tenuous and inadequately defined, as was pointed out by Ernest Gross on January 26, 1949. Gross was the State Department's legal advisor, and had been appointed coordinator for foreign assistance programs on January 3. In his January 26 memorandum Gross reported that "the development of the military assistance programs and underlying policies are fairly well off the ground."[22] Despite that optimistic note, Gross expressed concern about the exact relationship between military assistance and article 3, and he predicted—accurately, as it turned out—future trouble in presenting the Military Assistance Program.

In his report Gross maintained that, in addition to giving a general picture of European supply requirements to Congress, it would be necessary for the Truman administration to "explain the relationship between the military programs, the Atlantic Pact, and the E.R.P. . . ." However, he pointed out that there would probably be serious difficulties since no effort had been made to give article 3 "any substance, content, or meaning. . . ." Gross did not know whether or not any such efforts were under way with the European countries; nor was he aware of how, or even if, article 3 was to be implemented. He did know that, until he received answers to his questions about article 3, he could not proceed with his work on military programs. He therefore requested that his job be terminated quickly and that responsibility for coordinating the relationship between the European Recovery Program, military assistance, and the North Atlantic Treaty be turned over to a deputy under secretary of state. If this were not done, Gross warned that there would be an "illusion of effective coordination" among the three programs and that they "will not properly be presented to Congress in true relationship."[23]

Shortly thereafter, on January 31, Paul Nitze—deputy to the assistant secretary for economic affairs—returned from talks with American officials in Europe with a report on the status of western European military requirements. His description of European defense clearly presented a dilemma to the United States.

According to Nitze, in order for European defense to be effective, larger and more up-to-date military forces would be required. However, because the Europeans were in the midst of economic recovery programs, they could not make the financial, manpower, and technical allocations necessary to build effective, self-sustaining defense establishments. This meant that any costs above the existing European efforts would have to be borne entirely by the United States. Of course, given the mood of Congress, Nitze knew that it would be impossible to ask the American taxpayer to foot the bill for European rearmament without first receiving "some tangible evidence of increased self help and mutual and reciprocal assistance on the part of the European countries. . . ."[24]

In order to avoid placing the entire burden for European defense on American pocketbooks, yet keeping in mind the difficulties faced by the Europeans, Nitze hit on a formula to solve the problem. Noting that American officials in Europe had suggested a "carrot and stick" approach, Nitze urged that "military assistance from the United States be made conditional upon increased military budget appropriations by the individual Western Union countries." Nitze hoped that this formula would create the sense of "participation and self sacrifice" necessary to develop the foundations of an effective defense program and that it would constitute the initial application of the "self help and mutual aid" provision of the North Atlantic Treaty.[25]

In essence the initial effort was to be very limited, aimed at laying the groundwork for future efforts. Clearly, even with U.S. military assistance, Nitze did not expect the Europeans to create quickly an adequate defense system against an all-out attack by the Soviet Union. He knew that this would be impossible during the period of the European Recovery Program. However, he did advocate an interim assistance package of between $1 billion and $2 billion that would help spur the Europeans to greater defense efforts. Rather than expanding European forces, this initial aid would be aimed at improving *existing* forces and encouraging future improvements. While such a program would not lead to the rapid completion of an effective defense structure, Nitze hoped that, "[i]f a start were made during the next three years on a rearmament program and if the European Recovery Program were a success, the foundations might . . . be laid for an adequate security program to be developed in subsequent years."[26]

Nitze hoped that the American interim aid package could be developed prior to March 1, 1949, in order to serve as a basis for discussions with the Europeans and to facilitate its presentation to Congress. The administration thereupon set out to develop the principles by which the proposed Military Assistance Program would be administered and through which effective coordination with the Europeans could be achieved, a task both very difficult and, in the long run, not altogether successful.

On February 16, 1949, the new secretary of state, Dean Acheson, communicated to Ambassador Douglas in London the ground rules for American participation in the military aid program. Essentially, these guidelines remained consistent with the formula developed for the European Recovery Program and subsequently envisaged for the North Atlantic Treaty: that of European initiative in the development of an organizational conduit through which the aid could be channeled. Secretary Acheson made it clear that the likelihood of Congress's passing a military appropriation for western Europe would depend on the ability of the Brussels Pact nations to develop such a program and to utilize their own resources to build more effective military establishments. Furthermore, Acheson, emphasizing that the principle of reciprocity would play an important role in the development of the Military Assistance Program, stated that the Truman administration was "not thinking in terms of 'lend lease' but of 'mutual aid.' " According to Acheson, this meant a "coordinated program" wherein each member would contribute "what it most effectively can in manpower, resources, productive capacity or facilities to strengthen the defense capacity of the entire group."[27]

Ambassador Douglas communicated these views to the British on March 1, 1949, and the next day he was able to report to Washington that Foreign Minister Bevin had responded favorably to the generalities of the U.S. proposal but had reservations about the idea of a European initiative. Bevin felt that the United States had to assume mutual responsibility in proposing the program because the Europeans considered themselves in the "front lines" and felt that they "had to be careful about seeming to go too far in the question of Europeans pushing rearmament."[28]

The next day Ambassador Caffery communicated a more detailed memorandum to French Foreign Minister Robert Schuman.[29] During the discussion between Caffery and Schuman, it became evident that the French were attaching a great deal of importance to the Military Assistance Program as a logical extension of the North Atlantic Treaty. Caffery reported that because of France's long-term interest in a program of military aid and because of domestic political considerations "Schuman treated MAP [Military Assistance Program] as something which he had long been awaiting and which he believed would be of assistance to [the] French Government in fighting Communist attacks." More to the point, Schuman explained to Caffery that "public knowledge of [the] existence of MAP would be most useful to him in presentation to [the] Assembly of [the] Atlantic Pact and of possibility of implementation of mutual assistance clause thereof."[30]

Both the French and the Americans were thus emphasizing the "self help and mutual assistance" provisions of the North Atlantic Treaty to their respective legislative bodies as a rationale for the treaty and Military Assistance Program. However, there was one fundamental difference. In the United States the treaty was viewed as the more important of the two programs; the mutual assistance provisions were used to win support for the program of military aid. On the other hand the Europeans— especially the French—viewed arms aid as being of primary importance and planned to use the promise of such assistance as a basis for signing and ratifying the treaty.

Consequently, the order in which the treaty and the Military Assistance Program were presented to the public on both sides of the Atlantic became critical. To reassure the French, Caffery informed Schuman that the Military Assistance Program "would, according to our present thinking, be presented to Congress following the presentation of the Atlantic Pact, but prior to completion of action on the pact," and he agreed with the French foreign minister that "this program must be presented as a part of our whole effort for peace and security."[31] However, as the United States and the western Europeans moved closer to signing the treaty, and as the representatives of the Western Union countries continued to work on a response to the American requirements for a military aid program, the relationship between the treaty and arms aid was questioned by the Senate Foreign Relations Committee. As the weeks passed this relationship proved to be a thorn in the side of the Truman administration, as well as the greatest threat to Senate approval of the treaty.

On March 8, 1949, Secretary of State Acheson appeared before the Senate Foreign Relations Committee with a final copy of the proposed North Atlantic Treaty. After discussing the various articles, the senators asked Acheson about the duration of the treaty and the costs to the U.S. taxpayer. Senator Bourke Hickenlooper opened the questioning by

requesting a "rough estimate within certain lower and upper limits of the
financial obligations entailed in the treaty." Walter George added that it
was impossible to "intelligently discuss this without knowing something
about what our obligation is going to be under it. We start out on a 20
year program here and I haven't any idea of what it will cost." Arthur
Vandenberg then stated his feelings about the costs of the treaty and the
Senate's right to be appraised of them before ratification took place.
The senator stated: "I think if the administration has any plans which
are to follow consecutively in line with this treaty we certainly are entitled to know what they are before we pass on the treaty."[32] However,
Vandenberg then stated that, in his view, the real value of the treaty for
the Europeans did not come through implementation, but rather through
the commitment implied in article 5. According to Vandenberg, a senator
could vote for the treaty "and not vote for a nickel to implement it"
because of the deterrent effect that article 5 would have on Soviet actions.
In the senator's own words: "I don't care if there were no subsequent
implementation, I would feel that this treaty had gone a long, long, way
in the direction of an insurance policy."[33]

Hickenlooper responded by stating that, while he agreed with its basic
deterrent value, he was certain "that once we sign this treaty the very
next step is going to be an appropriation for the implementation of this
treaty. . . ." In his response Secretary Acheson sought to tread the fine
line between linking the Military Assistance Program to the treaty and
disclaiming their connection. In order to calm the fears of the senators,
Acheson stated that he agreed "with what Senator Vandenberg has said
about this. This treaty is not an authorization act, nor does it require
that anything be done, or that any money be spent, in any war." Yet
Acheson went on to say that "the military assistance pact is a logical extension of what you are talking about in this treaty" and reported that
the planned cost for the program would be approximately $1.5 billion.
He then attempted to reconcile both points of view by maintaining that
"the Military Assistance Pact is something which Congress ought to be
considering whether or not you have this treaty. . . ."[34] Therefore, he
told the senators that, while both the treaty and the Military Assistance
Program were related, one did not naturally flow from the other, and no
obligation to implement the treaty accrued through military assistance.[35]

However, no matter how much the State Department tried to make a
distinction between the two programs, the intimacy of the interrelation-

ship between the treaty and the military aid was evident in talks between American and European officials. On March 15, 1949, Ambassador Douglas met with the Western Union Consultative Committee to discuss a European draft response to the U.S. position regarding military assistance.[36] One of the major points of contention at this meeting was the question of "mutual" versus "reciprocal" aid.

Basically, the Americans conceived that the European draft response to the U.S. position should include the principle of "reciprocity," whereas the Europeans did not wish to go beyond the principle of "mutual" aid as embodied in article 3. Ambassador Douglas reported Bevin's position as follows:

> Bevin said that they had difficulty on this point because they could not be sure what US means by "reciprocal aid," and also could not anticipate the signing of Atlantic Pact. It was a matter of most extreme political delicacy, and fact that our Congressional time table required acceptance of principle [of reciprocity] before Atlantic Pact was signed created a cart-before-horse situation. He, for instance, might have to make statement in Parliament on MAP in which he could handle mutual aid easily because it was already specific, but reciprocal aid would be different.[37]

Ambassador Douglas countered this view by maintaining that some explicit mention of the principle of reciprocity was necessary for a favorable congressional response to the European requests. He maintained, however, that it would be possible for the Europeans to "accept [the] broad principle" of reciprocity while leaving the details to be "worked out later." Bevin stated that the acceptance of even the general principle of reciprocity would be difficult and hoped that the United States would understand that the principle of "mutuality" was included in the Military Assistance Program. Ambassador Douglas then made a point of linking the treaty, the Military Assistance Program, and the necessity for congressional approval of these programs in order to spur the Europeans to accept the principle of reciprocity prior to presenting either program. In this regard Douglas "spoke of MAP being partial implementation of Atlantic Pact and said our problem was to reconcile problems raised by public opinion in Europe as against public opinion in US."[38]

While the issue of reciprocity versus mutuality was never agreed on, the Europeans clearly wanted the promise of implementation before they presented the treaty to their respective parliaments, while the U.S. government—because of its difficulties with Congress—hesitated to promise implementation without European acceptance of the reciprocity principle. Moreover, despite the fact that the State Department was aware of the European desire to link the treaty and the arms program, the opposition Acheson encountered during the March 8 meeting of the Foreign Relations Committee led him to move in just the opposite direction. On March 31 he informed officials from the Netherlands "that we had deliberately decided to handle the Pact and the MAP as two separate matters," maintaining that "while ratification of the Pact seemed assured, [he] could give no guarantee respecting the passage of the MAP legislation, it having already encountered considerable resistance."[39]

This resistance to the arms program intensified following the signing of the North Atlantic Treaty, on April 4, 1949. The next day the Foreign Relations Committee met in executive session to discuss the relationship between the treaty and the Military Assistance Program. Henry Cabot Lodge opened the proceedings by stating that, unless the military aid program was presented to Congress in a very carefully worked out manner, "we are going to get ourselves tied up in the worst ballup we have ever been in."[40]

At that point Chairman Connally reminded Lodge of the distinction between the treaty and the arms program and said that the aid program was not yet before the committee. Lodge agreed but noted that there was a "disposition in the Senate to hold off on the treaty until they see what the arms program is." Vandenberg quickly agreed with his Republican colleague, and Lodge called for "extended public hearings" on the arms program and other related issues. However, he cautioned that public hearings could adversely affect opinion in Europe, and he hoped that the State Department would begin to think "about this business of reconciling American public opinion and Congressional opinion on the one hand, and the needs of the situation on the other. We ought to be very careful about what we are doing."[41]

Unfortunately, the chance for effective coordination was past. Almost simultaneously with the meeting of the Foreign Relations Committee, the foreign ministers of the Brussels Pact countries—in Washington for the signing of the treaty—presented a request for military aid to the U.S.

government. In this request the Europeans stated that they had developed "a common defence programme" and had "reached the conclusion that if this defence programme is to be effective the material assistance of the United States Government is essential."[42]

In their request the Europeans affirmed that economic recovery should have precedence over the arms aid program and said that the Military Assistance Program would be in accordance with the mutual aid provisions of article 3. However, no mention was made of the principle of reciprocity. In this regard the Europeans felt that "each Party consistent with its situation and resources" would contribute "in the most effective form such mutual aid as could be reasonably expected of it."[43]

The presentation and publication of the European request did indeed raise the level of public protest over the arms program,[44] and this in turn raised the fears of the Europeans that the Military Assistance Program would be defeated by the Senate. If, for domestic reasons, it was soon to become difficult for the Truman administration to present the North Atlantic Treaty and military assistance as parts of the same package, it was very important that the Europeans, for their own domestic purposes, be able to link the two programs.

This was especially true in France, where the far Left was opposed to any increase in defense spending, and the Right, led by de Gaulle, argued that any French efforts would have to be supplemented by the United States or they would be useless. On April 7, 1949, Ambassador Caffery reported that signing the treaty was "only half the battle to defeat [the] basic feeling of insecurity" in France. The other half of the battle could only be won by the promise of immediate American military assistance. Clearly, the European leaders feared that, unless they could get assurances of such assistance, they faced defeat on the treaty by the combined forces of the far Left and Right.[45]

One week later the North Atlantic Treaty was submitted to the Senate for consideration, and the Foreign Relations Committee met with Ernest Gross, who was then serving as assistant secretary of state for congressional relations. The questioning of Gross was sharp, and the State Department came under considerable criticism from many senators for its handling of the European arms request.[46] Moreover, some senators began to question the advisability of considering the Military Assistance Program prior to ratifying the treaty.

On April 12, 1949, the questioning of Gross was opened by Senator Lodge, who continued to maintain that the best thing the State Department could do would be to present a figure to the public prior to Senate treaty debates so that other senators would have a clearer idea of the amount of money they would be called on to appropriate for European defense. Essential to Lodge's argument was the fact that many opponents of the treaty were releasing figures far beyond those considered within the government. In this regard Lodge felt that "the whole tendency of frankness and completeness will be to shrink this thing to some kind of size, because there are so many variables."[47]

However, Chairman Connally dissented, asking Lodge whether or not such frankness would "build up some opposition to the pact itself by frightening these fellows that do not want so much arms and all that, and will vote against the pact because they say: 'Here is what it means.' " Gross then gave the State Department's point of view on the timing of the presentation of the arms aid program, maintaining that his department faced a serious dilemma in balancing the needs of the Europeans against the requirements for congressional approval. He also informed the committee that the president had the aid program under consideration and that it was uncertain how much time Truman would devote to its review. Moreover, he disclosed that it had been the State Department's idea "to have the program tucked away in our own files in the executive branch, ready for discussion with the committee whenever the committee wanted to do so."[48]

Gross's statement raised the question of the relationship between the State Department and the Foreign Relations Committee; Lodge would charge later that many other senators accused the committee of being a "vermiform appendix of the State Department," and Connally could maintain that such an accusation was "not without reason." Lodge then pointed out the disadvantages to both the treaty and the Military Assistance Program unless the State Department was more forthright in its relations with the committee. He stated that unless State and the committee developed "the broad lines of this program" there would be a total loss of faith in the committee. According to Lodge, that would mean other senators and other committees would be less inclined to consider the administration's policies in an orderly, intelligent, and sympathetic fashion and would create serious problems for the success of the State Department's programs.[49]

Senator Vandenberg also was critical of the way the State Department handled the release of the European requests, charging that the "Foreign Ministers came over here incidentally to sign a document, and actually to get a contract for armed help."[50] He then leveled a blast at the administration's failure to consult with the Foreign Relations Committee prior to the public presentation of the arms request. The senator said that if such consultation had taken place the State Department would have been advised to leave treaty implementation "to entirely supplemental attention" and that it could have avoided the "pathetically untimely release of these foreign requests." Vandenberg concluded that the relationship between the military aid program and the North Atlantic Treaty "bears so completely on the success of the pact itself that I can't help but express my very deep regret that our advice was not sought on the total project instead of only half of it."[51]

Because of the temper of congressional opinion regarding the Military Assistance Program and its relationship to the treaty, Acheson appeared before the Foreign Relations Committee on April 21, 1949. Also appearing with the secretary of state were the new secretary of defense, Louis Johnson, and Economic Cooperation Act Administrator W. Averell Harriman. At this time Acheson viewed the treaty and the Military Assistance Program as inseparable and was prepared to "propose that the one be accompanied by the other."[52]

However, the public furor over the State Department's mishandling of the European arms request had raised so many questions about the relationships among military assistance, the North Atlantic Treaty, the fiscal 1950 defense budget, and the European Recovery Program that the senators were afraid that approval of the treaty itself would be delayed.[53] Therefore, they felt that the best possible course to follow would be to separate consideration of the treaty from that of the Military Assistance Program. Both Acheson and Johnson stressed the need for the arms program as a necessary supplement to the North Atlantic Treaty,[54] but statements such as the following convinced those present that the best tactic was to proceed with the hearings on the treaty and to deal with military assistance after approval and ratification. Vandenberg stated baldly that "if this North Atlantic Pact is going to take on the overriding character of a permanent military alliance . . . there just ain't going to be any North Atlantic Pact, because you won't get the votes for it."[55]

Thus, when hearings on the North Atlantic Treaty opened on April 27, 1949, a *de jure* separation between the treaty and the arms program had been made: each would be considered on its own merits. Perhaps this was how it should have been: the link between the treaty and the military aid had been established relatively late in the process, and no adequate coordination had taken place prior to presenting the European arms request on April 5. Moreover, each program was the product of different considerations. The North Atlantic Treaty was the instrument by which the United States hoped to provide the necessary sense of security for recovery in western Europe, reintegration of western Germany into the western European political system, and restoration of the balance of power on the European continent. On the other hand the Military Assistance Program was directed more precisely toward meeting the Soviet threat, and could have existed—as advocated by George Kennan— outside the framework of a formal treaty. Yet in a larger sense the two programs were products of the same process, that of a growing U.S. involvement in European and world affairs, and a real link—however ill-defined—existed between the two programs. As the cold war intensified during the next two years, it would be this link that changed the shape and scope of the North Atlantic Treaty, as well as the nature of America's commitment to European security.

West Germany and the North Atlantic Treaty

Since it is argued that the provisions of article 5—the "heart" of the North Atlantic Treaty—dealt with the question of European security in its broadest sense, and not exclusively in terms of the Soviet-American rivalry, it is necessary to examine the relationship between ratification of the treaty and other issues of European security, foremost of which would be the situation in Germany during the spring of 1949.

Briefly, throughout the last half of 1948 and the early months of 1949, the three western occupation powers had been working on plans for implementing the London Agreements. These efforts—which called for trizonal fusion, the lifting of occupation responsibilities, and the eventual creation of a west German state—were given impetus by the signing of the North Atlantic Treaty.

Even though the western allies were proceeding with their plans for western Germany, the question of the new Germany's role in Europe remained unanswered. This problem was addressed in late March 1949 by a State Department policy paper stating that, in order for the West to benefit from the economic strength and strategic potential of Germany and guard against future German militarism, western Germany should be integrated into a wider western European grouping. However, the paper raised the key point that such a grouping would "have to be large enough to contain adequate counterbalances to German potential power, otherwise [it] would be dominated by Germany."[56]

The role of the North Atlantic Treaty in moving the French toward final acceptance of the London accords cannot be minimized. The French had remained skeptical about the London Agreements, fearing that the British and Americans would go too far in relaxing the authority of the occupying powers in the western zones. They also feared over-centralization and continued to have reservations regarding the status of the Ruhr. However, when the representatives of the North Atlantic Treaty countries met in Washington to sign the treaty, American officials were able to report that "the French may go a considerable way toward an improvement in Military Government relations with the Germans," and they were supported in this view by the British, who said that "the French will be strongly influenced [on the German question] by the Pact."[57] When Ernest Bevin and Robert Schuman met with Dean Acheson in Washington to discuss Germany, Schuman expressed his gratitude to the secretary of state for the treaty, and the three leaders were able to agree rapidly on the creation of the Occupation Statute for a west German state and "future policy to bring about the closest integration of the German people under a democratic federal state within the framework of a European association."[58]

Much of the success of the western effort in Washington stemmed from the attitude of French Foreign Minister Schuman and the guarantees of the North Atlantic Treaty. Schuman was a native of Lorraine and a leader of the Catholic *Mouvement Républicain Populaire.* He was conscious of the tragic history of Franco-German relations, and he hoped to achieve a reconciliation between the two traditional enemies. Because of his own personal convictions, once he was assured that French security requirements would receive sympathetic consideration, he was prepared to move ahead with American plans for Germany.[59]

The creation of a western German state was, in fact, "a watershed in postwar European policy." It meant a new role for Germany in Europe and the world. Furthermore, the United States and its allies hoped that by restoring some sovereignty to western Germany, and by integrating it into western Europe, the German people would actively support the West against the Soviet Union.[60]

The relationship between the North Atlantic Treaty and Germany's future in the West also received attention during the hearings on the treaty. Although Truman administration spokesmen Harriman and Lovett played down the link between the German question and the North Atlantic Treaty,[61] both Arthur Vandenberg and John Foster Dulles (R.-N.Y.)—who had just returned from a European trip—emphasized the importance of an American commitment through the North Atlantic Treaty in shaping the role of Germany in Europe.

On May 2, 1949, Dulles told the Foreign Relations Committee that "the pact is needed to make it possible to solve the problem of Germany." Dulles believed that under existing circumstances Germany could be tempted to find a "bargaining position" between East and West and that it might even find it expedient to enter into a "temporary alliance" with the Soviet Union in order to regain lost territories in Poland. Dulles feared that a combination of German and Russian power would easily dominate the continent.[62]

As Dulles saw it the only solution was to integrate Germany, or at least a part of it, into the western European orbit. But he knew that, unless this western orbit was strengthened by the presence of the United States, the new Germany would dominate. This he viewed as the main advantage of the North Atlantic Treaty: because the Atlantic alliance would include the United States, "it will superimpose upon the Brussels Pact another western unity that is bigger and stronger, so that it does not have to fear the inclusion of Germany."[63]

This point was confirmed in an executive session of the Senate Foreign Relations Committee held on June 2, 1949. At that meeting Senator Walter George said that it would be impossible for Germany and Spain ever to become members of the Atlantic Pact because of French hostility. George also felt that this French attitude would defeat the very purpose of the treaty.[64]

Vandenberg, quick to take exception to that argument, said that the very purpose of the Atlantic Alliance was to resolve French fears of a revived western Germany. He strengthened his argument by pointing out that the French had been intransigent on the German question "from start to finish" but that suddenly there had been a "substantial reversal" of French policy. This newfound French cooperation was, to Vandenberg, "one of the results of even having written the North Atlantic Pact."[65]

Significantly, both Vandenberg and Dulles had been involved in the early stages of formulating the treaty, when the issue of whether or not to use a treaty framework was still in doubt. The fact that both men expressed early reservations about the treaty concept and later defended it, emphasizing its role in achieving a settlement of the German problem, is yet another indication of the impact of the German question on the decision to pursue the treaty formula. Moreover, Dulles, going even further than Vandenberg, linked French cooperation in Germany to the receipt of arms aid as well as to the existence of the treaty.

Because Dulles was regarded as the Republican heir apparent to the position of secretary of state, he had accompanied Marshall to the Moscow Foreign Ministers Conference in the spring of 1947 and was well aware of the importance of the German question to European security. He understood French fears of a revived Germany and felt that if France could receive substantial arms from the United States and rebuild its army with modern equipment, French morale would improve "and they probably would be more sensible when it came to talking about the problem of Germany and so forth."[66]

The final report of the Senate Foreign Relations Committee on the North Atlantic Treaty adopted the position of Vandenberg and Dulles. Noting the ever-present European fears of potential German aggression and concerns that the Germans might be tempted to strike a deal with the Soviets unless given some future in the West, the report concluded that America's "European partners might be reluctant to accept Germany if it were not for the additional unity and security which the pact will afford."[67]

The newfound western unity on the German question was reaffirmed at the Council of Foreign Ministers meeting in Paris that began on May 22, 1949. The Soviets had proposed the meeting on March 21, and the western allies agreed to participate while at the same time continuing to move ahead on trizonal fusion and the North Atlantic Treaty.[68] The conference was held in the Rose Palace, and once the Soviets presented their proposals for Germany, it soon became clear that no progress would be made.

The Russian plan was merely a reiteration of their previous position on Germany: they wanted four power administration of the Ruhr, restoration of the Allied Control Council, and the creation, from existing economic bodies in both the eastern and western zones, of an All German State Council. The three western powers rejected those proposals because they viewed them as a Soviet attempt to disrupt western unity by turning the clock back to Potsdam and by creating four power machinery without any substance. Clearly, the mere reconstitution of the Allied Control Council would not eliminate the deep political differences dividing East and West. Acheson charged that the Soviets were hoping to capitalize on progress already made in the western zones and argued that the three allies would have to know in advance what would happen to the system they had set up in western Germany. However, he stated that the Soviet plans were so barren that "no reasonably prudent man" could accept them.[69]

If anything, the British and the French were more opposed to the Soviet initiatives than was the United States. Clearly, the lingering fears of German militarism combined with the potential for increased Soviet influence over a united Germany and made the Russian plan too much for them to accept. In fact a minor rift developed between the French and the Americans when James Reston of *The New York Times* suggested in an article on May 12 that the American position at Paris would be to secure a pullback of both Soviet and American forces in Germany.[70] The new American ambassador to Paris, David Bruce, had to assure the French that the United States had no such plans, and would do nothing with the occupation forces that would "weaken our influence in [the] European scene."[71] Clearly, the continued presence of the United States in a divided Germany integrated into a western Europe that was protected by the Atlantic Alliance was more important to France than a united Germany open to increased Soviet influence.

However, while the West was able to remain united in the face of these Soviet proposals for Germany, final implementation of the Washington agreements for West Germany would not take place until after ratification of the North Atlantic Treaty. And during the spring and summer of 1949, the treaty was coming under close examination by the U.S. Senate.

Ratification of the North Atlantic Treaty

When the public hearings on the treaty opened on April 27, 1949, the first witness before the Foreign Relations Committee was Secretary of State Dean Acheson. In a brief statement prior to questioning by the senators, Acheson attempted to link the provisions of the treaty with traditional American foreign policy, the Monroe Doctrine, the United Nations, and strong executive-legislative cooperation.[72] He then discussed the individual articles and the relationship between the treaty and military assistance. This was Acheson's most difficult task: he had to tread the fine line between giving the impression that the treaty and the Military Assistance Program were irrevocably linked and denying that acceptance of the obligations inherent in article 3 altered an individual senator's freedom of action when dealing with the question of appropriating money for the arms program. Acheson told the senators that, while they were not committed to voting for the Military Assistance Program proposed by the administration, ratification of the treaty did commit them to "the principle of self help and mutual aid."[73]

According to Acheson, the U.S. government was in a position where it could and should provide military aid to western Europe, and he earnestly hoped that Congress would see fit to do so. However, he pointed out that the treaty did not bind congressmen to reach the same conclusions as the administration because it did "not dictate the conclusion of honest judgment. . . ." Moreover, he stated that the treaty and the Military Assistance Program "should be considered separately and on their own merits."[74]

Shortly thereafter, when he was pressed on these points by Senator Connally, Acheson came much closer to acknowledging that the North Atlantic Treaty and the Military Assistance Program were, in fact, inseparable. The secretary of state told the senators that once the treaty was approved an individual senator would be forced to exercise his judgment on the arms program "less freely than he would have exercised it if it had not been for this treaty." Clearly, it was Acheson's understanding that even though a senator did not have to vote in favor of specific assistance programs he would be committed—by article 3 of the treaty—to the principle of "self help and mutual aid."[75]

It is clear from Acheson's forthright statements that, through the treaty, the United States would undoubtedly be committed to a mutual assistance program with western Europe. This meant a program for military aid, and in voting on an aid bill an individual senator would have to exercise his judgment less freely than before the existence of the treaty.

These facts seemed open to effective criticism from those isolationist senators who were worried about "entangling alliances" and the obligations they imposed. However, Acheson was criticized on the link between article 3 and the Military Assistance Program from such senators as Vandenberg, who had already made up his mind to vote in favor of the treaty and who was willing to separate the two issues. Witness the follow-

ing exchanges between Vandenberg and Acheson after the latter's asser-
tion that ratification of the treaty did "preclude repudiation of the
principle or of the obligation of making honest judgment regarding
mutual aid."[76]

> Senator Vandenberg. Suppose a Senator who votes for
> this pact says, in his own honest judgment, that he prefers
> to let the general obligation involved in the pledge of "one
> for all and all for one" to stand as his commitment to do
> everything required of him when the crisis arrives. Is he en-
> titled to say that?
> Secretary Acheson. Well, of course he can say it, Senator.
> Senator Vandenberg. Has he violated your rule if he says
> that?
> Secretary Acheson. In my judgment I think he would
> have violated my rule. . . .
> Senator Vandenberg. I think that is pretty clear. I am
> not sure I subscribe to it, but certainly there should be no
> doubt on the subject. I must say that I think a Senator
> could logically say that he accepts this obligation when it
> arises under article 51 [of the UN Charter] without accept-
> ing an obligation to prepare in advance to implement article
> 51. However, you have made your answer and that stands.[77]

Therefore, article 3 and the Military Assistance Program escaped hostile
examination during the hearings and debates on the treaty largely because
consideration of the arms program had been postponed until after the
treaty had been approved. The postponement of those issues meant that
such senators as Vandenberg could—in spite of Acheson's "rule"—continue to believe that a vote in favor of the treaty would not necessarily
commit them to approving new and costly assistance programs in the
future. Instead, the opposition the administration received on the Atlantic
Alliance came primarily from those senators who questioned the nature
of the guarantee provided by article 5 and the effect of that article on
the respective constitutional powers of the president and the Congress.

Among the most antagonistic opponents of the treaty was Senator
Forrest Donnell, who, back in February, had "set a land mine off" under
the treaty—again over the question of article 5. Although Donnell admitted that the treaty did stipulate in article 11 that "constitutional

processes" should be observed in carrying out the provisions of the treaty, he maintained that there was "nothing in the treaty which says that this obligation, individually to take such action, to assist the parties by taking such action as it deems necessary, is conditioned on the judgment of Congress."[78] Donnell believed that since the president had the right to use military force to meet an attack on the United States without a declaration of war by Congress, the chief executive would have the same right to use military force in meeting an attack on a party to the treaty, thus usurping the role of Congress. Acheson declined to comment on the constitutional ramifications of article 5, maintaining that it was a question for the attorney general.[79]

Following the closing of the initial hearings on May 8, 1949, the Foreign Relations Committee attempted to address the impact of the treaty on the relative powers of the president and Congress. The preliminary report of the committee, completed by June 3, stated that, while it was true that the president's authority as commander in chief had "never been clearly defined," it was certain that, in light of expert testimony before the committee, "the President would have no more authority as a result of the treaty to repel an armed attack against Denmark or France than he already possesses under the Constitution. . . ." The report concluded by stating that the treaty contained no "automatic commitments to go to war or any new authority for the President to use the armed forces of the United States without Congressional approval."[80]

This interpretation upset Senator Walter George, who argued that the report was misleading since, in his mind, the president had "absolutely" no power under the Constitution to use force in meeting an attack against another country without congressional approval. He also asked for the removal of the word "new" from the report since there were no *existing* powers for the president to use the armed forces to meet attacks on foreign countries.[81]

George's point raised the question of whether or not the treaty actually decreased the powers of the president to use the armed forces.[82] The issue was never resolved, but Ernest Gross presented the State Department's opinion of the impact of article 5 on the power of the president to use the armed forces.

According to Gross, the existence of the treaty, if and when it was approved by the Senate, "would not enlarge or diminish the constitutional powers of the President of the United States." However, Gross and the State Department felt that the treaty would "bring something new into the situation." It was his view that the president's discretion in exercising his constitutional authority apart from the treaty would "be affected by the existence of the treaty." In other words because of the treaty the president would have to "apply different standards in determining whether or not it was essential and appropriate to the conduct of our foreign policy to use Armed Forces in a particular situation."[83]

When the Foreign Relations Committee submitted its revised report, it remained vague on the impact of article 5 on the powers of the president as commander in chief. The report stated that article 5 did not require the United States to respond to an attack on a European city in the same way it would to an attack on New York and, in the event of such an attack, that the president could not take "any action, without specific congressional authorization, which he could not take in the absence of the treaty."[84] Of course, the committee did not venture to define just what the powers of the president were when he took action outside of the framework of the treaty.

The treaty came before the full Senate in late June 1949, and both Acheson and his biographer David McLellan have pointed out the more ridiculous aspects of the debate, focusing particularly—and in many cases justly—on the Republican opposition.[85] Most of the debate centered on the implications of article 5 and the impact of the treaty on various hypothetical situations involving the use of the armed forces. However, two Republicans—Vandenberg and Taft—addressed the question of article 3 and its subsequent implementation through the Military Assistance Program, and their views went to the core of the matter: Vandenberg maintained that the "heart of the treaty" was, and would continue to be, article 5; on the other hand Taft felt that the implementation of the treaty through article 3 would constitute the main force behind the pact.

Speaking on July 9, Vandenberg maintained that, while the treaty might be "a literal departure from orthodox American diplomacy," it did not depart from "a philosophy of preventive action against aggression" that was completely in line with the Monroe Doctrine tradition of U.S. foreign policy. Although he was aware that some senators thought that the strength of the treaty lay in its "subsequent physical implementation," Vandenberg stated his long-held position that his interest in the treaty would greatly diminish if he thought that "its repressive influence for peace is measured by or dependent on any such implementation." Vandenberg concluded by stating that article 3 could not "measure the final authority" of the treaty: "The supreme authority for peace is in the potential of the treaty itself, it is in article 5 and not article 3."[86]

Taft took just the opposite view, holding that article 3 was the key provision of the treaty. He maintained that despite his reservations about article 5 he still would vote for the treaty if it did not contain article 3. He felt that article 3 committed the United States to the arming of all the other signatories to the North Atlantic Treaty and was, in fact, "an incitation to war." Taft shared Vandenberg's belief "that the arming of Europe is not essential to the purposes of the pact" but argued that the terms of article 3 and the circumstances of the treaty's negotiation contradicted Vandenberg's position. Therefore, Taft reluctantly concluded that the Military Assistance Program had to "be considered an integral part of the Atlantic Treaty."[87]

Taft made one other very important point: while many considered the Rio Treaty the model for the North Atlantic Treaty, he pointed out that the only substantive provisions included in the Atlantic Alliance, but not found in the Inter-American Treaty, were those of article 3.[88] It also is interesting to note that Taft, like all other critics, continued to view the pact only as it affected U.S.-Soviet relations and ignored (or were unaware of) the importance of the German question to the treaty.

Unfortunately for Taft, other senators who continued to have doubts about the treaty and its relationship with the Military Assistance Program followed Vandenberg's lead and on July 21, 1949, voted overwhelmingly in favor of the North Atlantic Treaty. The vote was 82 to 13, and as Marquis Childs wrote in June 1949:

> As most of us were aware in one degree or another, this
> was a final farewell to what had been and what could never
> be again. The illusion that we could live alone behind a
> barrier of oceans was at last being shed. Yet at the same
> time the nostalgia for a past that had seemed safe and secure
> was still strong.[89]

Conclusion

What emerges from examining Senate approval of the North Atlantic Treaty is the knowledge that the central issue—that of subsequent implementation of the treaty through the Military Assistance Program—was deliberately postponed in order to win passage of the treaty. Instead of concentrating on the long-term obligation of "effective self help and mutual aid" contained in article 3, the debates focused on the theoretical obligation of article 5. This suited the administration perfectly, as it could point to the changed role of the United States in world affairs and argue that the North Atlantic Treaty represented an adaptation of traditional American foreign policy to changed international circumstance. That the rationale behind that type of commitment presented a persuasive argument can be illustrated by Senator Taft, who, in the last analysis, was willing to accommodate his views to the changed nature of the postwar world and support the Monroe Doctrine-type commitment contained in article 5. The major point of Taft's opposition to the treaty, however, was the link between the treaty and its subsequent implementation through article 3 and the Military Assistance Program.

It is clear that the two programs had been linked prior to consideration in the Senate; it also is clear that the link stemmed from different sources and was ill defined. The European requirements for aid came from two sources. First, Europe faced an immediate problem of military weakness. This problem existed, not merely in the face of the Soviet threat but also was—and this was especially true in the case of France—related to the wider question of western European security in the face of the emerging role of western Germany. Second, the western Europeans were skeptical about the circumspect guarantee of article 5 and wanted more tangible evidence of U.S. commitment.

On the other hand, from the American point of view, the link between article 3 and the Military Assistance Program existed because, in order to receive congressional authorization, any aid program would have to be based on the principles of "self help and mutual aid" contained in article 3. The Defense Department also had a strong hand in making the link between aid programs and article 3. Defense's attitude became evident after President Truman rejected Secretary Forrestal's $17.5 billion budget request in favor of $14.4 billion. It was hoped that by connecting the Military Assistance Program and the treaty an additional linkage—that between the granting of military aid by the United States in exchange for foreign base rights in Europe—could be established through the mutual aid obligations of article 3.

Despite these facts, the actual connection between the treaty and the Military Assistance Program was tenuous at best, with no effective coordination among the Europeans, the State Department, and the Senate Foreign Relations Committee taking place prior to the untimely (from the American point of view) announcement of the European request for military aid on April 5, 1949. Moreover, the relationship between article 3 and military aid was never adequately defined.

This lack of definition helped to separate consideration of the treaty from that of the Military Assistance Program. The need to separate the two programs stemmed from an even greater uncertainty concerning the purpose of the treaty itself. For many the major purpose of the treaty was contained in the Monroe Doctrine effect of article 5. On the other hand many Europeans considered such a commitment an inadequate guarantee. The French were particularly forceful in pressing for a military aid program as evidence of a tangible commitment from the United States to European security.

The congressional emphasis on the Monroe Doctrine language of article 5 and the European demands for firm U.S. commitments naturally put the State Department in a difficult position and forced such officials as Acheson to walk a thin line in defining the obligations that the United States was assuming through approval of the North Atlantic Treaty. The success of the State Department in this effort is illustrated by the fact that in spite of Acheson's candor in admitting that ratification of the treaty did require the U.S. government (and individual senators) to accept the principle of "self help and mutual aid"—and despite incisive arguments presented by Senator Taft that such an obligation would lead inevitably to a military aid bill—the central focus of the debates on the treaty centered on the implications of article 5. In meeting opposition to article 5 administration officials relied on the support of such Republicans as Arthur Vandenberg, who argued that the Rio Pact-Monroe Doctrine traditions of the United States were actually preserved in article 5, "the heart" of the North Atlantic Treaty. In the end Taft stood out as a solitary figure opposed to the treaty on the issue of article 3, opposition to the provisions of article 5 was largely circumvented by the provisions for the observing "constitutional processes" in meeting an armed attack, and the treaty passed by an overwhelming majority.

Finally, it is important to note that agreement on the status of the western zones of Germany and trizonal fusion was intimately connected with the signing and ratification of the North Atlantic Treaty. Moreover, the treaty would continue to play an integral role in the reconstitution and reintegration of German power into western Europe.

Notes

1. McLellan, *Dean Acheson: The State Department Years*, p. 152.

2. Ibid., p. 149.

3. Ibid., pp. 148-49.

4. Ibid., p. 154.

5. Ibid., p. 151.

6. Lawrence Kaplan, *Recent American Foreign Policy: Conflicting Interpretations* (Homewood, Ill.: The Dorsey Press, 1972), p. 96.

7. *FRUS*, 1948, vol. 1, pt. 2, p. 597, n. 3.

8. Ibid., p. 586; Report to the President by the National Security Council.

9. Ibid., pp. 587-88.

10. Ibid., p. 590; Forrestal to the National Security Council.

11. Warner R. Schilling, "The Politics of National Defense: Fiscal 1950," in Warner R. Schilling, Paul Y. Hammond, and Glenn H. Snyder, *Strategy, Politics, and Defense Budgets* (New York: Columbia University Press, 1962), pp. 1-266; especially 190-93.

12. *FRUS*, 1948, vol. 1, pt. 2, p. 601; Royall to Marshall.

13. Ibid., p. 614; Marshall to Royall.

14. Ibid., pp. 659-60; Memorandum from the Joint Chiefs of Staff to Forrestal.

15. Ibid., p. 745; Forrestal to Marshall.

16. Ibid., p. 655; Marshall to Lovett.

17. Schilling, "The Politics of National Defense: Fiscal 1950," pp. 199-200; *FRUS*, 1948, vol. 1, pt. 2, pp. 669-72; Forrestal to Truman.

18. *FRUS*, 1948, vol. 1, pt. 2, pp. 674-76; Memorandum by the Joint Chiefs of Staff to Forrestal.

19. Ibid.

20. *FRUS*, 1948, vol. 3, p. 347; Forrestal to Lovett.

21. U.S., Department of State, *Foreign Relations of the United States*, 1949, vol. 4, Western Europe, pp. 38-39; Lovett to Forrestal. Hereafter cited as *FRUS*, 1949, vol. 4.

22. Ibid., p. 49; Gross to Acheson.

23. Ibid., pp. 49-50.

24. Ibid., pp. 54-55; Nitze to the Foreign Assistance Steering Committee.

25. Ibid., pp. 55-56.

26. Ibid., p. 57.

27. Ibid., pp. 110-11; Acheson to Douglas.

28. Ibid., p. 138; Douglas to Acheson.

29. Schuman, who had served briefly as prime minister—from November 24, 1947 to July 26, 1948—became foreign minister on July 27, 1948 and served as such until August 1953. For an analysis of his role as a Christian Democrat in building the European community, see R. C. Mowat, *Creating the European Community* (New York: Barnes and Noble Books, 1973), pp. 66-75.

30. *FRUS*, 1949, vol. 4, p. 147; Caffery to Acheson. For discussion of a possible Scandinavian pact, see ibid., pp. 79-81; Minutes of the Twelfth Meeting of the Washington Exploratory Talks on Security.

31. Ibid., p. 147; Caffery to Acheson.

32. *The Vandenberg Resolution and the North Atlantic Treaty*, pp. 158-59.

33. Ibid., p. 159. See also a similar statement by Senator Henry Cabot Lodge, ibid.

34. Ibid., pp. 159-60.

35. Acheson repeated those views on March 18 in an address to the nation on "The Meaning of the North Atlantic Pact." U.S., Department of State, *Bulletin*, March 27, 1949, pp. 384-88.

36. The American position is found in *FRUS*, 1949, vol. 4, pp. 110-13; Acheson to Douglas.

37. Ibid., pp. 230-31; Douglas to Acheson.

38. Ibid., p. 231.

39. Ibid., p. 259; Memorandum of Conversation by Acheson. The reason for Acheson's conversation with the Dutch was American opposition to the Netherlands colonial policies in the Dutch East Indies.

40. *The Vandenberg Resolution and the North Atlantic Treaty*, p. 169.

41. Ibid., pp. 169-70.

42. *FRUS*, 1949, vol. 4, p. 286; Requests from the Brussels Treaty Powers to the United States Government for Military Assistance.

43. Ibid.

44. For example, see *The New York Times*, April 6, 1949.

45. *FRUS*, 1949, vol. 4, p. 288; Caffery to Acheson.

46. In all fairness to Gross and the State Department much of the blame for inadequate coordination must be placed on the Europeans, who refused to allow American officials to sit with them during the preparation of the arms request and kept the State Department in the dark as to the timing of the release. Ibid., pp. 231-32; Douglas to Acheson.

47. *The Vandenberg Resolution and the North Atlantic Treaty*, p. 180.

48. Ibid., pp. 180-81.

49. Ibid., p. 183.

50. Ibid., p. 185.

51. Ibid., p. 187.

52. McLellan, *Dean Acheson: The State Department Years*, p. 164.

53. See the editorial by Arthur Krock, *The New York Times*, April 12, 1949, p. 28.

54. *The Vandenberg Resolution and the North Atlantic Treaty*, pp. 214-18.

55. Ibid., p. 242.

56. *FRUS*, 1949, vol. 3, p. 132; Paper prepared in the Department of State.

57. Ibid., p. 156; Memorandum of Conversation by Acheson; Also Acheson, *Present at the Creation*, p. 287.

58. *FRUS*, 1949, vol. 4, p. 265; Memorandum of Conversation by Acheson; Also, Acheson, *Present at the Creation*, pp. 289-90.

59. McLellan, *Dean Acheson: The State Department Years*, p. 157.

60. Ibid.

61. U.S., Congress, Senate, Committee on Foreign Relations, *The North Atlantic Treaty, Hearings Before the Committee on Foreign Relations, United States Senate*

on Executive L. 81st Congress, 1st session, 1949, 3 parts, pt. 1, pp. 200-04, 280-84. Hereafter cited as *North Atlantic Treaty Hearings.*

62. Ibid., pt. 2, p. 341.

63. Ibid.

64. *The Vandenberg Resolution and the North Atlantic Treaty,* p. 270.

65. Ibid., pp. 271-72.

66. *North Atlantic Treaty Hearings,* pt. 2, p. 361.

67. *The Vandenberg Resolution and the North Atlantic Treaty,* p. 385.

68. McLellan, *Dean Acheson: The State Department Years,* p. 156.

69. *FRUS,* 1949, vol. 3, p. 924; The United States Delegation to Truman and Webb.

70. Kennan, *Memoirs,* vol. 1, p. 445.

71. *FRUS,* 1949, vol. 3, p. 878; Bruce to Acheson.

72. *North Atlantic Treaty Hearings,* pt. 1, pp. 5-9.

73. Ibid., p. 12.

74. Ibid., pp. 12-13.

75. Ibid., p. 16.

76. Ibid., p. 23.

77. Ibid., pp. 23-24. Another reference to the implications of article 3 came from Senator Hickenlooper, who wanted to know if the United States would be required to send "substantial numbers" of soldiers to Europe as a "permanent contribution" to European defense. Acheson's unequivocal reply in the negative would come back to haunt him during the so-called great debate over the assignment of U.S. ground forces to Europe in 1951.

78. Ibid., p. 80.

79. Ibid., pp. 80-82.

80. *The Vandenberg Resolution and the North Atlantic Treaty;* George reading from the preliminary report, pp. 266-67.

81. Ibid.

82. Ibid., pp. 280-85.

83. Ibid., p. 286.

84. Ibid., p. 373.

85. Acheson, *Present at the Creation,* pp. 385-86; McLellan, *Dean Acheson: The State Department Years,* pp. 155-56.

86. U.S., Congress, Senate, Senator Vandenberg speaking for the North Atlantic Treaty, 81st Congress, 1st session, July 9, 1949, *Congressional Record,* vol. 95, p. 8894.

87. U.S., Congress, Senate, Senator Taft speaking against the North Atlantic Treaty, 81st Congress, 1st session, July 11, 1949, *Congressional Record,* vol. 95, p. 9207.

88. Ibid., pp. 9206-07.

89. Marquis Childs, "Washington and the Pact," *Yale Review* 38, 4 (June 1949): 577-87.

FIVE

Implementing the Treaty

Introduction

The implementation of the North Atlantic Treaty was a crucial step in determining the scope and nature of the American commitment to Europe. The first two steps in implementing the treaty were the development of the Military Assistance Program under article 3 and the creation under article 9 of the North Atlantic Treaty organizational structure—in essence, putting the "O" in NATO. These steps took place from September 1949 to June 1950 and were in response not only to an increased perception of threat from the Soviet Union but also to a corresponding need to integrate western Germany into western Europe and to define the Federal Republic's role in western defense.

This chapter will establish the links among the Military Assistance Program, the development of NATO, and the emergence of west Germany as a semi-sovereign state. It will be demonstrated that the U.S. government, on the demand of certain U.S. senators, viewed the creation of an organizational structure for the North Atlantic Treaty as a means whereby west Germany could be included in the land defense of western Europe, thereby minimizing the role of the United States in that particular endeavor. On the other hand the French saw the creation of the NATO Council as assurance that France would be on an equal footing with the United States and the United Kingdom, that French forces would receive the bulk of American aid, and that the United States would be more permanently integrated into European affairs to balance the emergence of west German power. However, because of the military implications of NATO, France did not view it as a means of integrating the Federal Republic into western Europe. In this regard it will be shown that the Schuman/Monnet Plan for the European Coal and Steel Community in May 1950 was designed as much to prevent German integration into the emerging NATO structure as it was to facilitate the integration of west Germany into western Europe.

Initial Implementation:
The Military Assistance Program

On July 25, 1949, Congressman John Kee (D.-W.Va.) introduced
H.R. 5748, and two days later Senator Connally introduced S. 2341.
The purpose of those bills was to "promote the foreign policy and pro-
vide for the defense and general welfare of the United States by furnish-
ing military assistance to foreign nations."[1] The Senate committees on
Armed Services and Foreign Relations began joint hearings on the Mili-
tary Assistance Program on July 29, 1949, the same day on which the
House Committee on Foreign Affairs began its hearings.

In his memoirs Dean Acheson wrote of the military conditions then
prevailing in Europe: two and a half British and three U.S. divisions dis-
persed throughout Germany, six divisions of poorly trained and inadequately equipped French soldiers, and a few Benelux divisions faced over
thirty divisions of Soviet troops in eastern Europe. While the U.S. nuclear
monopoly reinforced the theory that an American political commitment
would be sufficient to deter an armed attack or political subversion, the
Prague coup and the Berlin blockade had raised doubts.[2]

While planners in Washington felt that the magnitude of a program
designed to redress completely the imbalance of forces in Europe by
providing the Brussels Pact with enough arms to match Soviet strength
was impossible, an aid program was developed to "preclude any quick
victory of sudden marches, backed up by an American capability for
providing punishing blows against an aggressor's home territory. This
placed the emphasis on deterrence."[3]

The amount of aid requested by the administration was the $1.4 billion
figure discussed during the hearings on the North Atlantic Treaty, a figure
soon questioned by opponents of the program. Senator Taft, the most
articulate opponent of the treaty precisely because he had foreseen the
subsequent implementation through article 3 and military assistance,
argued that, although the amount was not large enough to do any good,
it was sufficient to start an arms race with the Soviet Union.[4] Taft was
supported by a number of senators who wished to see the American commitment to Europe remain purely political, as well as by the traditional
isolationists.

While this opposition was serious, a more important source of concern
for the administration was a group of Republicans—as well as a few Democrats—headed by Senator Vandenberg. Although in favor of a program of

military aid to Europe, Senators Vandenberg, Lodge, Dulles,[5] and George had strong objections to the scope and wording of the bill. Moreover, they felt that article 9 of the treaty, which called for the creation of a North Atlantic Council and a defense committee to consider matters of treaty implementation, especially of article 3, be established before Congress took action on the Military Assistance Program. Vandenberg and his allies were eventually victorious on both points, with the second issue being of fundamental importance in determining the shape of American participation in NATO.

The first objection encountered by the Truman administration was aimed at the language of S. 2341, especially the wording of section 3. Given the temper of Congress, the State Department's wording inexplicably authorized the president to furnish military aid to any country requesting assistance if the chief executive—acting independent of Congress—determined that doing so would further the purposes of the bill.[6] The administration quickly came under fire from those who felt that the wording of section 3 granted too much power to the president and from those who argued that military assistance should be limited to the countries of the Atlantic Alliance plus Greece and Turkey.

Vandenberg started the attack on the administration's position on July 29 when he charged that the wording of the bill made the president of the United States "war lord No. 1 of the earth."[7] Four days later, on August 2, 1949, Vandenberg again leveled a blast at the bill when he held that it gave the president "the greatest peacetime power that was ever concentrated in an Executive. . . ." This, he said, would make it easy for the opponents of the program to defeat it, and in Vandenberg's opinion, such a defeat "would be the top tragedy."[8]

According to Acheson, this problem was solved rather quickly as he and other State Department officials left the hearing room and went directly to Truman. They found that the president was not particularly concerned about the section of the bill granting him the wide discretionary powers, and it was agreed to write new legislation.[9]

The new bill (S. 2388) went to the joint Senate Committee on Armed Services and Foreign Relations on August 5, 1949, and the senators were pleased with the changes relating to the power of the president to distribute military aid. Not only was certain language permitting wide discretionary powers deleted, but provisions were included limiting potential aid to the Atlantic Alliance, Greece, Turkey, Iran, Korea, and the Philippines.[10] However, the revised bill did not deal with the second Vandenberg objection, which related to implementing the treaty under article 9 prior to the extension of any military aid by the United States.

Vandenberg first raised the question of prior implementation on August 2, the same day as his attack on the language of section 3. It must be remembered that Vandenberg believed that the chief benefit of the treaty rested in its deterrent value rather than in its implementation through the Military Assistance Program, but if there was to be an aid program, it is clear that he did not want the United States to enter into a long-term and indefinite commitment to provide military assistance. Therefore, he favored the setting up of the North Atlantic Council and the Defense Committee in order to get a better picture of the defense needs of the Europeans and to develop an aid package that would place realistic limits on America's continuing obligation.[11] Ironically, it is the organizational structure created under article 9 that provides the enduring evidence of a permanent U.S. commitment to western European defense.

The failure of the Truman administration to come to grips with Vandenberg's second objection in its revised bill resulted in a major "revolt" from bipartisanship by Vandenberg and Dulles. On August 15, 1949, the two Republicans announced their plan to cut military aid to $1 billion and to require that it be made available "only to assist common defense plans made by the treaty council." They favored authorizing a small amount of military assistance immediately, the rest only after the president had approved the council's defense plans.[12] The administration's position was made even more difficult by a group of southern Democrats who balked at the bill for purely financial reasons.[13]

While Vandenberg and Dulles appeared to the administration and its supporters to rely too heavily on organizational structure in responding to what was, after all, an immediate political/military problem,[14] there was a logical consistency to their position that dated back to their earliest connection with the issue of American involvement in Europe: the question of Germany's relationship to the rest of the continent.

One of the major features of the Military Assistance Program was the military strategy inherent in the arms aid project. According to Acheson, this strategy consisted of three elements: strategic bombing, naval operations, and the land defense of western Europe. In the administration's view the United States would have primary responsibility for strategic bombing and would share naval responsibilities with the British. On the other hand France would have primary responsibility for land defense. This meant that the bulk of military assistance would go toward modernizing and reequipping French ground forces.[15]

However, Vandenberg and Dulles viewed this as one of the major flaws of the program. They had little faith in France's ability to develop the type and number of ground forces capable of being the first line of western defense in Europe, and they did not want to see the United States committed to supporting such a strategy.

While Vandenberg did feel that the most attractive feature of the Military Assistance Program was that, in the long run, it was supposed to decrease U.S. defense spending, he was skeptical of the administration's reliance on France as the major land power in western Europe. As he viewed it, "Western Germany is the final key to our peace hopes in Western Europe, and to our final victory in case of war."[16] Consequently, he felt that obtaining western Germany's goodwill and confidence was more important than reequipping the French Army, a policy that would surely threaten and alienate potential U.S. allies in the new Germany.[17]

John Foster Dulles shared Vandenberg's concerns and was anxious to include west Germany in western defense plans. Dulles feared, as did many others, that there was a real danger of losing all the Germans to the Soviet Union. Therefore, Dulles contended that it was necessary to change the status of the occupation of west Germany so that Germans would come to believe that the allied forces were there to defend, not to occupy their country. Yet at the same time Dulles admitted that "to bring Germany into the West involves extremely complicated problems so far as the French are concerned."[18]

Dulles expanded on this point in an exchange with General Omar Bradley, who was appearing as an administration witness before the Joint Committee, and he stressed the importance of the North Atlantic Council in reconciling France and Germany. Dulles told the general that it appeared that a sound defense program could not be developed unless it considered the political problem of Germany's relationship to western Europe. Dulles understood the French political problems but wondered whether the United States could use the promise of military aid to the French to bring them to a more cooperative position on the German question. Bradley agreed with Dulles: such a course had definite potential.[19] Shortly thereafter, Dulles again stressed that the successful defense of western Europe was completely wound up in the very touchy political relationship between the western allies—especially France—and the new Federal Republic of Germany. Therefore, Dulles did "not see how it is possible to view a military planning of the defense area without getting into delicate political problems which . . . [he] had assumed were a function of the council under the Atlantic Treaty."[20]

Senator Walter George, one of the Democrats who was troubled by the cost of the bill, also saw much wisdom in the Vandenberg-Dulles argument in favor of creating a council and the development of a strategic program prior to the extension of military aid. It was his position that it would be impossible for the United States and the other North Atlantic Treaty countries to defend western Europe successfully without including west Germany in the defense plans. Moreover, the senator also felt that the west Germans would become extremely uncomfortable if they saw the United States rearming France while continuing to dismantle industries in the Federal Republic. He, too, suggested that this action might drive the Germans into the arms of the Soviets.[21]

It is difficult to assess the effect of this particular argument on the Truman administration's program. Although Dulles was successful in convincing Bradley of the wisdom of the Vandenberg-Dulles-George argument,[22] and given the administration's long-standing desire to bring west Germany into a working relationship with western Europe, it is possible that the effect might have been considerable. Whatever the cause for the change, the bill was rewritten again to conform to Vandenberg's specifications: interim aid to the tune of $100 million was provided until a North Atlantic Treaty organizational structure could be set up, with the remaining $400 million allocated subsequently.[23] On August 18, 1949, the House threw a wrench into the proceedings by passing a version of the bill that was cut almost in half, and it was not until President Truman announced on September 23 that the Soviets had exploded an atomic device that the Senate version of the bill (passed September 27, 1949) was finally accepted by both houses. The Mutual Defense Assistance Program was signed into law on October 6, 1949.

Thus, the first stage of treaty implementation had been completed. The United States had developed the Military Assistance Program in accordance with the provisions of article 3 of the North Atlantic Treaty. However, before the bulk of the money allocated by the program could be transferred to the countries of the North Atlantic Treaty, the second stage of implementation would have to take place—the creation of an organizational structure and the formulation of a joint defense plan under article 9. What is important is that this requirement was inserted in the bill by the administration at the insistence of senators whose efforts were largely directed at creating an acceptable framework for west German participation in European defense. This point is critical in understanding the development of NATO as it evolved in the next year and a half. Moreover, as the United States and the western European parties to the North Atlantic Treaty moved in the direction of implementing the treaty under article 9, the French apparently also were anxious to move in this direction, not so much to help speed the integration of west Germany into western Europe, but rather to ensure that France would be primarily responsible for the land defense of Europe and therefore receive the bulk of U.S. assistance.

Developing an Organizational Framework

The French concern about the structure of the North Atlantic Treaty Organization can be traced, once again, to their perpetual fear of German power and apprehension lest the realities of the rapidly developing cold war create conditions whereby the new west German state would be in a position to dominate western Europe. This concern was especially strong among Communists and Gaullists, whose considerable strength in the French Assembly was a constant thorn in the side of the French government, forcing it to take certain hard-line positions regarding Germany and NATO's structure. The French government opposed new membership in NATO without Assembly approval and made it clear that it expected to be a full participant in all the committees set up to deal with alliance issues and to receive the vast majority of military aid under the Military Assistance Program. It is therefore somewhat ironic that the French preference for the strategy of "forward defense" ultimately led to the inescapable conclusion that west German participation in western defense was inevitable and that the North Atlantic Treaty Organization provided the vehicle whereby this act was accomplished.

On July 27, 1949—two days after the North Atlantic Treaty was ratified in the United States and President Truman sent his version of the Military Assistance Program to Congress—the French Assembly approved the treaty but attached three interrelated reservations: first, French approval for the membership of new countries in NATO would be conditional on

Assembly agreement;[24] second, the French government was to "seek the necessary guarantees from the other signatories of the North Atlantic Pact regarding the composition of the subsidiary organisms and of the defense committee"; and third, the French government also was required to press for "modern arms and equipment from the United States to enable French forces to fulfill their obligations under the Pact."[25]

Throughout the Assembly debates, the Communists charged that the North Atlantic Treaty was merely a device to create common cause between the West and the Federal Republic of Germany and that west German admission into the organization was inevitable.[26] The Gaullists also were fearful that west Germany would become a part of NATO, and *Le Monde* commented that "the participation of Germany is contained in this pact like the germ in the egg."[27] In order to counter these points Schuman appeared before the Assembly on July 25 and argued that west German entry into the pact was not in the foreseeable future and could not take place at any rate until after the peace treaty had been signed.[28] Nevertheless, when the Assembly finally approved the treaty, by a vote of 398 to 187, it attached the reservation concerning French approval of future members.

Despite Schuman's assertions to the contrary and the reservations imposed by the Assembly, it is clear that the treaty was designed to (1) provide security against a renewal of German aggression and (2) to be the vehicle whereby west Germany could be brought into a stronger relationship with western Europe. These points were emphasized in a *New York Times* editorial on July 28, 1949, immediately following the Assembly's approval of the treaty.

The editorial stated the importance of the affirmative French vote because it meant French membership in an alliance designed both to prevent Soviet attack and "to provide a firm foundation for real European peace by guaranteeing France against future aggression by Germany."[29] The editorial then addressed the growing awareness of many Frenchmen that a western Europe that did not contain west Germany was doomed to failure and that the Atlantic Alliance offered a means through which a working relationship between western Europe and the new German state could be achieved. The column concluded: "If the pact does bring about this change it will perform a service as important as saving Western Europe from Soviet aggression."[30]

Yet if there was an awareness of the usefulness of the North Atlantic

Treaty in helping to bring west Germany into an acceptable relationship with the rest of western Europe, the method by which this was to be accomplished was not specified in the treaty itself. And if *The New York Times* was enthusiastic about the pact's ability to help reconcile France and Germany, *Le Monde* remained skeptical.

In an editorial that was quoted in *The New York Times*, *Le Monde* pointed out that west Germany would soon be joining the economic and political organizations that were being set up in western Europe. Noting this, the editorial questioned whether or not it would be reasonable for Germany to be included in those organizations "and at the same time be excluded from the military one?" Because Germany would receive the first shock of any Soviet attack, a shock the weak allied occupation forces would be unable to repel, the French wanted to know how Germany would fit into the defense picture, if at all.[31]

Because the treaty was silent on how western defense would be organized, the creation of a North Atlantic Council to develop military strategy assumed great importance for the French. They were especially concerned about Germany's future role in any North Atlantic Treaty organizational structure and feared that they soon might be pressured into accepting German rearmament. Therefore, the French hoped to strengthen their position in the North Atlantic Council, win acceptance of a military strategy recognizing France as the bulwark of Europe, and tie the United States more closely to the continent through the implementation of article 9 of the treaty.

In early August 1949 French Ambassador Henri Bonnet informed Secretary of State Acheson that he had been instructed by his government to transmit to the United States the concern of the French regarding military assistance and the implementation of the treaty through article 9. These French concerns would accompany their deposit of the instrument of ratification in Washington, D.C.[32]

On August 10, 1949, Acheson informed Schuman that the U.S. government would not object to such a transmission of views, but he pointed out that many congressmen might feel that France was pressuring Congress on the Military Assistance Program.[33] On August 15 Schuman told Acheson that, although he was aware of the secretary's difficulty with Congress, he had promised the French Assembly to make a declaration regarding treaty implementation through article 9 and the Military Assistance Program. Schuman therefore suggested that, after a quotation

of the text of the French Cabinet's resolution on the North Atlantic
Treaty, a motion by the cabinet be included responding to the profound
French belief that the effective functioning of the aid provisions of article
3 could not be assured "except by the rapid and adequate implementation of military assistance on the one hand and article 9 on the other."[34]

Ironically, the French position on implementation under article 9 was
the same as that of Vandenberg and Dulles, only for just the opposite
reasons: the French wanted to use North Atlantic Treaty machinery
to secure their preeminent position in continental defense strategy and
arms assistance, while the senators hoped to use the council and subsidiary organizations to promote another strategy, one that would
emphasize Germany's role in western defense. However, Acheson was
disturbed at the convergence of senatorial and French views on treaty
implementation, and he suggested to Schuman that the French motion
use language that would remove implications that implementation of
the treaty through the Military Assistance Program and article 9 was
dependent on passage of the two. Moreover, Acheson asked that the
French postpone delivery of their message until after the deposit of the
French instrument of ratification in order to avoid the impression that
France might not live up to its treaty obligations.[35] On August 18 the
American embassy in Paris reported that Schuman had agreed to
Acheson's suggestions, and the reservations of the Cabinet were com-
municated to the U.S. government on an informal basis on August 25,
1949, two days after the deposit of the instrument of ratification.[36]

Not only were the French concerned about securing their participation on the policymaking bodies of the North Atlantic Treaty Organization; they also were desirous of further integrating the United States
into the defense of the continent through its participation on the various
regional planning boards. The United States, however, preferred to stand
aloof. This attitude appears to have been the result of reluctance of the
Joint Chiefs of Staff to sanction further military participation in the
defense of western Europe. Not only did the American position cause
anxiety in France and in the other continental countries,[37] but it also
provoked considerable concern in the United Kingdom, where the
desirability of increased continental involvement was being questioned.[38]

The first meeting of the North Atlantic Council took place on September 17, 1949, in Washington. With the exception of Luxembourg, all of
the signatories were represented by their foreign ministers, and the chair-

man of the council was Secretary Acheson. This group set up the following subsidiary bodies: a Defense Committee, a Military Committee, a
Standing Committee, and five Regional Planning Groups.[39]

The Defense Committee was made up of the defense ministers of the
alliance members, and its purpose was to make recommendations for the
implementation of articles 3 and 5 of the treaty.[40] The Military Committee was composed of one military representative (usually the chief of
staff) from each party to the treaty, and its purposes were to provide
"general policy guidance of a military nature to the Standing Group"
and to advise the Defense Committee on matters pertaining to the "unified defense of the North Atlantic area."[41]

The Standing Committee, a more selective body, consisted of the
United States, the United Kingdom, and France. Its purposes were to
"receive general policy guidance from the Military Committee" and then
to pass on "specific policy guidance and information to the Regional
Planning Groups. . . ."[42] Because one of France's chief objectives had
been to be treated as an equal partner of the United States and Great
Britain in planning western defense, French inclusion in the Standing
Group represented a substantial success for them. By securing membership in that body they assured themselves a strong voice in determining
where, how, and by whom Europe would be defended. However, France
was less successful in obtaining American participation in the Regional
Planning Groups.

Although the security of the entire North Atlantic area was of general
concern to all members, it was felt that certain parties were more interested in, or could make a greater contribution to, the defense of specific
regions within the area. Therefore, five Regional Planning Groups were
established: North Atlantic Ocean, Canada-United States, western Europe,
northern Europe, and southern Europe-western Mediterranean.[43]

Of course, the French had hoped to secure U.S. participation in all
five groups. Because certain members (that is, the United States) were
vitally interested in, and able to contribute to, the defense of the entire
North Atlantic region, political, military, and geographical considerations
were supposed to govern membership in the planning groups. However,
it finally was decided that, because of "the difficulty of evaluating the
political and military considerations involved, the membership of the
Regional Planning Groups shall be established on a geographical basis."
As a result, the United States only became a full participant in the North

Atlantic Ocean and the Canada-United States groups. On the other hand despite a softening in attitude by the Joint Chiefs of Staff, who finally agreed to American "participation as appropriate,"[44] the United States only agreed to be a "consulting member" on the other three groups.[45] While this arrangement meant that it would be more than just an observer on those bodies, it demonstrated American reluctance to be committed to the land defense of Europe through membership in continental planning groups. Because the French had hoped to secure more tangible evidence of U.S. willingness to defend western Europe, the American reluctance to accept full membership in all Regional Planning Groups was a blow to France. Moreover, America's desire to stand aloof from the continent soon was matched by a similar attitude on the part of the British.

Britain and the Continent

The question of the "special relationship" between the British and Americans was a growing concern in France, as it did not want to feel "abandoned" on the continent. Again, of primary importance was the issue of French sensibilities about the future of West Germany.

The Federal Republic of Germany came into existence on September 21, 1949, and its first chancellor was seventy-three-year-old Konrad Adenauer. Adenauer, a Christian Democrat, had emerged victorious by the narrowest of margins (one vote—his own) in the parliamentary vote that brought him leadership of West Germany.[46] Because of his Christian Democratic background he, like Schuman of France, viewed the Rhineland as a natural bridge between Germany and France and sought to make Franco-German reconciliation and the integration of West Germany into western Europe the cornerstones of his foreign policy.[47]

Of course, the goal then became the creation of the European institutions designed to accommodate German membership. The two that existed at the time of the birth of the Federal Republic were the Organization of European Economic Cooperation (OEEC)—created in 1948 to coordinate Marshall Plan aid—and the Council of Europe—which, first meeting in August 1949, was designed to deal with a wide range of European economic and political (but not military) issues. Both organizations envisaged German membership, and France sought to strengthen their institutional structures to prevent German domination of the continent by integrating the Federal Republic into the economic and political structure of a broad European community. The problem was that Britain, a member of both organizations, refused to participate in any structures that implied "supranational" authority.[48] Chief among British objections were, first, opposition to continental economic policies that threatened their welfare state economy and, second, a reluctance to break what the British considered to be stronger ties with the Commonwealth and the United States.[49]

The relationship with the United States was of special importance, and it was clear that the British would not take steps leading to wider economic and political involvement on the continent unless the United States did likewise.[50] This attitude was even more apparent in the military field, where the U.S. *chargé* in London, Julius Holmes, reported on September 28, 1949, that the "British determination not to give advance commitment in troops for Continent has undoubtedly been strengthened by our non-participation as full members in European regional planning boards under AP [Atlantic Pact]."[51] The British attitude of remaining aloof from the continent and developing its "special relationship" with the United States set off a major crisis in the "Atlantic Community" during the fall of 1949 and had the effect of increasing NATO's role as an integrative catalyst in western European affairs.

Briefly, the crisis centered on Britain's desire not to participate in the growing movement toward economic integration in western Europe. The French, and other powers, hoped to use the Council of Europe and the OEEC as institutional structures for the integration process, and in doing so were encouraged by the United States. Moreover, many American officials, including Paul Hoffman, director of the Economic Cooperation Administration (ECA), felt that British leadership on the continent was necessary to resolve French concerns about West Germany.[52] Hoffman was supported in his position by high American officials in western Europe directly responsible for coordinating Marshall aid. These men included Ambassadors Bruce (France), Douglas (United Kingdom), Dunn (Italy), Kirk (Soviet Union), John J. McCloy (high commissioner for Germany), and Colonel C. H. Bonesteel and W. Averell Harriman of the ECA.[53] On October 22, 1949, they informed Acheson that "no effective integration of Europe would be possible without UK participation because of the belief (not without reason) held by western continental powers of potential German domination if such UK participation did not take place."[54] Finally, the fact that the United Kingdom devalued the pound—and caused a grave financial shock in Europe—at the same time that Anglo-American monetary leaders were meeting in Washington, revived French fears of a "special relationship."[55]

The crisis continued throughout the remainder of 1949, but by the end of the year the western allies had reached a relatively stable *modus vivendi.* First, Britain would enjoy a *de facto* "special relationship" with the United States, which would not push for greater British participation on the continent. Second, the United States would support French leadership for the western European integration movement despite the negative British attitude toward strengthening continental institutional structures.[56] This U.S. attitude was the result of Acheson's belief that western Europe's future depended on Franco-German reconciliation, which was, in turn, dependent on French initiative. Therefore, he viewed the British and American role as advising and assisting France, not as putting that country "in the position of being forced reluctantly to accept American or UK ideas."[57]

However, the U.S. desire to support French leadership on the continent also was a product of American awareness of the growing antipathy between Great Britain and West Germany. Konrad Adenauer and the ruling Christian Democrats felt that the British Labour government was supporting the opposition Social Democrats,[58] and given that situation the West Germans felt more comfortable working with like-minded French Christian Democrats, such as Robert Schuman. This Franco-German collaboration ultimately led to the Schuman Plan (the European Coal and Steel Community) and, somewhat paradoxically, to a more important role for NATO in the integration process.[59]

One of the first suggestions of NATO's new role in the integration process came during the October meetings of American officials in Europe to discuss Britain's role on the continent. Although most of the discussion dealt with the British problem, Harriman—then working for the ECA— made an important point about the U.S. role in encouraging integration and the importance of NATO in that process.

According to Harriman, the British were not facing the fact that their negative attitude was in direct opposition to the principle of economic cooperation embodied in the Marshall Plan. In Harriman's view this meant that the United States would have to increase its pressure for European economic integration and should locate "some area for [American] participation in order to accelerate this movement and give confidence to the Europeans." The area that Harriman identified as the one in which the United States and western Europeans had the most in common was security: "Much could be done by the U.S. under the security umbrella but the ways and means require careful consideration. In the first place, the security organization must not be considered simply a military problem."[60]

Harriman felt that expanding the role of the North Atlantic Treaty to include matters other than security would be very helpful in the area of Franco-German relations, where French fears of abandonment on the continent were preventing progress. Harriman argued that the North Atlantic Treaty and the Military Assistance Program offered strong evidence that France was not being left alone on the continent, and he felt that the "Atlantic Pact concept should be the umbrella under which all measures agreed upon should be taken; that security, not economic integration or political integration, should be the point of departure of our policy."[61]

Since the British were hesitant to participate on the continent and to help smooth the integration of West Germany into western Europe, that task would have to be assumed by the United States. Moreover, since security was the one field in which the United States was most directly committed—through the provisions of the North Atlantic Treaty—it offered the best vehicle for U.S. leadership. Tangentially, American leadership also would increase the likelihood of British participation in continental affairs.

The idea of using the North Atlantic Treaty as an integration mechanism was not altogether new. Indeed, movement toward integration had been one of the stipulations imposed by Congress in approving the Military Assistance Program. But the concept of the treaty as the prime mover in this process was an innovation. When the Defense Committee issued its "Strategic Concept for the Defense of Europe" following the November meeting of the North Atlantic Council, the first sentence of its preamble dealt directly with this issue: "The attainment of this objective of the North Atlantic Treaty requires the integration of the parties to the Treaty to those political, economic, and psychological, as well as purely military means, which are essential to the defense of the North Atlantic area."[62]

The "Strategic Plan," approved by the president on January 27, 1950, basically called for "each nation . . . [to] undertake the task, or tasks for which it is best suited. Certain nations, because of geographic location or because of their capabilities, will be prepared to undertake appropriate specific missions."[63]

Specifically, in the initial stages of blunting an enemy attack against any party or parties to the treaty, the plan stated that "the hard core of ground forces will come from the European nations." On the other hand the United States would have primary responsibility for strategic bombing and would share responsibility with the British in maintaining the air and sea lines of communications.[64] Truman's approval of this plan had the immediate effect of releasing the remainder of the $1 million appropriation contained in the Military Assistance Program for the countries of western Europe and the North Atlantic Treaty.

However, not only was the organization developing in a military sense, but the political implications of NATO's emerging structure were assuming increased attention. This was especially true with regard to the question of West Germany. Throughout the winter and spring of 1950, it became increasingly apparent that some method would have to be found to accommodate the Federal Republic in either a European or an Atlantic framework. This awareness developed from two main sources: first, the realization that the industrial and economic potential of West Germany would be of major assistance to the European allies; second, if western Europe were to be spared another "liberation" following a Soviet attack, the defense of the continent would have to begin in Germany. This meant that West Germany ultimately would have to join the western defense system and that the main purpose of allied troops in Germany would have to switch from occupation to defense.

As the allies moved toward a solution to the West German problem, two issues continued to pose obstacles: British reluctance to become too involved on the continent and French apprehension about German rearmament. If the United States hoped to restore Germany to a position of power in Europe, the French would have to be assured that the new Germany would not threaten them. The only way such French confidence could be obtained would be through the establishment of a European organization with enough strength to contain German dynamism.[65] Yet such a European framework could only be established if the

British agreed to further involve themselves on the continent, and their failure to accept a larger role in Europe presented a deeply troubling problem for the United States.

If Britain would not actively involve itself on the continent, the only structural solution capable of resolving French fears was an Atlantic one that would include the United States. However, the only existing Atlantic establishment was NATO, and the idea of using a military alliance—however broadened to include economic and political function—as an integrative mechanism for bringing West Germany into Europe was anathema to the French. The eventual solution to this problem was "one of the most revolutionary innovations of the twentieth century—the European Coal and Steel Community, first known as the Schuman Plan."[66]

NATO and the European Coal and Steel Community

On March 22, the American officials who had met in Paris the previous October recovened in Rome to exchange views on the situation in Europe. Chief among their concerns was the question of West Germany's relationship to the other continental powers and the need to balance German power with increased British and American participation on the continent. In this regard Ambassador Bruce indicated that "some French officials [were] keenly interested in clothing it [NATO] with considerable political powers" in order to involve the United States more closely in European affairs and to secure an influential role for France in the new organizational structure.[67] Ambassador Bruce also indicated that this growing disposition to move NATO away from purely military to economic and political areas would present serious difficulties to the United States.

Ambassador Bruce reported that, if the North Atlantic Treaty institutions could be expanded to include a political dimension, the continental powers would no longer have to fear a revived Germany because they would be assured of American and Canadian commitment to Europe. Yet while Bruce felt that this would make up for the loss of confidence in Britain, it would cause severe domestic political problems in the United States. But despite the internal difficulties that prevented the United States from advocating a North Atlantic Treaty Organization with expanded, possibly supranational, political powers, Bruce did say that the United States should continue to support NATO's "development in every practicable way and should immediately stress its need for civilian leadership and direction and not permit it to be only military in nature and intention."[68]

The ambassadors supported an institutionally expanded NATO because they were aware that French Foreign Minister Schuman was "balanced on a needle" domestically and that it was very difficult for him to move France toward a more liberal policy for Germany without closer continental involvement by the United States. There were, however, signs of hope. Bruce praised Schuman for France's acceptance of a new role for West Germany in Europe,[69] and Charles Bohlen reported that, despite traditional French distrust of Germany, there was "a growing realization that without West Germany as a member, a community of Western Europe, whether politically, economically, or militarily, has little real substance and therefore [little] chance of success."[70]

Interestingly enough, much of the support for involving western Germany came from the French military, which recognized the futility of defending Europe west of the Rhine. According to General André Beaufre, who served at Fountainebleu under Field Marshal de Lattre de Tassigny, the West, whether or not Germany was rearmed, could not defend Europe on German territory without the sympathy of the German people. Clearly, the allies would not enjoy such support if they planned to surrender immediately two-thirds of Germany and to conduct defensive operations along the Rhine. Therefore, the French called for a "forward strategy," which meant giving battle east of the Rhine, "as near as possible to the Iron Curtain."[71]

Field Marshal Bernard Montgomery, commander of the Brussels Pact forces, was even more direct in his assessment of West Germany's role in western defense. After an on-the-spot tour of western European defense arrangements, Montgomery concluded that the West would have to take "drastic steps" if it was to defend western Europe. He found that the Brussels Pact countries did not have the resources or the manpower to create an effective defense organization, and as early as January 1949, he told a startled Ernest Bevin that West Germany would have to be included in both the Western Union and NATO. By November of that same year he was preaching the same doctrine in the United States to the Joint Chiefs of Staff, President Truman, and General Dwight D. Eisenhower.[72]

Not only was the question of West Germany's role in military strategy a growing concern in Europe, but it also was receiving attention in the United States. On March 23, 1950, Secretary of State Acheson informed Ambassador Douglas in London that the State Department was "considering [in] a preliminary fashion various ways to achieve related objectives of . . . greater integration of Ger [Germany] into Western Eur [Europe] and lessened dependence of NATO mil [military] strength on U.S. financial and industrial resources." In this regard Acheson wondered whether or not "equipment deficiencies in European members of NATO [could] be met by use of available industrial capacity in Western Ger [Germany] without violating security prohibition."[73] Here, of course, was the classic statement of the dilemma faced by American policymakers during the entire early postwar period: the need to restore the power of western Germany in order to create a new balance of power in Europe without also creating an imbalance of power in western Europe. Ambassador Douglas' reply on April 14, 1950 indicated that any move such as the one advocated by Acheson would have to be preceded by some far-reaching political and economic steps. The ambassador maintained that there was "no realistic utility [in] attempting [to] propose [a] detailed factual statement as suggested . . . before seeing light re [regarding] financial and political solutions to the problem of Germany."[74]

In order to speed consideration of the German question by the western allies, Secretary of State Acheson proposed a meeting of the North Atlantic Council. The French hesitated, feeling that trilateral negotiations would be better suited for dealing with the German problem. However, Acheson felt that it would be more useful to have a full council meeting "so that the potentialities of the Pact, which have to date concentrated on military matters, may be more fully realized." According to Acheson, such steps would include a strengthening of the treaty's institutions by the development "of additional central machinery to assist in carrying out the purposes of the pact and of what might be done under article 2."[75]

Shortly thereafter, Acheson expanded on what he hoped to accomplish from a full council meeting. In a letter to John McCloy, U.S. high commissioner for Germany, he said that the United States was searching for ways to strengthen the West economically, politically, and militarily. The secretary told McCloy that the United States was hoping to deal with the German question in the treaty context and felt "that if real progress can be made on strengthening western organization, together with a decision to incorporate Ger [Germany] into such an organization, the main outline of our Ger [German] policy will be fixed."[76]

The French, who wanted to discuss the German question outside of the treaty framework, were aware of the American intention to include it and were frightened at the prospect of the Federal Republic associated with an organization that was primarily military in nature. On the other hand they were aware that West Germany had to be brought into closer association with the western allies. These two considerations were largely responsible for Georges Bidault's "Atlantic High Council for Peace" speech of April 16, 1950. The purpose of Bidault's plan was to involve the United States and the United Kingdom more closely with continental problems and to bring West Germany into the closest possible association with the interests of its western European neighbors. These goals were to be accomplished outside the framework of the North Atlantic Treaty.[77]

The State Department's view of Bidault's proposal was negative. Even before the French leader's speech, Acheson was on record as opposing the creation "of anything comparable to Standing Groups" because of the sensitivities of the smaller states in NATO. Moreover, he continued to believe that *existing institutions,* including the OEEC, the Council of Europe, and NATO, should be strengthened to integrate the new Germany into the political and economic life of western Europe.[78]

In addressing the points outlined by Acheson, Ambassador Bruce wrote on April 25, 1950, that he was assuming "that the U.S. Government is willing to go substantially further than it yet has committed itself in developing in concert with the other members . . . [of NATO] a comprehensive political and economic as well as military association."[79] Bruce also favored an easing of U.S. pressure on the Europeans to integrate and instead advocated "a broadening conception of an Atlantic Treaty Community that will comprise most of western Europe as well as the US, UK and Canada and eventually western Germany, that will function along political, military and economic lines."[80]

Therefore, by late April 1950 the North Atlantic Treaty Organization was assuming a degree of importance in areas that went beyond a military alliance. Rather NATO was increasingly viewed as the mechanism whereby the United States could be more closely associated with all aspects of western European affairs—economic, political, and military— in order to facilitate the integration of West Germany into the Atlantic community. This effort was necessary because of the need to bring the Federal Republic into the West as a counterweight to the power of the Soviet Union and because of Britain's reluctance to involve itself in continental affairs without a similar U.S. involvement.

During late April representatives of the United States, France, and the United Kingdom began to prepare for a May conference of foreign ministers of the three western powers to be held in London. Again, the subject of the preparatory talks was the organizational structure of NATO with a view toward providing a mechanism to accommodate a new role for West Germany. While all parties were in accord on the problem, there was a certain amount of division as to the solutions; again, the division occurred on Anglo-American versus French lines.

Basic to the problem was the French fear that, if NATO were to be the vehicle whereby West Germany was brought into the system, military concerns would inevitably outweigh those of a political and economic nature, and Germany would be rearmed. In this regard French Ambassador René Massigli reminded the British and Americans that, although the inclusion of the Federal Republic in the western camp had much utility in the context of the East-West confrontation, the German question was beyond cold war issues and was, at least for the continental powers, a serious problem in and of itself.[81] A fear was growing in France that, while America had substituted the Soviet Union for Germany as the chief threat to stability in Europe, inadequate attention was being devoted to the day "when the Russian danger might diminish and a stronger Germany would again have to be faced in geographical proximity."[82]

Jean Monnet, *commissaire-général* of the Plan for the Modernization and Equipment of France, in describing the feeling in France at that time, was especially troubled by the fact that, in the spring of 1950, "the danger was still Germany—not, this time, because she might initiate something, but because other countries were treating her as the stake in their power games." He feared that in the cold war climate of the day the Americans would soon try to bring the Federal Republic of Germany into the political *and military* system being set up in the West, and he knew that the Soviets would take steps to counter such a move. In that atmosphere of escalation French neuroses about Germany would increase.[83]

Monnet was aware that Schuman was scheduled to meet with Acheson and Bevin in London on May 10 specifically to discuss the German question, and he also knew that his foreign minister had "no concrete proposals to take with him." This would place France at the mercy of the United States and the United Kingdom, and Monnet feared that a "group will form around the United States . . . in order to wage the cold war with greater zeal." In Monnet's mind this would inevitably lead to the rapid development of Germany, and France would not be able to prevent her from being rearmed.[84] Therefore, Monnet began to search for a way to integrate Germany's industrial strength more closely with the other countries of western Europe and to avoid the necessity for German rearmament.

Clearly, such a plan would have to be designed to end the age-old rivalry between France and Germany and to give West Germany a stake in the future by integrating its economic and political system into western Europe. But it is apparent that, from the context of Monnet's thinking, his work also was timed to establish France as the leader of the European movement and to prevent the Anglo-Americans from taking steps in Germany that would be inimical to French interests.

Another reason for the French opposition to using NATO as the framework for integrating West Germany into western Europe was that there were some continental powers vitally concerned with European economic and political issues that were not members of the defense organization and that could not play a full role in policy if NATO assumed a greater political and economic role.[85]

The British, on the other hand, felt that a new body should be created within the framework of the North Atlantic Treaty Organization that would deal with political and economic questions only. This approach would allow the United Kingdom to play an important role in continental affairs, while preserving the essentially Atlantic nature of that relationship. The British felt that the distinction between the political and military functions of NATO would facilitate the "future associations" of such countries as "Sweden, Switzerland, West Germany and Austria." Moreover, at the preparatory meetings the British maintained that while it was "premature" to speak of German rearmament at that stage it was "impossible to speak of incorporation of Germany into [the] North Atlantic Community on a partnership basis without considering rearmament, and conversely that strengthening the North Atlantic Treaty had to be a forerunner of rearmament."[86]

Finally, the Americans felt that some way to integrate Germany had to be found quickly. There was real concern that West Germans would value the goal of unification more than they would continued association with the West, and it was pointed out that "Germany was recovering her independence in spirit and in fact so rapidly that we had possibly no more than another year in which to influence her course toward [the] West." The United States was obviously concerned with harnessing the potential of the Federal Republic in the confrontation with the Soviet Union; yet it had not formulated a definite position as to how this goal would be accomplished.[87]

These, then, were the positions of the three major NATO allies as the London meeting approached. On May 7, 1950, Secretary of State Acheson arrived in Paris prior to journeying to London for the conference. While in the French capital he met with Foreign Minister Schuman and received the stunning news of Schuman's (and Monnet's) plan to pool French and West German coal and steel. The Schuman/Monnet Plan involved—in Acheson's words—the integration of "the basic materials of Europe's industrial economy, coal and steel . . . under the supranational control of the participating European states, with governmental powers and clearly defined purposes."[88]

The Schuman Plan was kept secret by its creators, even from the French Cabinet, and Acheson also was sworn to secrecy. This placed him in a difficult position when he arrived in London on May 9 and met with Foreign Minister Bevin. When the plan was announced to the British that afternoon, the American secretary of state was open to charges of collusion with the French.[89]

Not only were the British upset at Acheson, but they also were generally unenthusiastic about the plan, and refused a French invitation to join in the formal negotiations that ultimately led to the European Coal and Steel Community.[90] Again, much of this opposition stemmed from the Labour government's fear of joining a supranational institution based on a "freely competitive system in the basic commodity of coal and steel" while at the same time attempting to "manage the rest of Britain's economy as a welfare state."[91]

The French proposals had important impacts on both the future of Europe and the structure of NATO. By pooling French and West German coal and steel resources under a common authority, the Schuman/Monnet Plan paved the way for the economic integration of West Germany into western Europe, removed the perennial political question of the status of the Ruhr and Saar, and provided a new context for any future discussion of the rearmament question.[92] Of course, the chief benefits of the proposal was to establish a new basis for Franco-German relations and to make war between those two traditional enemies impossible.

Moreover, the purely continental basis of the plan removed much of the impetus for giving NATO an increased economic and/or political role. Since the French remained steadfast in their opposition to any military role for Germany at that time, the plan did draw in sharp distinction the economic and political nature of the continental movement and the overwhelmingly military nature of the Atlantic relationship epitomized by NATO. Yet while NATO would no longer be directly involved in the economic and political integration of West Germany into western Europe, it would continue to provide the military "umbrella" under which the goal would be accomplished.

Because of the security "umbrella" effect provided by NATO for European integration, the French continued their efforts to see the organization strengthened. Basic to the French position was a desire to strengthen the "executive" role of the North Atlantic Council and to have equal status with the United Kingdom and the United States within this organizational structure. The chief French complaint was that the NATO Council of Ministers met only twice a year, and those meetings were not sufficient to coordinate defense plans effectively. As an alternative the French proposed a Council of Deputies that would "be able to devote all the time necessary, and as continuously as required, to the exercise of the Council's responsibilities."[93] The French proposal also called for movement toward standardization of arms, each country's acknowledgment "of the necessity for the maintenance of forces disposable for initial fighting," and the "creation of the necessary operational internal structure for the use of these military resources within this framework of common defense." Moreover, the French suggested that the deputies look at the questions of financing, the setting up of balanced and collective forces, and the creation of an "operational internal structure . . . created for the employment of these resources should war break out."[94]

Acheson initially was puzzled at the French proposals,[95] but after they had been rewritten, he reported to President Truman on May 18 that their substance "seemed sound," and they were recommended to the member states.[96] The French, after taking measures to assure that NATO would not be the primary organ responsible for integrating West Germany into Europe, were in the forefront of strengthening the institutional structure of NATO and their role within that structure. One important aspect of the French concern was to have a strong voice in planning and organizing the land defense of Europe, which, it became apparent at London, was going to take place in Germany.

One of the important outcomes of the London meeting was that the Federal Republic of Germany became more prominent in western defense plans. The most tangible evidence of this came in response to a request from Chancellor Adenauer that the allies clarify their position regarding the defense of West Germany. On May 22, 1950, the three high commissioners for Germany, after consulting with their respective governments, issued a communiqué stating that an armed attack on the western occupation forces in Germany would be considered as an armed attack on all parties to the treaty and that article 5 immediately would be brought into play. As long as the occupation forces remained, the Federal Republic was protected by the North Atlantic Treaty. As a further assurance, the high commissioners stated that "[t]he three Allied Powers have no intention in the present European situation of withdrawing their occupation forces from Germany."[97]

In addition, Secretary Acheson suggested "changing the emphasis and functions of our military occupation forces in Germany so that Germans will come to look upon them not as a symbol of coercion but as representing [an] outpost of defense of [the] West. . . ." This would mean that Germans would accept the cost of occupation as a "German contribution to Western defense rather than [as a] punitive cost of losing [the] war."[98] This amounted, in effect, to the *de facto* adoption of the "forward strategy" concept advocated by France and increased French concern lest "the immediate conduct of the battle for Germany [pass] under the direct influence of our allies."[99]

Following the London meeting, efforts to strengthen NATO's institutional structure stagnated as the U.S. government was slow to appoint its representatives to the Council of Deputies. On June 14, 1950, British Ambassador Sir Oliver Franks sent a message from Bevin to Secretary Acheson in which the British foreign secretary expressed his concern about the delay in appointing the American deputy.[100] The secretary of state responded on June 24 with the appointment of Charles Spofford as deputy U.S. representative to the North Atlantic Council.[101] Less than twenty-four hours later, North Korea invaded South Korea, starting a process that led to the final entanglement of the United States in European security.

Conclusion

Late 1949 and early 1950 saw the beginnings of a structural framework for the North Atlantic Treaty Organization. The allied efforts during this time produced notable, if somewhat limited, results. Robert Osgood wrote that by "the eve of the Korean War, NATO already embodied a degree of military collaboration that was unprecedented among peacetime coalitions."[102] However, Osgood also was quick to point out the deficiencies of the emerging organization:

> Significantly, this concept involved a type and degree of mutual specialization of military functions which, under existing or foreseeable capabilities, was far more congruent with a guaranty pact than with an integrated defense system for the protection of Europe; for the United States function was confined to strategic bombing and protecting the naval lanes, while Europe was to provide the "hard core of the ground power in being."[103]

Of course, the limited success in building an institutional structure for the Atlantic Alliance was a product of the limited consensus concerning the role of the new organization. While the United States required the implementation of article 9 and the development of an "integrated" defense plan in order to ensure the eventual utilization of West German resources—and thereby minimize the need for a long-term American commitment—it is clear that the French sought a formalized structure for just the opposite reasons: to integrate the United States into western defense and to keep West Germany out of NATO.

Again, the overriding concern stems from the question of West Germany's relationship to western Europe. As it became apparent to the allies that (1) the defense of Europe would have to begin in the Federal Republic and that (2) West Germany's industrial strength was necessary for a successful rearmament program, traditional French apprehensions *vis-à-vis* Germany became more and more manifest. In order to assuage these apprehensions West German power had to be counterbalanced.

Initially, it was hoped on both sides of the Atlantic that Great Britain would fill this balancing role. This viewpoint was especially strong among the U.S. representatives in Europe, who felt that British participation in continental integration plans was essential to the creation of a strong and stable western Europe as a counterbalance to the Soviet Union. One of the proposals to this end strengthened the Organization for European Economic Cooperation to the point that it possessed some supranational authority.

However, by late 1949 it became clear that Britain was not going to embark on a program of closer involvement on the continent for two reasons: First, the British still considered themselves a great power with worldwide security commitments and responsibilities. In this regard they felt attached to the Commonwealth and, more importantly, to the United States. The desire to maintain and foster this "special relationship" with America was certainly one of the most important aspects of the British reluctance to join any continental union movement. Second, the Labour government was opposed to linking Britain's developing welfare economy with the market economies of the continental countries. This position was mirrored by the West Germans, who disliked Britain's Labour government because of its support for the opposition Social Democrats in the Federal Republic.

When all parties realized in early 1950 that it would be fruitless to continue attempts to bring Britain into the continent without also securing U.S. participation, NATO assumed greater importance as an integrative factor. It was felt that because the United States and the United Kingdom both were members of NATO—the former was not a direct participant in the Organization for European Economic Cooperation—that the new organization could transcend its purely military function and would take on economic and political roles as well. This idea received serious consideration throughout the spring of 1950, but it too met defeat. In this case the opposition came from the French, who feared that, even if the Federal Republic were brought into an expanded NATO on purely economic and political grounds, it would be impossible to exclude it from the military field.

This situation was largely resolved at the May 7-13, 1950, London Foreign Ministers' Conference, during which the French unveiled their plan for a continental solution to the economic and political problems associated with integrating West Germany into western Europe and proposed strengthening NATO's institutional structure in the purely military field in order to provide the security "umbrella" under which western European integration could take place. In both efforts the French were largely successful, and the timing of the announcement of the European Coal and Steel Community and the strengthening of NATO's organizational framework is vitally important. Although the creation of the European Coal and Steel Community did reject the idea of using NATO as a complete integrative mechanism, it also established the intimate interconnection between military security and the European integration movement and clearly indicated that the development of NATO as an organization was in response to a series of issues that transcended the cold war and embraced questions of perennial importance in European politics: the Franco-German problem and the relationship of the "Atlantic partners" to the continent.

Thus, by the spring of 1950, only the important question of German rearmament had not come out in the open, and opposition to such a move remained widespread throughout the Atlantic community. However, the outbreak of the Korean war reawakened fears that had gripped Europe in 1946 and 1947 and brought the German rearmament issue to the forefront of alliance politics.[104]

Notes

1. U.S., Congress, Senate, Committee on Foreign Relations, *Military Assistance Program,* Joint Hearings held in Executive Session before the Committee on Foreign Relations and the Committee on Armed Services, U.S. Senate, 81st Congress, 1st session, on S. 2388, *Historical Series,* 1974, pp. 631-32. Hereafter cited as *Military Assistance Program Hearings.*

2. Acheson, *Present at the Creation,* p. 308.

3. Ibid. The basis of this plan was Nitze's report of January 31, 1949.

4. U.S., Congress, Senate, Senator Taft speaking against the Military Assistance Program, S. 2388, 81st Congress, 1st session, September 22, 1949, *Congressional Record,* vol. 95, pp. 13148-50.

5. Appointed to fill an unexpired term from New York.

6. *Military Assistance Program Hearings,* pp. 633-34.

7. Ibid., p. 5.

8. Ibid., p. 22.

9. Acheson, *Present at the Creation,* p. 310.

10. *Military Assistance Program Hearings,* pp. 648-63.

11. Ibid., pp. 22-23.

12. Acheson, *Present at the Creation,* p. 311.

13. Ibid. For an example of such reasoning, see *Military Assistance Program Hearings,* pp. 84-85.

14. For the opposing arguments, see *Military Assistance Program Hearings,* pp. 79-82, especially the exchange between Vandenberg and Millard Tydings of Maryland. Also see McLellan, *Dean Acheson: The State Department Years,* p. 165.

15. *Military Assistance Program Hearings,* p. 30.

16. Ibid., p. 391.

17. Ibid., p. 392.

18. Ibid., pp. 120-21.

19. Ibid., p. 122.

20. Ibid., pp. 123-24.

21. Ibid., pp. 401-02. A telling point in George's argument was that he simply did not want the defense of western Europe to be "dependent on the emotions of Frenchmen. . . ." Ibid., p. 401.

22. Ibid., p. 122.

23. Ibid., p. 681. This amount referred only to monies from the Treasury. The remainder of the almost $1.4 billion was allocated to Greece, Turkey, Iran, Korea, and the Philippines or was accounted for in surplus equipment not exceeding $450 million in value.

24. *The New York Times,* July 28, 1949, p. 1.

25. *FRUS,* 1949, vol. 4, p. 318, n. 1.

26. *The New York Times,* July 24, 1949, p. 1.

27. Ibid., p. 3; *Le Monde* quoted in *The New York Times.*

28. *The New York Times,* July 26, 1949, p. 3.

29. Ibid., editorial, July 28, 1949, p. 22.

30. Ibid.

31. Ibid., July 24, 1949, p. 3.

32. *FRUS,* 1949, vol. 4, p. 318, n. 3.

33. Ibid., Acheson to Bruce, August 10, 1949.

34. Ibid., p. 320, Bonbright to Acheson, August 15, 1949.

35. Ibid., p. 321; Acheson to Bruce, August 17, 1949. The revised French motion simply called for "the earliest possible establishement of machinery under Article 9."

36. Ibid., n. 1. See also *The New York Times,* August 26, 1949, p. 8.

37. *FRUS,* 1949, vol. 4, pp. 321-22; Acheson to Douglas.

38. Ibid., pp. 325-27; Memorandum of Conversation by Acheson. See especially Attachment A, *Aide-Mémoire,* p. 327.

39. Ibid., pp. 330-37. Report of the Working Group on Organization, to the North Atlantic Council.

40. Ibid., p. 332.

41. Ibid., p. 333.

42. Ibid., p. 334.

43. Ibid., pp. 335-36.

44. Ibid., p. 322; Johnson to Acheson.

45. Ibid., pp. 330-31; Report of the Working Group on Organization, to the North Atlantic Council; Organizational Chart.

46. Konrad Adenauer, *Memoirs, 1945-1953* (Chicago: Henry Regnery Company, 1965), p. 182. The vote took place on September 15, 1949.

47. Ibid., p. 202. See also Mowat, *Creating the European Community,* pp. 14-20.

48. Dalton, *High Tide and After,* pp. 313-27; Adenauer, *Memoirs,* pp. 203, 210-12, 249-54.

49. *FRUS,* 1949, vol. 4, pp. 330-40; Holmes to Acheson.

50. Kennan, *Memoirs,* vol. 1, p. 453.

51. *FRUS,* 1949, vol. 4, p. 340; Holmes to Acheson.

52. McLellan, *Dean Acheson: The State Department Years,* p. 240.

53. *FRUS,* 1949, vol. 4, pp. 472-73, Summary Record of a Meeting of U.S. Ambassadors at Paris.

54. Ibid., p. 343; Bruce to Acheson.

55. Ibid., pp. 338-39; Acheson to Webb; also, McLellan, *Dean Acheson: The State Department Years,* p. 242.

56. McLellan, *Dean Acheson: The State Department Years,* p. 246.

57. *FRUS,* 1949, vol. 4, pp. 338-39; Acheson to Webb.

58. Ibid., p. 487; Summary Record of a Meeting of U.S. Ambassadors at Paris. Statement of John McCloy.

59. For more detail on the "Atlantic Crisis" of 1949, see ibid., pp. 338-50, 367-496. See also McLellan, *Dean Acheson: The State Department Years,* pp. 249-52; and Acheson, *Present at the Creation,* pp. 322-25.

60. *FRUS,* 1949, vol. 4, pp. 489-90; Summary Record of a Meeting of U.S. Ambassadors in Europe. Statement of W. Averell Harriman.

61. Ibid., p. 494.

62. Ibid., p. 353; Strategic Concept for the Defense of the North Atlantic Area.

63. Ibid., p. 354

64. Ibid., p. 355.

65. McLellan, *Dean Acheson: The State Department Years,* p. 249.

66. Ibid., p. 250.

67. U.S., Department of State, *Foreign Relations of the United States,* 1950, vol. 3; Western Europe, pp. 797-98; Summary Record of a Meeting of U.S. Ambassadors at Rome. Hereafter cited as *FRUS,* 1950, vol. 3.

68. Ibid., p. 798.

69. Ibid. See also McLellan, *Dean Acheson: The State Department Years,* p. 247.

70. *FRUS,* 1950, vol. 3, p. 815; Summary Record of a Meeting of U.S. Ambassadors at Rome.

71. Beaufre, *NATO and Europe.* p. 26.

72. Sir Bernard Montgomery, *The Memoirs of Field Marshal the Viscount Montgomery of Alamein, K.G.* (Cleveland, Ohio: The World Publishing Company, 1958), pp. 457-58.

73. *FRUS,* 1950, vol. 3, p. 32; Acheson to Douglas.

74. Ibid., p. 52; Douglas to Acheson.

75. Ibid., p. 831; Acheson to Douglas.

76. Ibid., p. 833; Acheson to McCloy.

77. Ibid., pp. 63-65; Bruce to Acheson. One of the main criteria Bidault listed for future German membership in NATO was the availability of military supplies for the other allies. Ibid., p. 62.

78. Ibid., p. 59; Acheson to Bruce.

79. Ibid., p. 63; Bruce to Acheson.

80. Ibid., p. 64.

81. Ibid., p. 839; The U.S. Delegation to the Tripartite Preparatory Meetings to Acheson.

82. Robert McGeehan, *The German Rearmament Question* (Urbana: University of Illinois Press, 1971), p. 161.

83. Jean Monnet, *Memoirs* (Garden City, N.Y.: Doubleday and Company, Inc., 1978), p. 291.

84. Ibid., pp. 292-93.

85. *FRUS,* 1950, vol. 3, pp. 845-46; The United States at the Tripartite Preparatory Meetings to Acheson.

86. Ibid., p. 862. The British also proposed an "umbrella" organization, although not necessarily NATO, that would have embraced both the United States and West Germany.

87. Ibid., p. 883; The U.S. Delegation at the Tripartite Preparatory Meetings. See also, ibid., pp. 697-701.

88. Acheson, *Present at the Creation,* pp. 382-85.

89. Ibid., pp. 385-86.

90. Mowat, *Creating the European Community,* pp. 103-12.

91. Acheson, *Present at the Creation,* p. 385; Dalton, *High Tide and After,* pp. 334-35.

92. Mowat, *Creating the European Community,* p. 93.

93. *FRUS,* 1950, vol. 3, p. 1104; French Draft Resolution on the Organization of the Mechanism of the Treaty.

94. Ibid., p. 1105; French Draft Resolution on the North Atlantic Council.

95. Ibid., p. 1054; Memorandum of Conversation by Jessup.

96. Ibid., pp. 124-25; Acheson to Truman.

97. Ibid., p. 1085; Paper Approved by the Foreign Ministers. The word "present" was subsequently deleted.

98. Ibid., p. 1016; Acheson to Webb.

99. Beaufre, *NATO and Europe,* p. 27.

100. *FRUS,* 1950, vol. 3, pp. 128-29; Franks to Acheson.

101. Ibid., p. 129; Acheson to Certain Diplomatic Offices.

102. Robert Osgood, *NATO: The Entangling Alliance* (Chicago: University of Chicago Press, 1962), p. 47.

103. Ibid.

104. McLellan, *Dean Acheson: The State Department Years,* p. 256.

SIX

Final Implementation: The Assignment of Ground Troops

Introduction

French General André Beaufre has recorded that, in the view of many Europeans, "above all else NATO was a means of integrating the Americans into our defense system. This was a political necessity because of the vagueness of the terms of the treaty. . . ."[1] At no stage of treaty implementation was Beaufre's analysis more correct than during the assignment of American ground forces to Europe as an integral component of General Dwight D. Eisenhower's NATO command structure; a policy decision that sparked what became known as "the great debate" in American foreign policy.

The assignment of American troops to NATO and the creation of an integrated command structure with Eisenhower in charge took place under the provisions of article 3 of the North Atlantic Treaty and gave tangible evidence of the U.S. commitment to European security. With the stationing of "hostage" troops in Europe, no longer could there be any doubt that the United States would participate in the initial defense of western Europe in case of a Soviet attack, nor could there be any doubt that a profound and fundamental departure had taken place in the conduct of American foreign policy.

It is important to realize that, until the creation of the NATO structure and the assignment of U.S. ground forces to that organization, none of the American policies for Europe—as revolutionary as they were—implied permanent American involvement in continental affairs. Indeed, both the Marshall Plan and the Military Assistance Program were meant to strengthen western Europe and to restore a balance of power in Europe so that U.S. involvement would not be necessary. That neither of these programs was likely to permanently entangle the United States in Europe is made evident by the facts that the Marshall Plan was terminated in the early 1950s and that the Military Assistance Program reached its peak in the same period, eventually being discontinued after long years of decline.

The North Atlantic Treaty itself was viewed by American policymakers as providing the political support necessary to supplement the economic and military assistance given by the two programs mentioned above. The treaty did not require or include plans for the creation of a military organization with an integrated command structure, a supreme commander, or troop contributions from the member states. In fact, Secretary of State Acheson insisted at the Senate hearings on the treaty that it would not be necessary for the United States to deploy large numbers of troops in Europe.[2] It was the leap from the treaty to the organization (NATO) that led to the permanent entanglement of the United States.

The transformation from a political treaty to a permanent military alliance was the result of the Korean war. The North Korean invasion on June 25, 1950, raised western fears about the adequacy of their defense preparations. In order to counter such fears it was decided to take two important steps: first, to strengthen the American commitment to western Europe by assigning additional U.S. troops to the continent; second, to increase the defense capabilities of the western European countries themselves. However, both steps raised delicate political questions. On the one hand a decision by the Truman administration to assign additional forces to Europe would surely encounter partisan political opposition in the United States; on the other hand increasing the military capabilities of western Europe would necessarily bring the extremely sensitive issue of German rearmament out in the open.

The increased perception of military threat from the Soviet Union came when the long-term relationship between the United States and western Europe was ill defined and when European fears of German power were still fresh. It is argued here that the Korean war led to the creation of a NATO structure that was designed to counter the Soviet threat by giving concrete evidence of the American political-military commitment to western Europe and by providing the framework for the eventual rearmament of West Germany.

The fact that the creation of NATO was tied to the questions of assigning additional American troops to Europe under article 3 of the treaty as well as to German rearmament has been the subject of works by other authors,[3] but what has not been analyzed is the effect of the dual nature of NATO on long-term U.S. foreign policy. It is argued here that—because American troops were assigned to an integrated NATO command structure first to counter a perceived military threat from the Soviet Union but also to provide the necessary counterweight to German rearmament—the U.S. commitment to western Europe assumed a "depth and permanence" that have not been realized. Yet the fact that the American commitment to western Europe through NATO clearly had a dual purpose, and must be viewed in light of the German question, as well as in that of the Soviet threat, remains the enduring legacy of postwar U.S. foreign policy.

Defining the Problem:
The United States, Germany, and the Defense of Europe

The outbreak of hostilities in Korea on June 25, 1950, confirmed the worst western fears regarding the intentions of the Soviet Union and raised doubts about the defense of western Europe. At that time western forces consisted solely of the American and British occupation forces in Germany and the poorly armed and ill-trained Benelux and French divisions scattered throughout Germany and western Europe, the bulk of the French regular army being tied down in Indochina. Moreover, preliminary NATO planning of a western defense strategy had been initiated only shortly before the Korean invasion, which then gave urgency to defense planning and raised serious questions for the Truman administration: Could Europe be successfully defended? If so, what should the American contribution be? And what would be expected of the NATO allies?

In answering these questions American policymakers concluded that it would be possible to defend western Europe if the United States contributed substantial numbers of troops to the continent and if the Europeans increased their defense capabilities, including, importantly, the military participation of the Federal Republic of Germany.

The question of linking German and American military contributions to western defense dominated both the internal formulation of and the international negotiations about the U.S. commitment to Europe. While many in the Truman administration, especially in the Defense Department, felt that German rearmament should proceed immediately, they soon encountered difficulties with the Europeans, especially the French, who did not wish to provide the means of war to a country that so recently had been a powerful and ruthless enemy.

American interest in German rearmament clearly predated the Korean war, but that conflict provided the impetus for bringing the rearmament issue to the forefront. German rearmament had been discussed within the Pentagon as early as 1947, and by 1948 "the Joint Chiefs of Staff were alert to the importance of a possible German armed force." In addition, on May 20, 1948, Secretary of the Army Kenneth Royall reported that the Joint Chiefs felt that any future commitment of American troops to Europe allowed for the eventual inclusion of German and Spanish forces as well.[4] The year 1949 also brought calls for German rearmament: the strategy of "forward defense," Field Marshal Montgomery's assessment of Western Union defense capabilities, and the creation of a 60,000 man paramilitary East German "police force" all led to behind-the-scenes discussions of rearming the West Germans.[5]

Moreover, additional interest in German rearmament was sparked by the completion of a reassessment of American foreign and security policy that had been initiated in the wake of the successful Soviet atomic explosion during the summer of 1949. This reassessment, entitled NSC 68, was completed by April 1950; it argued that there was a "sharp disparity between our actual military strength and our commitments" and that, on balance, "our military strength is becoming dangerously inadequate." In order to rectify this inadequacy, the report recommended that the United States "[d]evelop a level of military readiness which can be maintained as long as necessary as a deterrent to Soviet aggression" and increase the military capability of allies and friendly nations.[6]

Although NSC 68 did not advocate immediate German rearmament, it did suggest that the United States make "separate arrangements with Japan, Western Germany, and Austria which would enlist the energies and resources of these countries in support of the free world."[7] The Joint Chiefs of Staff, painfully aware of the inadequate status of western defense forces in Europe and supported by the conclusions of NSC 68, urged that German rearmament be discussed at the May 1950 NATO meeting in London.[8]

However, the State Department had long been opposed to any discussion of German rearmament with the allies. This was because of State's belief that the political problems associated with any such discussion would outweigh whatever military advantages might be obtained. Secretary Acheson was acutely aware of French sensitivities about Germany, and he knew that France hoped to permanently exclude Germany from NATO. He feared that any plans to associate Germany with the Atlantic Alliance would undermine the whole structure of western defense by running the risk of alienating France.[9] Thus, throughout 1949 and early 1950 Acheson took pains to offer public assurances that the

United States was not considering opening the German rearmament question.[10]

With the outbreak of the Korean war, the State Department discovered that it could no longer delay, and Acheson quickly found himself in a debate with the Defense Department over questions of how quickly the United States should seek German rearmament; whether such rearmament should coincide with, precede, or follow the commitment of U.S. forces to Europe; and how German troops should be integrated into a western defense structure. During July and August 1950, the battle lines were drawn between those who favored the simultaneous commitment of American troops to Europe and the rearming of West Germany and those who believed that American forces should be committed to NATO prior to opening the rearmament issue.

Only two and a half weeks after the North Korean invasion, U.S. ambassador to the United Kingdom, Lewis Douglas, reported his views on the impact of the Korean war on U.S. defense policy in Europe. According to Douglas, the United States had been slow in facing its responsibilities concerning "the establishment within the mutual defense structure of specific command relationships in Europe, and American involvement therein, and the question of commitments of U.S. forces planned to be made available to NAT[O] defense in case of an emergency." He felt that American slowness in accepting these responsibilities had resulted in a "curious, unnecessary, and somewhat detrimental schizophrenia which exists as between the NATO and Western Union." In order to correct that situation Douglas suggested that there should be a "genuine merging of the military side of [the] Western Union with the Western European Regional Groups of the NATO."[11]

Douglas hoped that if the United States would "join up to the hilt" in European defense efforts it would help persuade the French "to put their military house in order." Of course, France was then engaged in a costly war in Indochina, and the human and material drain of that conflict simply made it impossible for them to make an effective contribution to European defense.[12] Douglas felt that if the French could be assured of a strong American commitment to European defense, including troops, they would be more likely to improve their own defense efforts. Moreover, Douglas believed that it was vital that the military potential of Germany be included in western defense preparation, but concluded that this could not be accomplished until France had been given assurance of an American troop commitment and had time to modernize its own forces.[13]

Shortly thereafter, on July 22, 1950, Acheson informed various diplomatic offices that the United States was planning to increase its own defense effort and that the president was going to ask Congress for $10 billion toward that end. A large portion of that amount, between $4 and $6 billion, would be for the NATO countries, and it was hoped that such assistance would lead to the "attainment and maintenance of our common strength at an adequate level as soon as it is possible to determine what each nation will need to do." Acheson went on to say that the United States would require, by August 5, the "firmest possible statement from [the] European countries of [the] nature and extent of increased effort, in terms of increases in both forces and military production, they propose to undertake."[14]

Clearly, the United States was hoping to use the promise of increased military assistance to spur the NATO allies to greater efforts, but the picture from Europe was bleak. On July 26 Spofford met with French and British political and military leaders and reported to Acheson on the weakness of the Western Union forces, the inadequate levels of training in the French Army, and the deficient command structures on the continent. The French officials had explained to Spofford that because of the "bleeding which was resulting from Indochina" and domestic political and economic problems, they were having difficulty maintaining their armed forces and were fearful of becoming the "infantry of Europe."[15] Spofford also reported to the secretary of state that, after hearing these views, he interjected the substance of Acheson's message about increased military expenditures and urged the British and French to give the "strongest evidence possible" of their defense plans to assist the president in formulating the necessary appropriations.[16]

However, it soon became clear that what the French wanted was not U.S. military assistance but American troops. On July 28 Spofford reported that the French were insisting that the line of western defense be drawn as far east as possible and that all members of NATO agree to this strategy. Moreover, the French argued that additional British and American troops be sent to Germany to ensure the success of western defense.[17]

This view was supported the same day in a telegram from American ambassador to Paris David K. Bruce. Bruce reported that the French still had strong memories of the interwar years "and even of 1914" when they had felt abandoned militarily on the continent, and he argued that in order for France to make a meaningful defense effort some assurance had to be made that "French soldiers would be dying for something that has a chance to survive." Such assurance could only be achieved through "the united armies of an Atlantic group."[18]

On the question of German participation in western defense, Bruce maintained that "[a]side from all the other advantages of a really 'common NATO defense,' *the problem of Germany is enough in itself to compel such action.*" The ambassador felt that West German participation in the defense of Europe was essential, but he reported that it would be "politically impossible" to take steps toward rearming the Federal Republic "as long as the European peoples see in such action the risk of a resurgence of German military might. A truly common effort is the only way out." Bruce felt that one solution to the German problem would be the creation of a "European Army" in order to remove fears of strictly national German military forces, but concluded that some association of this European Army with the Atlantic Community and NATO would be preferable.[19]

Secretary of State Dean Acheson also was very conscious of the requirements of European defense, including U.S. and German participation. Although as late as June 5, 1950, he had responded negatively to suggestions of German rearmament, the Korean war quickly changed his thinking. Acheson believed that the strategy of forward defense required West Germany's emotional, political, and military involvement, and he now was prepared to move ahead. However, in his view the "real question was not whether Germany should be brought into a general European defense system, but whether this could be done without disrupting everything else we were doing and giving Germany the key position in the balancing of power in Europe." Acheson felt that the West had time to set up an integrated Atlantic defense system, including the participation of U.S. troops, that would be strong enough to contain a resurgent West Germany. Moreover, he felt that pressing for immediate German rearmament would cause political problems with the European allies and only delay eventual German participation.[20]

However, a strong lobby in the U.S. government favored the immediate inclusion of the Federal Republic in western defense. On August 3, 1950, John McCloy, the American high commissioner in Germany, sent cable

#962 to Acheson in which he called for an "effective defense to prevent invasion by the Soviets" and maintained that "this objective cannot be achieved merely by strengthening [the] national armies of the Western European countries." McCloy based his view on "evidence that even France lacks the capacity, if not the will, to build a national army able to carry the brunt of the defense of Western Europe."[21]

In order to counter the deficiencies of European defense, McCloy called for "real contributions of German resources and men," and maintained that they should be integrated into a "European Army." Although McCloy was "absolutely opposed" to the creation of a German national army, he urged the western powers to move rapidly in the direction of a European army, arguing that it was "the only way to achieve effective defense and that any other course, even if vigorously followed, [would] not do so." Significantly, McCloy made no mention of a prior American commitment of forces to offset the recruitment of German manpower and, in this regard, was at variance with Acheson's thinking.[22]

McCloy's desire to see West Germany rearmed was motivated, at least in part, by the growing strength of the East German paramilitary police force, and his views on German rearmament soon began to receive increased attention in Washington. One of those who became convinced of the wisdom of McCloy's thinking was Henry Byroade of the German office of the State Department, and it quickly became clear that Acheson and those who favored a gradualist approach to German rearmament were outnumbered.[23] This state of affairs led to a major debate over the questions of U.S. participation in European defense and German rearmament within the Truman administration during August 1950.

Defining U.S. Policy: August 1950

On July 31, 1950, Secretary Acheson communicated the State Department's thinking on the German question to President Truman. Acheson explained that, in order to accomplish the goal of rearming West Germany without at the same time creating an imbalance of power in western Europe, West Germany's military power would have to be integrated into a larger framework, a framework that would have to include the United States. Truman "expressed his strong approval of this line of thought" and directed Acheson to proceed along the lines of a European army that would include German units and "follow the decisions reached in accordance with the North Atlantic Treaty procedures."[24]

Prompted by Truman, Acheson immediately began work on a plan to lay the groundwork for eventual West German participation in a European army strengthened by an American commitment to Europe. In early August 1950 he approached the Pentagon with the idea of sending U.S. troops to Europe in order to lay such a groundwork for the creation of a European army and German integration into that army, and he quickly ran into opposition.

While the military did not have to be persuaded that European defense needed "beefing up" or that this would require increased numbers of allied troops, additional American forces and military assistance, the inclusion of German armed forces, and the creation of a unified command to integrate the common effort, "they wanted all of these elements in . . . 'one package.' "[25] Therefore, the first two weeks in August 1950 was a period of debate between Acheson and those who followed his gradualist approach to German rearmament and a "united and immovable Pentagon," which insisted that any commitment of U.S. troops to Europe be accompanied by the *simultaneous* rearmament of West Germany.[26] Moreover, the Pentagon's view quickly gained support from U.S. representatives abroad.

On August 9 Admiral Alan Kirk, ambassador to the Soviet Union, cabled Washington that a decision on German rearmament could not be "postponed until France and Belgium are strong enough to match a re-armed Germany."[27] McCloy also continued to press for rapid rearmament, arguing that even though German participation in European defense was dependent on French acquiescence time was too precious to permit the United States to delay arriving at a definite stand in favor of German rearmament. The French, he believed, "will not oppose prompt action within a European army structure."[28] Only Ambassador Bruce continued to support the gradual approach to German rearmament, preceded by the assignment of more American and British troops to Europe and the strengthening of French armed forces.[29] For this view, Bruce and his colleagues in Paris were criticized for representing French views with "excessive vigor."[30]

A turning point for American decision makers came in mid-August. Charles Spofford had been meeting with European representatives in London for weeks and had been urging them to make greater defense efforts. He had been handicapped in his deliberations by his inability to assure them of greater U.S. troop commitments to European defense. As a result the Europeans were reluctant to make decisive decisions regarding their own defense programs, and their replies to American requests for estimates of increased defense plans were disappointing. Therefore, on August 9, 1950, Spofford flew back to Washington to urge that the United States quickly make a substantial contribution of American ground forces to Europe. Spofford felt that unless the United States was prepared to do this NATO would stagnate.[31]

Added to this pressure for an American commitment of troops came increased calls for German participation. On August 11 the Consultative Council of the European Assembly of the Council of Europe—with West German representatives participating for the first time—called "for the immediate creation of a unified European Army, under the authority of a European Minister of Defense, subject to proper European democratic control and acting in full cooperation with the United States and Canada." This European army proposal was sponsored by Winston Churchill and included provision for a German contribution.[32]

On August 16, 1950, Acheson's gradualist approach suffered another blow when Deputy Under Secretary of State H. Freeman Matthews sent a paper to the Defense Department supporting "the formation of a European Defense Force of [the] United States, U.K. and Continental military contingents, including those from Germany, under a Supreme Commander with full command authority and supported by an international general staff."[33] Matthews held that the supreme commander should be an American because such an appointment would "be a clear indication of the full commitment of the U.S."[34] Matthews stated that "the keystone of European defense will center around what is now the Western Union grouping and which will be augmented by U.S. and German contingents." Matthews' plan envisioned the integration of German forces at division level into the European army and eventual West German membership in NATO.[35]

Although Matthews felt that Acheson was "in general agreement with the concept advanced in this paper," the secretary of state had not reviewed the paper, and was not aware of the particular conclusions and recommendations put forward by his lieutenants.[36] However, any paper that called for joint U.S.-German participation in European defense could only weaken Acheson's position and increase his sense of isolation within the U.S. government on the rearmament issue.[37] Moreover, it could not help but add fuel to the Pentagon's adamant view that American participation in the initial defense of Europe be accompanied by the simultaneous inclusion of West German troops so that in the event of a Soviet attack American forces would not run the risk of being isolated and destroyed.[38]

Not only was Acheson under pressure at home, but the French also began to pressure the United States to clarify its position regarding European defense. On August 5 French Premier René Pleven informed Ambassador Bruce of a French three-year rearmament program in an attempt to move the administration ahead with its military aid programs for Europe. However, the French made it clear that their increased military effort would not occur without increased financial aid, larger military efforts by other NATO members, and the creation of a unified command.[39]

On August 17, 1950, the French proposed to augment the NATO legal framework by creating a general staff or High Command, establishing a joint budget, adopting a comprehensive "general program" for European defense, and securing full American participation in NATO's Regional Planning Groups. The French government declared that it was "extremely anxious" to learn of the American response to these proposals. It is apparent that the French plans differed significantly from U.S. thinking in that they did not address the problem of German rearmament, but sought instead to bind the United States—through military assistance and NATO—to the defense of France.[40]

Faced with both domestic and international pressure, Acheson and the State Department were hard pressed to develop a policy regarding the stationing of American troops in Europe and the rearmament of Germany. The fact that the NATO foreign ministers were scheduled to meet in New York on September 12, 1950, added to the sense of urgency.

On August 26, in an effort to resolve the issue prior to the September 12 meeting, President Truman directed Acheson and Secretary of Defense Louis Johnson to prepare recommendations in response to a series of questions concerning American and German participation in the defense of Europe. These questions are crucial to understanding the confusion and uncertainty that continued to surround U.S. policy in Europe. Even at this late date, after two months of discussion within the administration and only two weeks before important negotiations with allies, Truman asked questions revealing that a further American commitment to Europe was not taken for granted and that if such a commitment were made its form was far from having been decided. Truman's questions included:

—Are we prepared to commit additional United States forces to the defense of Europe;
—Are we prepared to support, and in what manner, the concept of a European defense force, including German participation on other than a national basis;
—Are we prepared to look forward to the eventuality of a Supreme Commander for the European defense forces;
—Are we prepared to consider full United States participation in European defense organs. . . ?[41]

These questions had been debated throughout the summer of 1950, and as shown above, a number of plausible answers had been advanced by various American policymakers. Thirty years later, it is difficult to envision a world without NATO in its present form. In the late summer of 1950, however, it was by no means clear how American policy would turn out.

On September 8 Acheson and Johnson delivered their responses to Truman's questions. They agreed on the earliest possible commitment of additional American forces to the defense of Europe "in order that any doubts of American interest in the defense, rather than the liberation of Europe, will be removed, thus increasing the will of our allies to resist."[42] The two secretaries believed that the development of a European army within the framework of the North Atlantic Treaty appeared to be the best way to obtain "the maximum contribution from [the] European nations and to provide as well a framework in which [a] German contribution of a significant nature could be realized." They pressed for the early creation of an integrated European army capable of defending western Europe (including the Federal Republic of Germany) and advocated the appointment of a supreme commander.[43] Acheson and Johnson also recommended that "we should proceed without delay with the formation of adequate West German units. . . ."[44]

This, of course, marked the administration's acceptance of the Defense Department's "package plan." The next day President Truman made public his intention to send additional American ground troops to Europe. He indicated that the embarking of troops would depend on other NATO countries making similar efforts, but he did not discuss the

link that existed between German rearmament and the stationing of
U.S. forces in Europe,[45] a link that America's allies were only faintly
aware of, if at all. The acceptance of the "package plan"—requiring the
simultaneous integration of American and German units into European
defense—put the United States on a collision course with the French;
a collision that would occur when Acheson met with Schuman and Bevin
in New York beginning on September 12, 1950.

After the "package plan" was accepted, the focus of attention shifted
from the internal deliberations to international discussions with the NATO
allies. What is important about the internal discussion within the U.S.
government is that it demonstrated the centrality of the German rearmament issue in the Truman administration's consideration of how to
respond to the Soviet threat to western Europe. Having formulated a
U.S. policy based on the "package plan," the next task was to convince
the Europeans to accept that policy. It turned out to be an impossible
task, for, in contrast to American perceptions, German rearmament was
not viewed in a favorable light by the European members of NATO.

The Collision with France, September 1950

As U.S. policy was being defined in response to Truman's queries,
it became apparent that conflict with France was incipient. On September 2 Acheson informed the French that, although no clear policy regarding a European army had been developed, the State Department
felt that the creation of such a force would lead to the establishment of
a supreme commander with an integrated staff, "and that in this event,
it should be possible to integrate into such a Force German units in a
controlled status without thereby creating a German national army."
To calm French apprehensions over German rearmament, Acheson said
"that if these steps are to be effective larger participation by the US
both in troops in Europe and in the direction of the unified force might
be required."[46] These assurances were not enough for the French, and
Foreign Minister Schuman replied on September 5 that the upcoming
ministers meeting would probably result in a significant "divergence of
views on certain problems, notably concerning that of German rearmament. . . ."[47]

It is therefore clear that the French had warning that the United
States planned to open the German rearmament question in New York.
Added confirmation of this is offered by Jean Monnet. According to

Monnet, he met with Schuman just before the latter's departure for New York and told the foreign minister that he would be unable to prevent discussion of German rearmament in his meetings with the Americans.[48]

Monnet feared that any discussion of creating national German forces would take the whole question of Franco-German relations out of the context of the Schuman Plan for Coal and Steel and allow the Germans greater freedom of action to operate independently between East and West. Therefore, he hoped Schuman would be prepared to discuss German rearmament only within the context of the Schuman Plan and argued that to be forewarned was to be forearmed.[49]

However, Schuman informed Monnet that he was going to follow the French government's simple position "that there can be no question of rearming Germany at all." Accordingly, Schuman told Monnet that he preferred to believe that the German rearmament question would not arise in New York. As a result, when he received word from President Truman that the United States planned to open the rearmament question during the upcoming meetings, the French foreign minister was caught off guard. This information reached Schuman while he was in transit between Paris and New York, and as soon as he landed he, and British Foreign Secretary Ernest Bevin, had to cable home for instructions.[50]

While the British soon were able to accept the American position, it quickly became clear that the French were going to remain adamant in their opposition to German rearmament. On September 14 Schuman said that public opinion in France would not allow German rearmament when the French themselves were in such desperate need of military assistance. He said that the French parliament would veto any moves that would lead toward rearming Germany, and he could not understand why the United States was in such a hurry to proceed in that direction. Instead, he wanted the United States to integrate its command structure into NATO in order to lay the groundwork for eventual German participation.[51]

In an effort to find a compromise solution Acheson suggested that an agreement on the "basic principle of the program" and a "decision to keep German rearmament lagging behind that of the other powers" might be more acceptable to the French. Again, Schuman was negative, maintaining that the inevitable news leaks on any agreement—if only in principle—would be interpreted in France "as an irrevocable decision which would result in German units receiving materials which France itself needed and France would be on the same footing as Germany."[52] In order to keep the pressure on, the United States continued to maintain that U.S. forces could not be assigned to Europe without German rearmament, but to no avail, and the discussion of the German question as well as additional U.S. troop assignments was postponed until September 22, 1950, when the French, British, and American defense ministers would join the talks.[53]

By the time of the joint defense and foreign ministers meeting, all of the NATO allies except France were in favor of the American proposal.[54] Moreover, Secretary of Defense Johnson had been replaced in mid-September by former Secretary of State General George C. Marshall, whose working relationship with Acheson was excellent.[55] This newfound cooperation between Defense and State added an element of flexibility to the American position, and the United States began slowly to back off from its advocacy of rapid German rearmament. Instead, the Americans continued to press for an "agreement in principle on the German question."[56] However, the French position became more rigid with the arrival of Defense Minister Jules Moch (a Socialist) from Paris.

In anticipation of trouble from Moch, Acheson had informed President Truman that, although Schuman was flexible, the real "difficulty lay in Paris, and specifically in the Socialist Party and even more specifically in Moch."[57] A vigorous anti-Stalinist, Moch had demonstrated his toughness during the Communist-sponsored labor riots during 1947, when, as minister of interior, his effective use of the wide police powers granted him by the Ramadier government was instrumental in quelling the violence. However, he also had been an active member of the Resistance, and his son had been tortured by the Nazis during the war. As a result he was vehemently opposed to German rearmament.[58]

Because of Moch's attitude, the second round of September meetings was devoted to convincing him of the wisdom of German rearmament in order to gain his support before the French Assembly. In this effort the United States received help from British Defense Minister Immanuel Shinwell, who also was a Socialist.[59] On September 23 Shinwell pointed out to the French that it would "be fatal not to take advantage of [the] US offer of troops" by rejecting the principle of German rearmament, and he emphasized that for psychological reasons alone the West Germans had to have a stake in their own defense.[60] While Moch would later admit that the promise of American troops was a telling point for French-men,[61] he argued that the role of NATO "was not to defend Germany as such but to preserve freedom in Europe and to take advantage of our occupation of Germany to fight further from the bulwarks of our own frontiers."[62]

Secretary of Defense Marshall also sought to influence the French by linking future arms aid from the United States to the rearmament ques-tion. He told the French that "there would be no problem of priorities for NATO countries if the US can plan on the participation of Germany now." However, he pointed out that if "the US Administration cannot assure Congress that all available means in Germany would be utilized to achieve an effective European force there would be serious problems regarding the appropriations for defense."[63]

Although Schuman and Moch were opposed to division-sized units for the West Germans, pressured the Americans for a rapid commitment of money and men, and counseled delay on the German rearmament question, there was some flexibility in their position. While they could not accept even the principle of German rearmament, they did not want to reject it outright or prohibit discussions of the problem.[64]

The flexibility of the French position also was in evidence on Septem-ber 23. After Marshall explained the difficulties that the Truman admin-istration would encounter with Congress unless German contributions to NATO defense forces could be assured, Moch offered hope to the Ameri-cans. Although he doubted that the French Assembly would support German participation in western defense, he added that "there was a chance of getting a 'package' sold to the Parliament."[65] It was clear that Moch's idea of a "package" had to "include precise information of what [the] French [could] expect from the United States under the aid program and how many and at what date U.S. divisions would arrive in Europe."[66] In order to exploit this flexibility, Acheson informed Truman that Moch "needed much ammunition if he is to sell this package to his Parliament, but he was willing if the ammunition is forthcoming."[67]

The September 23 meeting was something of a breakthrough for the allies. At its conclusion the three powers agreed—at the suggestion of Moch—to postpone a proposed meeting of defense ministers (scheduled for October 16) until October 28, "in order to attempt to get favorable French parliamentary action" on the principle of German rearmament.[68]

Yet even after the September 23 meeting, Acheson continued to convey to the French a rather inflexible attitude. According to Moch, the secretary of state told him that if, during the October meetings, France continued its irrevocable opposition to the rearmament of Germany, the United States would have to rethink its position and find a new solution.[69] But the sincerity of Acheson's posture toward the French was undermined by the impression he gave to the British. He told Bevin that if the French parliament did not approve the principle of German participation "he would have to consider going ahead anyway," but was, in fact, optimistic about the possibility of French approval.[70] In light of subsequent American flexibility, Acheson apparently was trying at this point to pressure the French into acquiescence by appearing more rigid than he really was. This tactic did not succeed because the French did not really believe the American threats.[71]

By September 25, 1950, the U.S. position began to show increased signs of flexibility. On that date the assistant secretary of state for European affairs, George Perkins, wrote to Under Secretary of State James Webb about a proposed resolution of the North Atlantic Council regarding the appointment of a supreme commander. According to Perkins, the original resolution prepared by the Council of Deputies stated that the "Supreme Commander will be appointed as soon as sufficient national forces in being *have been committed* to the integrated Force to enable the latter to be reasonably capable of fulfilling its responsibilities." However, when that draft was shown to the Defense Department, the Pentagon suggested a slightly different wording: "The Supreme Commander shall be appointed as soon as there is assurance that sufficient forces *will be provided* to the integrated Force to enable the latter to be reasonably capable of fulfilling its responsibilities."[72]

According to Perkins, the significance of the changed wording was that it would permit the appointment of an American supreme commander prior to the organization of a European army. This had been the State Department's view all along, and the fact that the suggested revision came from the Defense Department demonstrated its newfound willingness to cooperate with State.[73]

On September 26, 1950, the North Atlantic Council adopted a resolution that included the revised paragraph mentioned above as well as two paragraphs calling for:

(a) The establishment at the earliest possible date of an integrated force under centralized command and control composed of forces made available by governments for the defense of Western Europe;
(b) The full authorization of manpower and productive resources available from all sources. . . .[74]

Moreover, the Defense Committee was requested "to make specific recommendations regarding the method by which, from the technical point of view, Germany could make its most useful contribution to the successful implementation of the plan" for the defense of Europe, bearing "in mind the unanimous conclusion of the Council that it would not serve the best interests of Europe or of Germany to bring into being a German national army or a German general staff."[75]

Therefore, at the conclusion of the second round of September talks in New York, the United States and France were beginning to search for ways to close the breech that had opened over the question of the American "package plan" linking German rearmament to the assignment of U.S. troops to Europe. Although the U.S. government maintained that it could not assign a commander or station its troops in Europe as part of an integrated European defense plan unless German units were included, this position was not so rigid as it appeared. On the French side, although they continued to reject the notion of any form of German rearmament— even in principle—it was clear to all concerned that this position also was subject to change. Acheson was even able to report that Moch appeared to have "changed from an opponent to an advocate."[76]

An indication of what the next round of negotiations would look like came at the end of the New York meetings. Schuman had told Acheson that "he [Schuman] was thinking personally of taking [the] initiative in re [regarding] Ger[man] participation in [a North Atlantic] force. He realized [the] importance [of] France not being 'dragged along' and was considering what he cld [could] do to bring about some sort of Franco-German agreement."[77]

The Pleven Plan

After October 1, 1950, the initiative clearly was with the French to come up with a plan whereby German contributions to the defense of western Europe could be accepted. Acheson, despite his private signs of flexibility, placed the burden on France for developing new ideas, and the French clearly had to play for time.[78] Added to pressure from the United States, the French were suffering financially, the war in Indochina made their dependence on U.S. assistance all the greater, and they feared losing the leadership in Europe over the German rearmament question.[79]

On the American side, the Defense Department, especially the Joint Chiefs of Staff, continued to oppose any integrated force that did not include the participation of German units. On October 13 the Joint Chiefs informed Acheson that, if no agreement were reached on the issue of immediate German participation in the defense of Europe during the defense ministers meeting at the end of October, "the United States course of action for the conduct of a war against the USSR, including the magnitude and extent of the United States contribution to the defense of Western Europe, should be reexamined by the United States."[80] Although the Joint Chiefs had expressed their willingness to appoint a supreme commander for the integrated army on the "assurance that sufficient forces will be provided," the assurance they demanded was evidence of German participation.

Acheson reviewed the Joint Chiefs' statement, and his reply to Marshall on October 16 indicated that differences between State and Defense still existed and that Acheson was increasingly aware that compromise with the French would be necessary. While he agreed that it was essential that West Germany participate in western defense and that such a condition be precedent to American support for the European efforts, he suggested "that we leave open the possibility of a reexamination of our position on this matter as time proceeds." The secretary of state argued that, if the United States continued too long in its policy of linking American support for an integrated army with the simultaneous rearmament of West Germany, "we will rather quickly arrive at a situation where we must . . . delay our moves for support of the integrated force." Acheson cautioned that such a delay "will not appear to be in the best interests of the United States." Moreover, Acheson felt that "[t]his would be particularly true if we were convinced by that time that the French Government would be able, within a relatively short period of time, to agree to German participation in that force."[81]

Acheson's flexibility was tested when he received word of the Pleven

Plan (named for the French premier, René Pleven) for a European Defense Community.[82] Essentially, the Pleven Plan, which the French parliament approved on October 24 by a vote of 343 to 225, envisaged the creation of a European army into which German units "at the smallest possible level" would be integrated. The European army would come into being only after a European institutional framework was established—including a European minister of defense, a European parliament with the power to vote a European defense budget, and a European council of defense ministers—to oversee the whole project. In addition, Pleven maintained "that the proposal for a European army should in no way interfere with the establishment of the integrated NATO force . . ." and thereby "sought to gain the benefits of the American package proposal minus German rearmament."[83]

Most American officials regarded the Pleven Plan as merely a delaying action by the French. The problem, from the American perspective, was that the Pleven Plan saw German rearmament as an eventual rather than as an immediate concern that would be faced only *after* the European political and military superstructure was in place. The Americans saw the plan as an attempt to avoid rather than to confront the problem of German rearmament. An additional American fear was that the Pleven Plan would greatly diminish American influence on the German rearmament process. As Ambassador Bruce reported to Acheson: "It might turn over to a purely European (probably continental) group the responsibility without US participation for the vital question of German military contribution to European defense and should the study and the negotiations envisaged in this study bog down, it might be difficult for us to intervene successfully."[84]

Although the American reaction was cool, Acheson saw reason for hope within the Pleven proposal. He explained that, even though the French would deny that the proposal constituted their acceptance of the principle of German rearmament, "we were considering whether or not, without stating it, to proceed on that basis."[85] Following the conclusion of the defense ministers' meeting a few days later, Acheson would begin to do just that.

On the eve of the defense ministers' meeting, Jules Moch met with Secretary Marshall in order to outline the French position. The French defense minister told Marshall that their plan envisaged the immediate appointment of a supreme commander and included the stipulation that "all troops that can be made available will be placed under the Supreme Commander at once." Moch also stated that the European defense minister could not be appointed until after the completion of the Schuman Plan for the European Coal and Steel Community, "perhaps in 1951," and only then would the Europeans develop a "special experimental force with German units" included.[86]

However, Marshall responded that "until [the] US knows what arrangements will be agreed [to] by NATO on [the] contribution of Germany to [the] defense of [Western Europe] including Western Germany, it is not possible to give final form to command and [military] structure for [the] integration force."[87] Given these opposing positions, the October meeting ended in deadlock and some acrimony.

Although the meeting of the defense ministers was completely unproductive, it cleared the air and made future progress possible. Following these meetings, Acheson and Marshall began to modify the American position on the one package proposal.

On November 3 Acheson cabled Ambassador Bruce in Paris expressing his displeasure over Moch's "quasi dictatorial" attitude during the October meeting with Marshall and instructing Bruce to inquire whether Moch's position was in accord with that of the French government.[88] He also told Bruce that, if the French did not demonstrate that they were "willing to use all available means" to organize western European (including French) defense, the American people could not be expected to contribute substantial amounts to the western military program. Acheson informed Bruce that French attitudes in the Military Committee and the Council of Deputies would be used to measure their sincerity, adding that he attached a great deal of importance to achieving a workable defense program before the end of the year.[89]

Bruce reported on November 4 that he had conferred with Pleven. The French premier had indicated that he was aware of Moch's intransigence and felt that he would be able to "handle" his defense minister. Pleven also agreed that the French representatives on the Military Committee and on the Council of Deputies could discuss any plans "affecting [the] contribution of German armed forces to the defense of the West."[90] It is apparent that Pleven, as well as Acheson, was anxious that agreement on the German rearmament question be reached before the end of the year.

The Spofford Compromise

The scene then shifted to the Council of Deputies and the Defense Committee, where the French were willing to discuss the various plans for German rearmament. By mid-November Charles Spofford was able to report that the "French would like to accept something close to the American plan on condition that we can take some action toward European integration and in so doing save [the French government's] political face." He also reported to Washington that French military thinking was generally close to that of the Americans and that with some pressure the French might be willing to drop their requirement that a European political superstructure precede moves toward German rearmament. However, Spofford cautioned that if too much pressure were applied the French government would fall.[91]

On November 16 Ambassador Douglas reported that he, Bruce, McCloy, and Spofford agreed that, as long as the final solution to the rearmament problem came within the NATO framework, the United States "should ... accept in principle and take a benevolent attitude toward the concepts of continental political institution provided their development is not permitted to delay or weaken development of [an] integrated North Atlantic defense."[92]

On November 18 the first tangible evidence of progress was seen in a report to the Military Committee by a special Standing Group on the "Military Aspects of German Participation in the Defense of Western Europe." This report (designated MC 30) reflected the growing tendency to find a "transitional" arrangement regarding German rearmament that would breach the gap between American and French policy. The report noted the desirability of creating an integrated European defense force under political supervision by a European political superstructure but held that "its achievement must not delay the contribution of Germany." However, the report maintained that, if the effort to create a European army failed, "Germany would contribute units directly into an integrated NATO defense force." MC 30 also called for the immediate recruitment of German troops and recommended that the size of the German contributions be limited to regimental combat teams of approximately three thousand men.[93]

Four days later, on November 22, Spofford wrote a memorandum that said that, while work was proceeding on solving the political problems associated with the development of a European army and German re-armament, certain steps, "upon which there already exist large measure of agreement," should be taken immediately. Therefore, Spofford proposed to separate the long-term political problems from the immediate military necessities with a "transitional period." During that period, the allies would proceed immediately with the essential features of military organization and begin to recruit German manpower "under strong provisional controls pending [the] development of [a] more permament system." This would allow the "broader political problems to be dealt with concurrently but freed from pressure of military urgency."[94]

Not only did the work of the Council of Deputies and the Military Committee spur the French and Americans toward reaching a compromise, but the situation in Germany itself also dictated caution to the Americans. Throughout the entire negotiations on German rearmament, it had been assumed that the Germans would willingly participate in the framework of a European army. However, beginning with negotiations on the Pleven Plan in early October, John McCloy began to send disturbing reports to Washington from Frankfurt informing State Department officials that, even if the French and Americans were to agree immediately on the rearmament question, it would take at least a year before the Germans would be ready to contribute troops to western defense efforts.[95]

At the root of the delay was the necessity to "psychologically" prepare the Germans for rearmament. To many Germans—as McCloy was finding out—psychological preparation meant giving the Federal Republic a stake in the defense of the West by assuring them that they would participate in that defense as equal partners with the other western allies and that all of West Germany would be defended by NATO.[96]

Moreover, strong elements in Germany, mostly Socialists under the leadership of Kurt Schumacher, valued reunification with East Germany more than integration into the western economic and defense structures. Domestic opposition to Adenauer's acceptance of the European Coal and Steel Community was growing, heightening Adenauer's demand that West Germany be treated by the allies as an equal.[97]

For the western allies, meeting the German demands would have meant an end to the Occupation Statute and the restoration of more sovereignty to the Federal Republic, steps they were unprepared and unwilling to take without considerable thought. There was genuine fear that the Germans were demanding too much; her neighbors had to be reassured.

So it was decided not to press for rapid German rearmament but to let it follow as a matter of course.[98]

November 1950 also brought a reversal of fortunes for American forces in Korea, increasing European fears of the adequacy of western defense efforts on the continent.[99] This made it all the more necessary for the United States to give western Europe added assurances of armed support. As a result of these mounting pressures Acheson wrote Schuman on November 29 urging him to accept the compromise submitted by Spofford. Acheson also informed him that the supreme commander should be appointed immediately "as a tangible step to give form and impetus to our military effort."[100] Of course, since the appointment of a supreme commander carried with it the implication that troops would necessarily follow, this marked Acheson's abandonment of the "package plan."

The letter Acheson sent to Schuman is very enlightening for another reason: it gave a clear picture of the reasoning behind the evolution of the U.S. commitment to Europe. Acheson told the French foreign minister that the United States "has given every evidence in statements, actions, and treaties, of the *depth and permanence* of its interest in Europe, its support for closer European association, its willingness to cooperate with Europe. . . ." He also stated that "the Atlantic Community is an essential part of the free world structure, whether it be from the point of view of global security or of *permanently ending the threat of German domination.*" Acheson pledged that the United States would continue working with France to strengthen NATO and that such cooperation was "an essential corollary to an orderly progression from German cooperation in defense, to European integration, *and thus final solution of the problem of relations with Germany.*"[101]

Of course, the final agreement to reject the "package plan" needed the approval of the Defense Department. This was obtained on December 6, 1950, in a White House meeting of the British and American heads of government, foreign ministers, and military leaders. At this meeting Acheson asked Marshall if the French would approve the Spofford compromise and if the Defense Department would agree to the appointment of a supreme commander. Marshall replied that "[i] f a reasonable basis was established, they would go ahead . . . in the approval of the appointment of a Supreme Commander."[102] Acheson had already informed those in attendance that the French cabinet had agreed to accept the Spofford proposals, subject to their receipt of Acheson's letter to Schuman—then in the hands of Ambassador Bruce. The next day Ambassador Bruce delivered the letter to Schuman and set in motion the final acceptance of the Spofford Plan and the principle of German rearmament.

By December 12 the NATO Military Committee and the NATO Council of Deputies approved the creation of a European Defense Force as long as it did not delay the addition of German manpower to the defense of the West.[103] The Military Committee recommended the establishment of a Supreme Headquarters Atlantic Powers in Europe and the appointment of a supreme commander who "should be a U.S. Officer and should be appointed forthwith."[104]

These proposals were formally accepted by the French on December 15, and on December 17 the North Atlantic Council met in Brussels to finalize the compromise agreement. At that time Acheson announced that President Truman—as per council request—had appointed General Dwight D. Eisenhower as supreme commander, and would shortly increase the number of American troops "under the command of the Supreme Commander."[105]

The acceptance of the Spofford compromise represented a bargain in which the United States agreed to trade support for a European defense structure and a decoupling of American troop commitments from immediate German rearmament while the French accepted the idea that the commitment of American troops to Europe was part of a larger plan that included German rearmament in the not-too-distant future. With this compromise, both sides could feel that they had achieved their essential objectives. The United States had gained French adherence to at least the idea of German rearmament. The French gained an immediate American military commitment to the defense of Europe while delaying the rearming of Germany. The operational impact of this compromise was American participation in an integrated NATO command structure and the deployment of American troops to Europe. This last step, taken before German rearmament and in fulfillment of the provisions of article 3 of the North Atlantic Treaty, touched off what became known as the "great debate" on American foreign policy.

The Great Debate

Although it made a good deal of sense from a purely military/strategic viewpoint to create an integrated command structure for NATO in response to the Korean war, the fact that this structure also was created to contain a rearmed Germany had important implications for future American foreign policy. Clearly, and in Acheson's own words, the fact that Europe (and especially France) had to be helped to become reconciled to a rearmed West Germany gave the American commitment to the Atlantic Alliance a "depth and permanence" that had not previously been contemplated.

The American decision to send troops to Europe did in fact lead to a permanent commitment to European security and is interesting in light of the great debate on American foreign policy that took place during the winter of 1951, when the wisdom of the Truman administration's steps was questioned in the Senate.[106] What strikes one about the debates is that the links among German rearmament, the American troop commitment to NATO, and assurances to the French were never publically acknowledged by the administration. This was despite the fact that the chief spokesman for the opposition—Robert Taft—did not object to the stationing of additional troops in Europe in response to the Korean invasion, but rather to their assignment to an integrated NATO command structure, a structure created to integrate the United States into the continent and to provide a framework for eventual German rearmament.

The focus of the great debate was Senate Resolution 8, introduced by Senator Kenneth Wherry on January 8, 1951, which stated:

> *Resolved,* That it is the sense of the Senate, that no ground forces of the United States should be assigned to duty in the European area for the purposes of the North Atlantic Treaty pending the formulation of a policy with respect thereto by the Congress.[107]

Basically, two distinct sets of questions were involved in the great debate. One set dealt with the military feasibility of the administration's actions: How many troops were to be sent to Europe? What would their ratio be to European forces? Could Europe be defended by ground troops? What was the proper role for the United States in western defense? The other set of questions involved constitutional issues: Was President Truman overstepping his powers as commander in chief by assigning American forces to NATO? What role did Congress have in implementing the North Atlantic Treaty?

One of the first questions about the military feasibility of the decision to send troops to Europe concerned the exact number of such troops. Since President Truman had only announced his intention to increase substantially the strength of U.S. forces in Europe, estimates of the troop increases ranged from five to fifteen divisions.[108] This question was settled on February 15, when Secretary Acheson informed a joint session of the Senate Armed Services and Foreign Relations Committees that the administration was planning to send four additional divisions to Europe to augment the two already on occupation duty in Germany.[109]

The opposition then argued that the defense of Europe by a land army against the forces of the Soviet Union could not be carried out by the limited forces available to the West—even with American help.[110] Therefore, they felt it was a mistake to send four more divisions to Europe since, if western defenses collapsed, it would be almost impossible to rescue American troops stationed on the continent.[111]

Rather than send additional ground units, the Republican opposition felt that the United States should continue in its traditional role of supplying the strategic bombing potential necessary to "pulverize Russia."[112] Taft and others also raised questions regarding the administration's policy on the grounds that the United States had "no definite assurance of support from the European nations to be defended."[113] Moreover, Taft felt that, although the Truman administration had announced plans to send only four divisions to Europe, the strong possibility existed that more would be sent in the future.[114]

The administration countered these arguments by emphasizing the deterrent effect of the four additional divisions and by arguing that their purpose was not "to win a war after it gets started, but . . . to prevent it. . . ."[115] In his testimony before the joint committee Acheson maintained: "An adequate initial defense is an essential part of our efforts to deter an attack against Western Europe, and this initial defense can come only through having forces in being in Europe."[116]

One of the telling points to the administration's arguments was that the bulk of the land forces would come from the Europeans themselves. Secretary of Defense Marshall stated that the main purpose of sending the troops to Europe was to boost the morale of the Europeans and to spur them to greater defense efforts.[117] He also stressed the fact that one of Eisenhower's main responsibilities would be to ensure "that all members of the North Atlantic Treaty contribute the maximum amount of strength which their geographic, economic, and manpower situations permit."[118] In his testimony Eisenhower concurred with Marshall, saying that if it appeared the Europeans were not doing their share the United States should take "another look" at its commitments.[119] Moreover, both Eisenhower[120] and Marshall[121] suggested that, when the Europeans had built up their strength and the security situation had improved, the United States might be able to withdraw troops from Europe.

The administration's arguments were effective, and by the end of February the opposition was losing ground and support; so much so that the only ones who continued to object to the stationing of troops in Europe were the bedrock isolationists from the pre-World War II days who had consistently opposed any form of U.S. involvement in Europe.[122]

However, Senator Taft continued to object to certain aspects of the administration's policy. Although Taft had opposed the North Atlantic Treaty precisely because it might involve long-range commitments under article 3, even he had accepted the necessity of stationing four additional divisions in Europe in order to demonstrate U.S. support for European defense and to encourage the Europeans in their own efforts.[123]

Yet, although he could accept the military wisdom of sending more troops to Europe, Taft maintained that the president had overstepped his constitutional powers when he—without obtaining congressional approval—announced his decision to assign additional U.S. troops to NATO under Eisenhower's command. In responding to this criticism the administration pointed out that it was within the power of the president as commander in chief to deploy American forces as he saw fit to ensure the security of the United States, and administration witnesses cited numerous precedents to support their claim.[124]

Yet for Taft that argument only touched the surface of his objections. Taft maintained that he was not questioning the power of the president to station troops abroad, but rather to assign them to an "integrated army" in fulfillment of the provisions of article 3 of the North Atlantic Treaty. Specifically, he feared that the president would not be able to withdraw the troops at a later date once they became integrated into an international army.[125] Thus, while Taft could support the stationing of troops in Europe to build the confidence of the western Europeans, he was opposed to their presence in NATO as part of a *permanent* U.S. commitment.[126]

Taft's arguments did, in fact, find considerable sympathy in the Senate. Just as there could no longer be any doubt in Europe that the United States would be an initial participant in the defense of the continent, there could no longer be any doubt in the United States that a fundamental departure had taken place in the conduct of American foreign policy. In this respect the provisions of article 5—which had been so hotly debated in 1949 and which included constitutional safeguards— were now superseded by the provision of article 3, which—through the stationing of U.S. troops in Europe as part of NATO—firmly locked the security of the United States with that of western Europe. Given this situation, many felt that new rules would have to be developed for the conduct of American foreign policy.

Senator Vandenberg, on his deathbed, wrote to Senator Wherry on February 17, 1951 and stated that the Senate should recognize the president's power as commander in chief as well as the U.S. obligation to NATO. But he also hoped that any Senate resolution would "restate the great responsibility of Congress in decisions of this character and it should urge the president to submit his recommendations under Article 3 to the Congress when not incompatible with the public interest. . . ."[127]

Under the leadership of Senators Connally and Richard Russell (D.-Ga., Chairman of the Armed Services Committee), the joint committee began work on a resolution designed to meet many of the issues raised by Vandenberg, Taft, and others, yet without taking the strident stand proposed in Wherry's Resolution.[128]

The result of these efforts was the nine paragraph Senate Resolution 99, which began by approving the appointment of Eisenhower and accepting the principle that the security of the North Atlantic required the stationing abroad of "such units of our Armed Forces as may be necessary and appropriate to contribute our fair share to the forces needed for the joint defense of the North Atlantic area. . . ." Moreover, regarding any future commitment of troops, S. 99 held that "it is the sense of the Senate that no ground troops in addition to such four divisions should be sent to Western Europe in implementation of article 3 . . . without further Congressional approval."[129]

The Senate Resolution also clearly stated the determination of the Congress to ensure that the Europeans were doing their fair share. It approved "the understanding that the major contribution to the ground forces under General Eisenhower's command should be made by the European members of the North Atlantic Treaty. . . ." Moreover, it reiterated the need for the Europeans to "give full, realistic force and effect to the requirement of Article 3 . . . specifically insofar as the creation of combat units is concerned."[130]

The resolution passed the Senate on April 4, 1951, exactly two years after the signing of the North Atlantic Treaty. The vote was 69-21, with Taft voting with the majority and Wherry against. Its approval marked the final recognition and acceptance by the Senate that a fundamental departure had taken place in American foreign policy. As Senator Connally said at the time: "We have now approached the time when it is necessary for us to carry out the authorizations of the treaty. . . ."[131]

Almost as an afterthought, S. 99 included the following paragraph:

> 9. It is the sense of the Senate that consideration should
> be given to the revision of plans for the defense of Europe
> as soon as possible so as to provide for utilization on a vol-
> untary basis of the military and other resources of Western
> Germany and Spain. . . .[132]

This last-minute inclusion is curious in that—despite the fact that the future role of Germany in the defense of western Europe had played such a major role in shaping the nature of the American commitment to Europe through the North Atlantic Treaty, the Mutual Defense Assistance Program, and the assignment of ground forces—the German question was hardly discussed during the great debate. This is all the more curious since opposition to Truman's decision to send troops to Europe as an integral component of an integrated command structure focused on the two areas where the German issue had played such an important role: the military feasibility of assigning American troops to Europe without increased European (German) efforts, and the creation of an integrated NATO force to accommodate the eventual participation of German units without running the risk of destroying the western European balance of power.

The first hint that the administration was going to avoid the German question came when General Eisenhower returned from a preliminary inspection tour of Europe and addressed a joint session of Congress on February 5, 1951. The general said that he was not going to mention the several conversations he had in Germany about German rearmament for the specific reason that a political platform had to be established before German participation could be contemplated. He said that he wanted no mercenary Hessians in his command and that "until the political leaders, the diplomats, and the statesmen, find the proper answer, it is not for a soldier to delve in too deeply."[133]

Eisenhower's attitude set the tone for administration military witnesses during the hearings on Senate Resolution 8. When he was called to testify, Eisenhower maintained: "There is no hope as of today to start arming Germans. There is a tremendous political platform to be established before this could come about."[134] Secretary of Defense Marshall, who had indicated to the French that Senate opposition to the stationing of American troops in Europe would increase without the assurance of German participation as an indication that Europe was doing its share, was somewhat more encouraging, but he too maintained that a good deal of time would have to pass before Germany could be included in the active defense of the West.[135] General Bradley, while maintaining that the United States was looking forward to a German contribution, was as circumspect as Eisenhower and Marshall.[136]

Clearly, no one in the administration wanted to admit to a Congress that had strong questions about the wisdom of stationing U.S. troops in Europe, and especially about the capacity of America's allies to do their share, that the United States had just lost a political battle with France over the question of German rearmament. This was especially true since many powerful senators had been consistent advocates of bringing West Germany's military potential into the picture. Moreover, there could be no question of admitting to Congress that, in stationing troops in Europe to lay the groundwork for *eventual* German participation, the U.S. commitment had assumed a "depth and permanence" that had never been contemplated in previous administration policies or statements.

Equally interesting, the senators—apparently placated by the promise of a European army containing German units—did not press the administration for further clarification. The inclusion of paragraph 9 of Senate Resolution 99 was literally a last-minute insertion, taking place on April 4, 1951, the same day that the resolution was approved by the Senate.[137] On the surface this lack of senatorial probing into the German rearmament question is curious because the debate between the United States and France on this issue had received widespread news coverage, especially in *The New York Times*. However, because of the secrecy surrounding the discussions with the French, the press was unable to report on the debate *within* the American government over German rearmament or that the commitment of U.S. ground forces to Europe in an integrated command was the essential ingredient in creating the platform for German rearmament.[138] Therefore, despite a general awareness that a serious rift had developed between the United States and France over the question of German rearmament, the senators who participated in the great debate had an incomplete picture of the issues involved in the assignment of American ground forces to NATO.

However, one senator did challenge the administration's presentation of the German question. Not surprisingly, that senator was Joseph McCarthy (R.-Wisc.)—one of the supporters of paragraph 9—who charged that General Eisenhower "was barred at the present time from using the manpower of Western Germany, and would be barred from using it until the diplomats and politicians worked the problem out." McCarthy supported the idea of including a paragraph relating to Germany in the Senate resolution because he did not want to "tie General Eisenhower's hands." He added: "However, as of today we are tying his hands just as definitely as we are tying the hands of General MacArthur in Korea."[139]

Therefore, it is clear that when the Senate voted to approve Senate Resolution 99 and sanction the dispatch of American forces to NATO, the senators were unaware of the important implications of the German question in determining the scope and structure of the American commitment and, in that important aspect, the so-called great debate was incomplete. By ignoring a major reason for the American commitment to European security, the great debate failed to come to grips with the permanent nature of that commitment.

Conclusion

Throughout internal and international discussions, the assignment of American ground forces to Europe was linked to the question of German rearmament. In this sense the question was not whether West Germany would participate in the military defense of western Europe, but when and how. The American "package plan," developed in August and September 1950, sought to bring in German units immediately and attempted to tie the stationing of American troops to the simultaneous inclusion of German formations in a NATO force. The French Pleven Plan, developed in October, sought to delay the German contribution by making such a move dependent on the prior commitment of American troops and the creation of a European army with a European political superstructure. In the compromise Spofford plan the principle of German rearmament was accepted by the French, while the United States agreed to deploy four additional divisions to Europe as part of an integrated command framework designed to accommodate German units should the concept of a European army fail.

Had American policymakers not assumed that German rearmament was necessary, the shape of the U.S. commitment to Europe might very well have been much different. The United States could have responded to the Soviet threat by simply increasing its military assistance programs and by strengthening the occupation forces in Germany. Nothing in the North Atlantic Treaty required participation in a unified command structure or the deployment of American troops to Europe in an integrated defense arrangement. These structures, it is argued, were greatly influenced by the American desire to gain French acceptance for German rearmament, thereby giving the U.S. commitment a shape and permanence it might otherwise not have assumed.

The role of Germany in shaping the American commitment to Europe is doubly interesting in light of the secrecy that surrounded that issue during the great debate on American foreign policy during the winter of 1951. The reason behind this secrecy appears to be twofold: first, it is apparent from Marshall's statements to the French that he feared an adverse domestic reaction to the stationing of American troops in Europe if he could not assure the Congress that such a move would be accompanied by an increase in European (including German) military potential. Obviously, knowledge of the fact that the Defense Department itself questioned the wisdom of sending American troops to Europe without the simultaneous rearmament of Germany would have added fuel to the opposition's arguments. Second, and perhaps more important, by concentrating exclusively on the Soviet threat as a reason for assigning troops to Europe, the administration could present that action as a temporary commitment that could be reduced and eventually eliminated as the perceived threat from the Soviet Union was reduced. By ignoring the more complex and permanent implications of the American commitment, the administration was able to avoid strengthening the isolationist sentiment opposing its policy and could postpone discussion of the implications of

the German question for American policy until after the political groundwork had been more firmly established in Europe.

Notes

1. Beaufre, *NATO and Europe*, p. 28.
2. *North Atlantic Treaty Hearings*, vol. 1, p. 47.
3. Laurence Martin, "The American Decision to Rearm Germany," in Stein,
ed., *American Civil Military Decisions*, pp. 643-66; McGeehan, *The German Rearmament Question*; McLellan, *Dean Acheson: The State Department Years*, pp.
327-46.
4. Martin, "The American Decision to Rearm Germany," p. 646.
5. Ibid., p. 647.
6. U.S., Department of State, *Foreign Relations of the United States*, 1950,
vol. 1, National Security Affairs; Foreign Economic Policy, p. 261; Lay to the
Nation Security Council (NSC 68).
7. Ibid., p. 275.
8. Martin, "The American Decision to Rearm Germany," p. 650.
9. Ibid., p. 648.
10. Acheson, *Present at the Creation*, p. 436.
11. *FRUS*, 1950, vol. 3, p. 131; Douglas to Acheson.
12. Ibid., pp. 131-32.
13. Ibid.
14. Ibid., p. 138; Acheson to Certain Diplomatic Offices; McLellan, *Dean
Acheson: The State Department Years*, p. 327.
15. *FRUS*, 1950, vol. 3, p. 143; Spofford to Acheson.
16. Ibid., p. 144.
17. Ibid., p. 148; Spofford to Acheson.
18. Ibid., p. 158; Bruce to Acheson.
19. Ibid., pp. 157-58.
20. Acheson, *Present at the Creation*, pp. 436-38.
21. *FRUS*, 1950, vol. 3, p. 181; McCloy to Acheson.
22. Ibid. For earlier statements by McCloy regarding German Rearmament,
see Acheson, *Present at the Creation*, p. 438.
23. Acheson, *Present at the Creation*, p. 438.
24. *FRUS*, 1950, vol. 3, pp. 167-68; Memorandum of Conversation by Acheson.
25. Acheson, *Present at the Creation*, p. 438.
26. Ibid.
27. *FRUS*, 1950, vol. 3, p. 193; Kirk to Acheson.
28. Ibid., p. 206; McCloy to Acheson.
29. Ibid., pp. 194-95; Bruce to Acheson.
30. Martin, "The American Decision to Rearm Germany," p. 654.
31. Ibid., p. 655; McLellan, *Dean Acheson: The State Department Years*, p. 328.

32. *FRUS*, 1950, vol. 3, pp. 207-08: Douglas to Acheson, especially no. 3, p. 207.
33. Ibid., p. 214; Matthews to Burns.
34. Ibid., p. 215.
35. Ibid., p. 214.
36. Ibid., p. 211.
37. Acheson, *Present at the Creation*, p. 438.
38. McLellan, *Dean Acheson: The State Department Years*, pp. 328-29.
39. Martin, "The American Decision to Rearm Germany," p. 655. For a summary of the French memorandum, see *FRUS*, 1950, vol. 3, p. 1386; Bruce to Acheson.
40. *FRUS*, 1950, vol. 3, p. 221; Bruce to Acheson.
41. Ibid., p. 250; Acheson to Truman.
42. Ibid., p. 273; Acheson to Johnson and Truman.
43. Ibid., p. 274.
44. Ibid., pp. 275-76.
45. For the text of Truman's speech, see *The New York Times*, September 10, 1950.
46. *FRUS*, 1950, vol. 3, p. 261; Acheson to Bruce.
47. Ibid., p. 267; Bruce to Acheson.
48. Monnet, *Memoirs*, p. 341.
49. Ibid.
50. Martin, "The American Decision to Rearm Germany," p. 658.
51. *FRUS*, 1950, vol. 3, pp. 294, 299; Minutes of a Private Conversation between Acheson, Schuman, and Bevin; for reports on the change in the British position, see ibid., p. 336; Acheson to Truman. Within a year, the British "Third Force" headed by Aneurin Bevan would strongly criticize British defense policies, including agreement to the rearmament of Germany. See Foot, *Aneurin Bevan*, vol. 2, pp. 344-46; also Aneurin Bevan, et al., *One Way Only* (London: Tribune Publications, 1951), p. 16. For the French view, see Monnet, *Memoirs*, p. 342.
52. *FRUS*, 1950, vol. 3, p. 299; Minutes of a Private Conversation between Acheson, Schuman, and Bevin.
53. McLellan, *Dean Acheson: The State Department Years*, pp. 330-31.
54. *FRUS*, 1950, vol. 3, pp. 327-29; Acheson to Webb.
55. Acheson, *Present at the Creation*, pp. 441-42; *FRUS*, 1950, vol. 3, p. 336; Acheson to Truman.
56. McLellan, *Dean Acheson: The State Department Years*, p. 331.
57. *FRUS*, 1950, vol. 3, p. 336; Acheson to Truman.
58. Monnet, *Memoirs*, p. 341.
59. *FRUS*, 1950, vol. 3, p. 336; Acheson to Truman.
60. Ibid., p. 340; Acheson to Webb.
61. McLellan, *Dean Acheson: The State Department Years*, p. 331.
62. *FRUS*, 1950, vol. 3, p. 342; Acheson to Webb.
63. Ibid., p. 341.

64. Ibid., p. 342.
65. Ibid., p. 1392; Memorandum by Battle.
66. Ibid., p. 344; Acheson to Webb.
67. Ibid.
68. Ibid.
69. McLellan, *Dean Acheson: The State Department Years,* p. 332; McGeehan, *The German Rearmament Question,* pp. 59-61.
70. *FRUS,* 1950, vol. 3, p. 344; Acheson to Webb.
71. McGeehan, *The German Rearmament Question,* p. 60.
72. *FRUS,* 1950, vol. 3, p. 345; Perkins to Webb. Emphasis added.
73. Ibid., pp. 345-46.
74. Ibid., p. 350; Acheson to Webb. Any specific mention of "German army units" was deleted from the text at French insistence. McGeehan, *The German Rearmament Question,* p. 61.
75. *FRUS,* 1950, vol. 3, p. 350; Acheson to Webb.
76. Ibid., p. 353; Memorandum of Conversation by Acheson.
77. Ibid., p. 357-58; Webb to Bruce.
78. Monnet, *Memoirs,* p. 343.
79. Ibid., pp. 343-46.
80. *FRUS,* 1950, vol. 3, p. 377; Matthews to Webb, including a memorandum by the Joint Chiefs of Staff.
81. Ibid., pp. 381-82; Acheson to Marshall.
82. Ibid., pp. 377-80; Bohlen to Acheson.
83. McGeehan, *The German Rearmament Question,* pp. 64-66; Monnet, *Memoirs,* pp. 346-48.
84. *FRUS,* 1950, vol. 3, p. 380; Bohlen to Acheson.
85. Ibid., p. 404; Memorandum by Acheson.
86. Ibid., p. 411; Acheson to Bruce.
87. Ibid., p. 423; Acheson to Bruce.
88. Ibid., pp. 427, 430; Acheson to Bruce.
89. Ibid., p. 430.
90. Ibid., p. 433; Bruce to Acheson.
91. Ibid., pp. 457-59; Spofford to Acheson.
92. Ibid., p. 460; Douglas to Acheson.
93. Ibid., p. 518; Marshall to Burns.
94. Ibid., p. 480; Spofford to Acheson.
95. Ibid., pp. 394-95; Acheson to McCloy, especially n. 1; McLellan, *Dean Acheson: The State Department Years,* p. 335.
96. Adenauer, *Memoirs,* pp. 311-12.
97. Ibid., pp. 375-81.
98. McLellan, *Dean Acheson: The State Department Years,* p. 335.
99. Adenauer, *Memoirs,* p. 304.
100. *FRUS,* 1950, vol. 3, p. 497; Acheson to Bruce.
101. Ibid., p. 498. Emphasis added.

102. Ibid., p. 1750; The United States Minutes, Truman-Attlee Conversations.
103. Ibid., p. 547; Report by the North Atlantic Military Committee.
104. Ibid., p. 557; Report by the North Atlantic Military Committee to the North Atlantic Defense Committee.
105. Ibid., pp. 595-96; United States Delegation Minutes of the Second Meeting of the Sixth Session of the North Atlantic Treaty Council with Defense Ministers.
106. For the record of the great debate, see U.S., Congress, Senate Committees on Armed Services and Foreign Relations, *Assignment of Ground Forces of the United States* to Duty in the European Area, Joint Hearings Before the Committee on Foreign Relations and the Committee on Armed Services, U.S., Senate, 82nd Congress, 1st session, on S. Con. Res. 8, 1951. Hereafter cited as *Assignment of Ground Forces;* U.S., Congress, Senate, Committee on Foreign Relations, *Executive Sessions of the Senate Foreign Relations Committee,* vol. 3, pt. 1, 82nd Congress, 1st session, 1951, *Historical Series,* 1976. Hereafter cited as *Executive Sessions,* vol. 3, pt. 1.
107. *Executive Sessions,* vol. 3, pt. 1, p. 559.
108. U.S., Congress, Senate, Senator Taft speaking on the European army, 82nd Congress, 1st session, March 20, 1951, *Congressional Record* vol. 97, p. 2660.
109. *Assignment of Ground Forces,* p. 40.
110. Ibid., p. 709.
111. Ibid., p. 683-84.
112. Ibid., p. 695.
113. Ibid., p. 608.
114. U.S., Congress, Senate, Senator Taft speaking for S. Con. Res. 8, 82nd Congress, 1st session, March 20, 1951, *Congressional Record* vol. 97, p. 2600.
115. *Assignment of Ground Forces,* p. 78.
116. Ibid., p. 80.
117. Ibid., pp. 40-41.
118. Ibid., pp. 42-43.
119. Ibid., p. 24.
120. Ibid., p. 19.
121. Ibid., pp. 49, 55.
122. Acheson, *Present at the Creation,* p. 495.
123. U.S., Congress, Senate, Senator Taft speaking for S. Con. Res. 8, 82nd Congress, 1st session, March 20, 1951, *Congressional Record* vol. 97, p. 2653.
124. *Assignment of Ground Forces,* pp. 89-93.
125. Ibid., p. 640.
126. Robert Taft, *A Foreign Policy for Americans* (New York: Doubleday & Co., 1951), p. 100.
127. Vandenberg, ed., *The Private Papers of Senator Vandenberg,* p. 571; see also p. 572.
128. *Executive Sessions,* vol. 3, pt. 1, p. 1; editor's note.
129. U.S., Congress, Senate, Text of S. Res. 99, 82nd Congress, 1st session, April 4, 1951, *Congressional Record,* vol. 97, p. 3282.

130. Ibid., p. 3283.

131. Ibid. The House never took action on its version of S. 99.

132. Ibid.

133. U.S., Congress, House, General Eisenhower speaking before a joint session of Congress, 82nd Congress, 1st session, February 21, 1951, *Congressional Record,* vol. 97, p. 874.

134. *Assignment of Ground Forces,* p. 21.

135. Ibid., p. 50.

136. Ibid., p. 140.

137. U.S., Congress, Senate, senators speaking on the inclusion of paragraph 9 in S. Res. 99, 82nd Congress, 1st session, April 4, 1951, *Congressional Record,* vol. 97, pp. 3254-62. Among the supporters were Senators George, Case, McCarthy, and Brewster.

138. See *The New York Times,* September-December 1950.

139. U.S., Congress, Senate, Senator McCarthy speaking on the inclusion of paragraph 9 in S. Res. 99, 82nd Congress, 1st session, April 4, 1951, *Congressional Record,* vol. 97, p. 3260.

Conclusion

Two conditions dominated the early postwar world: the collapse of
western Europe as a center of international economic, political, and
military power and the emergence of the Soviet-American rivalry. It
was the interplay of these two conditions that shaped the scope and
structure of the American commitment to western Europe through the
North Atlantic Treaty and NATO.[1] Yet because of the emphasis on the
cold war and the Soviet-American rivalry, the American effort to reconstitute the old international system is an often-neglected factor in analyses
of American participation in European security.

However, the process of shaping the American commitment to Europe
was complicated and witnessed serious disagreements across the Atlantic,
between the Truman administration and Congress, and within the administration itself. Moreover, from the first, the evolution of the American
commitment involved factors other than those defined by the relatively
limited parameters of the cold war, chief among which was, of course,
Germany's status in the postwar world. It has been argued throughout
that—because of the failure to reach four power agreement on the status
of Germany and because of Germany's importance to the balance of
power in Europe—the American commitment assumed a more permanent
character than would have been necessary merely to meet the threat posed
to western Europe by the Soviet Union.

Briefly, the formulation and implementation of the North Atlantic
Treaty clearly were American responses designed to reconcile French
fears of a resurgent Germany to the realities of the cold war that—from
the American point of view—demanded western German participation
in the recovery and defense of western Europe. This reconciliation
process was evident at every stage of the evolution of the American commitment and forged an alliance structure responsive to European security
in its most general sense.

Therefore, the period between 1947 and 1951 was marked by American efforts to give France the sense of security and certainty about the American commitment to Europe necessary to achieve French agreement on the utilization of German resources in the cold war. It is clear that the Marshall Plan was designed to "dovetail" German economic recovery with a wider program for European recovery. Moreover, such steps as the Brussels Pact, the Vandenberg Resolution, the North Atlantic Treaty, the development of NATO, and the assignment of American ground forces to Europe as a part of an integrated NATO command were all greatly influenced by the dual goal of integrating western Germany into the western state system and providing security against German domination of that system.

This is not to say that these steps were taken completely outside the sphere of the cold war and the Soviet-American rivalry. Indeed, there can be no doubt that at critical junctures Soviet policies and actions, such as the Prague coup, the Berlin blockade, the testing of atomic weapons, and the North Korean invasion of South Korea, served as catalysts for western agreement on the shape and structure of the evolving Atlantic relationship. By increasing the general sense of insecurity in the West, Soviet policies made it easier for France to accept the American view of the cold war (and the corresponding need to bring Germany into the picture) and facilitated increased American involvement in European security.

But even as the United States and western Europe began to structure the North Atlantic Treaty, it was clear that their approaches to European security stemmed from different philosophical roots. At the end of World War II the western Europeans were aware of their own weakness, the immediate threat posed by the Soviet Union, and the centuries-old problem of Germany. Therefore, they required an American commitment that would help them get back on their feet, contain Soviet communism, and prevent a renewal of German aggression.

On the other hand the United States was just emerging from a century and a half of isolation and tended to view world affairs exclusively in terms of Soviet-American relations. Its chief foreign policy goal was to contain Soviet Communism by restoring the balance of power in Europe, and the best method for accomplishing that goal was to utilize German resources to counterbalance Soviet power. Moreover, because of its lingering isolationist tradition, the United States was wary of becoming entangled in a permanent alliance.

These differing American and European foreign policy traditions
clashed during the formulation of the North Atlantic Treaty. Because of
their more complex security requirements, the western Europeans favored
an Atlantic Alliance based on the models of the Dunkirk Treaty (1947)
and the Brussels Pact (1948). From the European perspective, these
treaties offered two advantages: first, each party assumed an "automatic"
commitment to help defend against an armed attack on another signatory
by using "all the military and other means" available; second, both the
Dunkirk and Brussels treaties were specifically directed against a renewal
of aggression by Germany. It is clear that the Europeans wanted an alliance
framework containing automatic commitment in order to entangle the
United States more firmly in continental security and sought guarantees
against a renewal of German aggression prior to agreeing to American
plans for including western Germany in recovery and defense programs.

On the other hand the United States envisaged a more limited commitment based on the Monroe Doctrine tradition of American foreign policy.
This tradition, which found prior expression in the Inter-American Treaty
of Reciprocal Assistance (1947), merely required each signatory to regard
an attack on one as an attack on all and to take whatever measures it
deemed necessary in meeting that attack. Moreover, the obligation was
"open ended" in that it was not directed at any particular country and
remained in effect in case one party to the treaty attacked another.
Indeed, at an American request specific mention of Germany had been
deleted from the operative article of the Brussels Pact (but not from the
preamble) in order to conform to the Rio Pact model and to facilitate
eventual American association with (and German membership in) western
European security efforts.

When the North Atlantic Treaty was finally signed on April 4, 1949,
it represented almost complete acceptance of the American formula. Due
to Senate opposition to stronger language, article 5—the so-called heart
of the treaty—conformed to the tradition of Monroe Doctrine and
the Rio Pact in that an attack on one was considered to be an attack on
all and the appropriate response was left to the individual signatories.
As some concession to the Europeans the phrase "including the use of
armed force" was inserted to clarify American intentions.

However, because of the vagueness of article 5, the Europeans turned
from the guarantee provided by the treaty itself and concentrated on
entangling the United States in European security through the subsequent
implementation of the treaty under article 3, which was the most unique

provision of the treaty, having no precedent in the Dunkirk, Rio, or Brussels pacts, but rather tracing its origins to the Vandenberg Resolution of June 1948. Interestingly enough, its original purpose was to ensure that the Europeans did their fair share in mutual defense efforts by insisting on the principle of "continuous and effective self help and mutual aid." It is therefore somewhat paradoxical that the Europeans viewed article 3 as a means of obtaining a permanent American commitment to Europe. Yet as the American commitment continued to evolve, it was the provisions of article 3 that led to the progressive involvement of the United States in an entangling alliance.

Therefore, as a result of these differing philosophical traditions, the North Atlantic Treaty contained two different foci: first was the vague "Monroe Doctrine" guarantee of article 5 designed to appeal to isolationist sentiment in the United States; second was the promise of subsequent implementation under article 3 used by the Europeans to progressively involve the United States in the full range of continental security issues. That both those appeals were successful is illustrated by the fact that the North Atlantic Treaty was approved in the Senate by the overwhelming majority of 82-13 on August 21, 1949, and simultaneous with the signing of the treaty, France agreed to trizonal fusion and the Occupation Statute for the Federal Republic of Germany—agreements that came into effect only after ratification of the pact.

However, the philosophical differences as to the meaning of the treaty continued to exist side by side as the NATO structure was developed throughout 1949 and into the spring of 1950. There can be no doubt that the United States sought to use the North Atlantic Treaty Organization as a way to include the Federal Republic of Germany in the defense of western Europe while at the same time to remain aloof from increased involvement on the continent. Pursuing just the opposite course, France sought to prevent West German association with NATO (witness the Schuman/Monnet Plan for the European Coal and Steel Community) and was actively seeking increased American integration on the continent through NATO's Regional Planning Groups.

It was not until after the outbreak of the Korean war, on June 25, 1950, that the United States and western Europe (especially France) started to reconcile their philosophical differences and that the American commitment to Europe began to assume a more tangible and permanent character. Again, the issue at hand was West Germany's role in western defense, and the most important treaty provisions were those of article 3.

The Korean invasion, by raising fears about Soviet intentions in Europe, forced the western allies to move in the direction of constructing a viable defense against the possibility of Soviet aggression. Everyone agreed that such a defense would have to include an increased number of U.S. troops in Europe, but from the perspective of the Defense Department, even the assignment of additional American troops would not be sufficient to repel a Soviet attack unless it was accompanied by the simultaneous inclusion of German units in a European army. However, the specter of German rearmament, even within the framework of a European army associated with NATO, was unacceptable to France. Therefore, the summer and fall of 1950 witnessed intense and often acrimonious debate both within the Truman administration and across the Atlantic on the relationship between the assignment of American ground forces to Europe and the rearmament of West Germany. It was not until the United States agreed to assign additional forces to an *integrated* NATO command structure without the simultaneous inclusion of German troops that France would agree even to the *principle* of eventual German rearmament through the European Defense Community. In short the United States had finally come to accept the fact that in order to restore a balance of power and prevent Soviet domination of Europe it would have to participate in that balance to prevent German domination of western Europe.

President Truman's December 19, 1950, announcement that he was sending additional troops to Europe in fulfillment of article 3 and as a part of an integrated NATO command structure unleashed a storm of criticism and inaugurated the great debate on American foreign policy during the winter of 1951. Because there could no longer be any doubt that the United States would participate in the initial defense of Europe, the constitutional safeguards written into the treaty no longer applied. Although the vast majority of senators—through S. 99 (April 4, 1951)— ultimately faced up to the new responsibilities of the cold war and approved Truman's action, it was clear that a great departure had taken place in the conduct of American foreign policy; from then on, the security of the United States was unmistakably linked with that of western Europe.

Curiously, the so-called great debate never really focused on the impact of West German rearmament in shaping the American commitment to NATO. This is most interesting because Congress had long favored utilizing West German resources to restore the European balance and to contain Soviet communism. It is clear that Congress viewed such programs as the Marshall Plan, the North Atlantic Treaty, and the creation of NATO as methods of bringing West Germany back into the western state system and of minimizing the U.S. commitment. It is doubtful that many senators would have approved the assignment of six U.S. divisions to NATO if they had been aware of the serious opposition voiced by the Defense Department to such a course of action without the simultaneous inclusion of West German forces.

Therefore, it is becoming increasingly apparent that the Truman administration deliberately withheld information regarding the impact of the German question in structuring the American commitment. One reason for such action was to avoid public discussion of the serious rifts that had developed between the western allies and within the administration itself over the link between the assignment of U.S. forces to NATO and West German rearmament. Another influence on administration policy also must have been the fact that, because the question of West German rearmament could only be resolved through the prior assignment of American troops to an integrated command structure, the U.S. commitment to western Europe had assumed—in Acheson's words of assurance to Robert Schuman—a "depth and permanence" not previously envisaged.

Indeed, it was not until June 1952 that the Senate linked the presence of American troops in Europe to the West German rearmament question. At that time the Senate Foreign Relations Committee was examining the contractual agreements that would govern relationships among the Federal Republic of Germany, the European Defense Community, and the western allies. During his testimony, Acheson was questioned on the measures that would be taken if the Federal Republic attempted to withdraw from the European Defense Community and pursue unilateral rearmament or reunification. Acheson replied that such an eventuality would lead to consultations under article 4 of the North Atlantic Treaty on how best to deal with such a problem.[2] Moreover, it was clear that any such attempt on the part of the Federal Republic would call into play allied forces, which—although they were no longer occupation forces—continued to be stationed on West German territory.[3] Such knowledge led to the following statement by Senator Guy Gillette (D.-Iowa).

> Now, since the only really effective guarantee of the
> integrity and unity of the EDC [European Defense Com-
> munity] will be these troops, we can properly ask and we
> should ask what would happen to the EDC if Germany's

relationship—what would happen if our troops were no
longer there and she decided to withdraw.

Now that is the effective guarantee we have and, I think,
Mr. Chairman, that we must recognize it. I am willing to
recognize it. It is a price that, I think, we have to pay for
bringing her in, her armed forces into, the EDC, but I cannot read into this anything other than the only guarantee
against withdrawal and, Mr. Chairman, a guarantee of a
changed situation—every member of this Foreign Relations
Committee knows that the German people want to be united,
they know that they will—and our accepting this only as
an interim arrangement. . . .

All of these contingencies are ahead of us, and there
is nothing in any of these treaties as a guarantee against
those contingencies excepting the presence of United
Kingdom and U.S. troops there, and our commitment to
use those troops for the security of Europe, and I do not
want to say these things out on the floor; I do not want
to oppose this treaty . . . but we must recognize that it is
a transition proposal . . . and it has no substance except the
troops, no substance or guarantees or perpetuity or value.[4]

Therefore, in order for western Europe to accept the reconstruction of
a West German state and its integration into the recovery and defense
programs for western Europe, the United States clearly had to involve itself in a security framework designed to meet the more complex needs
of its European allies. In essence, in order to reconstitute a balance of
power against the Soviet Union, the United States had to become a part
of a more intricate balance designed both to contain the Soviet threat and
permanently to end the threat of German domination of western Europe
by integrating the western portion of that divided country into a larger
Atlantic framework.[5] It is this complex structure that remains the enduring legacy and that stands as the hallmark of postwar American foreign
policy.

Of course, the fact that the U.S. commitment to western Europe was in
response to questions surrounding the status of West Germany as well as
to the Soviet-American rivalry has important implications for current
U.S. foreign policy. Any discussion of arms control or troop reductions
must take into account the fact that the American presence in Europe

has two purposes: to offer western Europe security against Soviet policies and to prevent German domination by securely binding the Federal Republic of Germany to larger European and Atlantic frameworks. Any substantial reduction of the U.S. commitment to Europe would inevitably challenge those relationships and raise anew the questions of German reunification and possible dominance.

Notes

1. McLellan, *Dean Acheson: The State Department Years,* p. 380.
2. U.S., Congress, Senate, Committee on Foreign Relations, *Executive Sessions of the Senate Foreign Relations Committee,* vol. 4, 82nd Congress, 2nd session, 1952, *Historical Series,* 1976.
3. Ibid., pp. 505-06.
4. Ibid., pp. 506-07.
5. Ibid., p. 472.

Bibliography

Books

Acheson, Dean. *Present at the Creation.* New York: W. W. Norton & Co., 1969.
———. *Sketches From Life of Men I Have Known.* New York: Harper & Brothers, 1961.
Adenauer, Konrad. *Memoirs, 1949-1953.* Chicago: Henry Regnery Co., 1965.
Aron, Raymond. *The Imperial Republic.* Englewood Cliffs, N.J.: Prentice-Hall, 1974.
Backer, John. *The Decision to Divide Germany.* Durham, N.C.: Duke University Press, 1978.
Beaufre, André. *NATO and Europe.* New York: Vintage Books, 1966.
Bohlen, Charles. *The Transformation of American Foreign Policy.* New York: W. W. Norton & Co., 1969.
Clay, Lucius. *Decision in Germany.* New York: Doubleday and Co., 1950.
Dalton, Hugh. *Memoirs.* vol. 3: *High Tide and After.* London: Frederick Muller, 1962.
Dulles, John Foster. *War or Peace?* New York: Macmillan, 1950.
Foot, Michael. *Aneurin Bevan, A Biography.* 2 vols. New York: Atheneum, 1974.
Furniss, Edgar. *France: Troubled Ally.* New York: Harper & Row, 1960.
Gaddis, John Lewis. *The United States and the Origins of the Cold War: 1941-1947.* New York: Columbia University Press, 1972.
Gilbert, Felix. *To the Farewell Address.* Princeton, N.J.: Princeton University Press, 1970.
Gimbel, John. *The American Occupation of Germany.* Stanford, Calif.: Stanford University Press, 1968.
———. *The Origins of the Marshall Plan.* Stanford, Calif.: Stanford University Press, 1976.
Godson, Roy. *American Labor and European Politics: The AFL as a Transnational Force.* New York: Crane, Russak, 1976.
Hoopes, Townsend. *The Devil and John Foster Dulles.* Boston: Little, Brown and Co., 1973.
Hunter, Robert. *Security in Europe.* Bloomington and London: Indiana University Press, 1972.
Jones, Joseph. *The Fifteen Weeks.* New York: Viking Press, 1955.
Kaiser, Robert. *Cold Winter, Cold War.* New York: Stein and Day, 1974.
Kaplan, Lawrence. *Recent American Foreign Policy: Conflicting Interpretations.* Homewood, Ill.: The Dorsey Press, 1972.

Kennan, George Frost. *Memoirs.* 2 vols. Boston: Little, Brown and Co., 1967-71.

Kolko, Joyce and Kolko, Gabriel. *The Limits of Power.* New York: Harper & Row, 1972.

Krock, Arthur. *Memoirs: Sixty Years on the Firing Line.* New York: Funk and Wagnalls, 1978.

Lafeber, Walter. *America, Russia and the Cold War, 1945-1975,* 3rd ed. New York: John Wiley & Sons, Inc., 1976.

Laqueur, Walter. *The Rebirth of Europe.* New York: Holt, Rinehart and Winston, 1970.

Macridis, Roy C., ed. *Foreign Policies in World Politics.* Englewood Cliffs, N.J.: Prentice-Hall, 1976.

McGeehan, Robert. *The German Rearmament Question.* Urbana: University of Illinois Press, 1971.

McInnis, Edgar. *The Shaping of Postwar Germany.* New York: Frederick A. Praeger, 1960.

McLellan, David. *Dean Acheson: The State Department Years.* New York: Dodd, Mead & Company, 1976.

Millis, Walter, ed. *The Forrestal Diaries.* New York: Viking Press, 1951.

Montgomery, Sir Bernard. *The Memoirs of Field Marshal the Viscount Montgomery of Alamein, K.G.* Cleveland, Ohio: The World Publishing Company, 1958.

Monnet, Jean. *Memoirs.* Garden City, N.Y.: Doubleday and Company, Inc., 1978.

Mowat, R. C. *Creating the European Community.* New York: Barnes and Noble Books, 1973.

Osgood, Robert. *NATO: The Entangling Alliance.* Chicago: University of Chicago Press, 1962.

Perkins, Dexter. *A History of the Monroe Doctrine.* Boston: Little, Brown and Co., 1963.

Pfaltzgraff, Robert, Jr. *The Atlantic Community: A Complex Imbalance.* New York: Van Nostrand Reinhold Company, 1969.

Price, Harry Bayard. *The Marshall Plan and Its Meaning.* Ithaca, N.Y.: Cornell University Press, 1955.

Schilling, Warner R. *Strategy, Policy and Defense Budgets.* New York: Columbia University Press, 1962.

Shulman, Marshall. *Stalin's Foreign Policies Reappraised.* Cambridge: Harvard University Press, 1963.

Stein, Harold. *American Civil Military Decisions.* Birmingham: University of Alabama Press, 1962.

Taft, Robert A. *A Foreign Policy for Americans.* New York: Doubleday and Co., 1951.

Vandenberg, Arthur H., Jr., ed. *The Private Papers of Senator Vandenberg.* Boston: Houghton Mifflin Co., 1952.

Willis, F. Roy. *France, Germany and the New Europe, 1945-1953.* Stanford, Calif.: Stanford University Press, 1965.

Wolfe, Thomas. *Soviet Power and Europe, 1945-1970.* Baltimore: Johns Hopkins University Press, 1970.

Yergin, Daniel. *Shattered Peace.* Boston: Houghton Mifflin Co., 1977.

Articles

Art, Robert. "America's Foreign Policy: In Historical Perspective." In *Foreign Policies in World Politics,* edited by Roy C. Macridis. Englewood Cliffs, N.J.: Prentice-Hall, 1976: 339-84.

Childs, Marquis. "Washington and the Pact." *Yale Review* 38, 4 (June 1949): 557-87.

Gaddis, John Lewis. "Was the Truman Doctrine a Turning Point?" *Foreign Affairs* 52, 2 (January 1974): 386-402.

Hammond, Paul Y. "Directives for the Occupation of Germany: The Washington Controversy." In *American Civil Military Decisions,* edited by Harold Stein. Birmingham: University of Alabama Press, 1962: 311-464.

Henrikson, Alan K. "The Map as an 'Idea': The Role of Cartographic Imagery During the Second World War." *The American Cartographer* 2, 1 (1975): 19-53.

Martin, Laurence. "The American Decision to Rearm Germany." In *American Civil Military Decisions,* edited by Harold Stein. Birmingham: University of Alabama Press, 1962: 645-63.

Rubin, Alfred P. "SEATO and the American Legal Obligation Concerning Laos and Cambodia." *International and Comparative Law Quarterly* 20, 3 (July 1971): 500-18.

United States Department of State Publications

U.S. Department of State. *Foreign Relations of the United States.* Conferences of Cairo and Tehran, 1943.

——. *Foreign Relations of the United States.* Conference on Berlin, 1945, vol. 2.

——. *Foreign Relations of the United States.* 1946, vol. 2, Council of Foreign Ministers.

——. *Foreign Relations of the United States.* 1946, vol. 6, Eastern Europe; The Soviet Union.

——. *Foreign Relations of the United States.* 1946, vol. 7, The Near East and Africa.

——. *Foreign Relations of the United States.* 1947, vol. 1, General; The United Nations.

——. *Foreign Relations of the United States.* 1947, vol. 2, Council of Foreign Ministers; Germany.

——. *Foreign Relations of the United States.* 1947, vol. 3, The British Commonwealth; Europe.

——. *Foreign Relations of the United States.* 1947, vol. 6, The Near East and Africa.

——. *Foreign Relations of the United States.* 1948, vol. 1, part 2, General; The United Nations.

——. *Foreign Relations of the United States.* 1948, vol. 2, Germany and Austria.

——. *Foreign Relations of the United States.* 1948, vol. 3, Western Europe.

——. *Foreign Relations of the United States.* 1949, vol. 1, National Security Affairs, Foreign Economic Policy.

——. *Foreign Relations of the United States.* 1949, vol. 3, Council of Foreign Ministers; Germany and Austria.

——. *Foreign Relations of the United States.* 1949, vol. 4, Western Europe.

——. *Foreign Relations of the United States.* 1950, vol. 1, National Security Affairs; Foreign Economic Policy.

——. *Foreign Relations of the United States.* 1950, vol. 3, Western Europe.

——. *Act of Chapultepec.* Treaties and Other International Acts Series 1543, Pubn. 2679 (1946).

——. *The Inter-American Treaty of Reciprocal Assistance.* Treaties and Other International Acts Series 1838, Pubn. 3380 (1949).

——. *North Atlantic Treaty.* Treaties and Other International Acts Series 1964, Pubn. 3635 (1950).

——. *Germany, 1947-1949: The Story in Documents.* European and British Commonwealth Series 9, Pubn. no. 3556 (1959).

——. *Bulletin,* May 11, 1947.

——. *Bulletin,* May 18, 1947.

——. *Bulletin,* March 27, 1949.

Congressional Publications

U.S. Congress. House. Committee on Foreign Affairs. *Hearings Before the House Committee on Foreign Affairs on H.R. 2616,* 80th Congress, 1st session, 1947.

——. Committee on International Relations. *Selected Executive Session Hearings of the Committee, 1945-1950.* Vol. 5, part 1, Mutual Defense Assistance Act of 1949. *Historical Series,* 1976.

U.S. Congress. Senate. Committee on Armed Services and Foreign Relations. *Assignment of Ground Forces of the United States to Duty in the European Area. Joint Hearings Before the Committee on Foreign Relations and the Committee on Armed Services on S. Con. 8,* 82nd Congress, 1st session, 1951.

——. Committee on Foreign Relations. *European Recovery Program. Hearings Before the Committee on Foreign Relations, United States Senate on United States Assistance to European Economic Recovery,* 80th Congress, 2nd session, 1948.

——. *Executive Sessions of the Senate Foreign Relations Committee,* vol. 1, 80th Congress, 1st and 2nd sessions, 1947-1948. *Historical Series,* 1976.

——. *Executive Sessions of the Senate Foreign Relations Committee,* vol. 2, 81st Congress, 1st and 2nd sessions, 1949-1950. *Historical Series,* 1976.

——. *Executive Sessions of the Senate Foreign Relations Committee,* vol. 3, part 1, 82nd Congress, 1st session, 1951. *Historical Series,* 1976.

——. *Executive Sessions of the Senate Foreign Relations Committee,* vol. 4, 82nd Congress, 2nd session, 1952. *Historical Series,* 1976.

——. *Legislative Origins of the Truman Doctrine.* Hearings held in Executive Session Before the Committee on Foreign Relations, United States Senate, 80th Congress, 1st session, on S. 938, 1947. *Historical Series,* 1973.

——. *Military Assistance Program.* Joint Hearings held in Executive Session Before the Committee on Foreign Relations and the Committee on Armed Services, United States Senate, 81st Congress, 1st session, on S. 2388, 1949. *Historical Series*, 1973.

———. *The North Atlantic Treaty. Hearings Before the Committee on Foreign Relations, United States Senate, on Executive L*, 81st Congress, 1st session, 1949, 3 parts.

———. *The Vandenberg Resolution and the North Atlantic Treaty*. Hearings held in Executive Session Before the Committee on Foreign Relations, United States Senate, 80th Congress, 2nd session on S. 239 and 81st Congress, 1st session on Executive L, The North Atlantic Treaty. *Historical Series*, 1973.

U.S. Congress. *Congressional Record*. 80th through 82nd Congresses.

Miscellaneous

Great Britain. Parliament. *Parliamentary Papers*, 1946-1947. Cmnd. 7217. Treaty of Alliance and Mutual Assistance Between His Majesty in Respect to the United Kingdom and Northern Ireland and the President of the French Republic, March 4, 1947.

United Nations. Treaty Series. *Treaties and Other International Agreements Registered or Filed and Reported with the Secretariat of the United Nations*, vol. 19, no. 304 (1948). "Treaty for collaboration in economic, social and cultural matters, and for collective self defense [The Brussels Treaty]," 17 March 1948, p. 51.

Index

European Minister of Defense,
proposal, 192, 202-3
European Recovery Program
(Marshall Plan), 23, 31, 48-50,
53-54, 58, 60, 66-67, 70, 74-75,
127-29, 136, 164-65, 183, 226;
interim aid under, 53

Flanagan, Stephen, ix
Fletcher School of Law and
Diplomacy, ix
Foreign Affairs, 26, 40
Foreign Assistance Act of 1948,
122
Forrestal, James, 30, 59-60,
122-26, 147
Forward defense, strategy, 158, 169,
176, 186, 188-89
Four Power Treaty on the Disarmament and Demilitarization of
Germany, draft proposal,
19-21, 57, 63, 67, 74, 88
France, 6, 9-11, 16, 22, 30-31,
33-34, 41, 75, 113, 121, 129,
144, 152, 172; army, 102, 107,
113, 153, 156, 159, 169, 176,
185, 187-88, 201; Cabinet, 158,
161, 174; Christian Democrats,
16, 165; Communists, 18, 52,
54, 65, 130, 158-59, 197; defense
policy, 124, 130, 134, 187-88,
191, 193; and European defense,
103, 156, 160, 163, 176, 204;
and European integration,
164-65, 173-74; and Germany,
16-18, 23, 42, 49-50, 52-53,
55-58, 60-63, 70-72, 74-75, 81,
85, 87-88, 91-92, 94-102,
108-9, 111-13, 120, 138-41,
152, 156-60, 163, 165-75,
177-79, 187-89, 191, 193,

195-203, 206-7, 214-15, 221-22,
224; and Marshall Plan, 48, 52;
Ministry of Foreign Affairs, 96;
*Mouvement Republicain
Populaire*, 16; National
Assembly, 97-98, 100, 130,
158-60, 196, 198, 202; and
North Atlantic Treaty, 80, 87,
100, 102, 110, 112; and North
Atlantic Treaty Organization,
158-59, 161, 168, 172, 175-78,
188-89 191-93, 195-208,
214-16, 221-22, 224-25; politics,
49, 51-52, 54, 70, 97, 134;
*Rassamblement du Peuple
Français* (Gaullists), 16, 97, 158;
Socialists, 16, 97, 197; Treaty of
Mortefontaine, 4; Truman Doc-
trine, 25, 27. *See also* Germany;
Great Britain; United States
Franks, Oliver, 176

Gaddis, John Lewis, 27
Gaulle, Charles de, 16, 51, 134
George, Walter, 28, 120, 131, 139,
144, 154, 157
Germany, 4-6, 9-20, 30-31, 41-42;
division of, 13-15, 18-19, 22;
and France, 16-18, 23, 42; and
Marshall Plan, 32-36; reparations, 13-16, 18-20, 50, 55, 58
Germany, eastern, 63, 69, 109,
186, 190
Germany, Federal Republic of, 152,
157, 159, 203, 205, 221, 224-27;
and European defense, 156-58,
160-61, 163, 167, 169-70,
176-77, 184-85, 188-89, 200;
and European integration,
163-69, 171-74, 177; and
France, 156-60, 163, 165-67,

ABOUT THE AUTHOR

Timothy P. Ireland is an adjunct assistant professor at the Fletcher School of Law and Diplomacy and coordinator of the International Relations Program at Tufts University in Medford, Massachusetts.